D1613779

PERSPECTIVES ON ELEMENTARY EDUCATION

A Casebook for Critically Analyzing Issues of Diversity

STACEY NEUHARTH-PRITCHETT

University of Georgia

BEVERLY D. PAYNE

University of Georgia

JUDITH C. REIFF

University of Georgia

Boston ■ New York ■ San Francisco
Mexico City ■ Montreal ■ Toronto ■ London ■ Madrid ■ Munich ■ Paris
Hong Kong ■ Singapore ■ Tokyo ■ Cape Town ■ Sydney

Series Editor: *Traci Mueller*
Series Editorial Assistant: *Krista Price*
Marketing Manager: *Elizabeth Fogarty*
Production Administrator: *Michael Granger*
Editorial-Production Service: *Omegatype Typography, Inc.*
Manufacturing Buyer: *Andrew Turso*
Cover Administrator: *Jill Winitzer*
Composition and Prepress Buyer: *Linda Cox*
Electronic Composition: *Omegatype Typography, Inc.*

For related titles and support materials, visit our online catalog at www.ablongman.com.

Copyright © 2004 Pearson Education, Inc.

All rights reserved. No part of the material protected by this copyright notice may be reproduced or utilized in any form or by any means, electronic or mechanical, including photocopying, recording, or by any information storage and retrieval system, without written permission from the copyright owner.

To obtain permission(s) to use material from this work, please submit a written request to Allyn and Bacon, Permissions Department, 75 Arlington Street, Boston, MA 02116 or fax your request to 617-848-7320.

Library of Congress Cataloging-in-Publication Data

Neuharth-Pritchett, Stacey.
    Perspectives on elementary education : a casebook for critically analyzing issues of diversity / Stacey Neuharth-Pritchett, Beverly D. Payne, Judith C. Reiff.
        p. cm.
    Includes bibliographical references and index.
    ISBN 0-205-36661-9 (alk. paper)
      1. Multicultural education—United States—Case studies.   2. Education (Elementary)—Social aspects—United States—Case studies.   I. Payne, Beverly D. II. Reiff, Judith Campbell.   III. Title.

LC1099.3.N48 2004
370.117—dc21

                                                                          2003052431

Printed in the United States of America

10   9   8   7   6   5   4   3   2   1   08   07   06   05   04   03

Photo Credits: p. 2: Will Hart; p. 7: Will Hart; p. 15: Will Hart; p. 42: T. Lindfors; p. 60: Will Hart; p. 85: T. Lindfors; p. 91: T. Lindfors; p. 102: Robert Harbison; p. 128: T. Lindfors; p. 142: Comstock; p. 153: Brian Smith; p. 159: Will Hart; p. 170: Nancy Sheehan Photography; p. 192: Tony Freeman/Photo Edit.

Dedicated with love to John and Maggie
—Stacey Neuharth-Pritchett

Dedicated to David (Mio marito, mio amante, mio amico)
—Beverly D. Payne

In loving memory of my mother and father
—Judith C. Reiff

CONTENTS

CHAPTER FIVE
Social Issues 125

CHAPTER SIX
Special Needs 151

PREFACE

In the field of teacher education, there has been an increased focus in the past fifteen years on the integration of culturally responsive approaches to teaching in preparation programs. Since we entered the new millennium and societal demands for incorporating diverse perspectives into nearly all of our interactions have increased, teacher educators have been confronted with an imperative to prepare new teachers for teaching in this diverse world. The multicultural education movement has particular relevance because of the increasing diversity of ethnic, cultural, religious, and socioeconomic groups in public schools (Diaz, 2001). These changing demographics present challenges that should highlight the need to prepare teachers whose training meets the needs of all children in society. Along with changes in societal demographics, the public schools are undergoing a shift that involves a more diverse and increasing proportion of students enrolling in schools from groups previously underrepresented. At the same time the proportion of White teachers is increasing (Campbell, 1996; Fox & Gay, 1995; Olmedo, 1997). This phenomenon increases the likelihood that teachers in the public schools will be teaching students whose cultural backgrounds differ greatly from their own.

This book is a collection of cases that explore a wide range of diversity issues. The cases were written by teacher educators, public and private schoolteachers, administrators, graduate students, undergraduate preservice teacher education students, student teachers, psychologists, clinicians, social workers, and parents. The case approach was chosen because cases foster discussion-based, active learning designed to guide students in problem analysis and problem solving. This approach centers on organizing discussions around defining problems, identifying alternatives, and proposing solutions to the issues presented in the case. The goal is the reader's ability to learn how to analyze situations, evaluate a variety of solutions, and evaluate the consequences of those solutions, rather than simply to develop one right answer. The use of cases in classroom teaching often sways the teacher from didactic presentation; instead the teacher serves as a facilitator to foster understanding, ask questions, provide bridging statements, sustain the flow of discussion, and recognize students' contributions.

The design of this book is intended to promote its use as a basic or supplementary text in early childhood education, elementary education, child development, educational psychology, curriculum, special education, and multicultural education courses. We perceive the text mainly to be used at the undergraduate level but would also consider it applicable to alternative teacher education programs at the graduate level (e.g., teacher certification programs for students whose undergraduate degrees are in noneducation fields). The text could serve as a professional reference for college educators, public school personnel, and staff development personnel. Additionally, the text would also be appropriate for social science-related disciplines such as child care, early intervention, social work, nursing, law, counseling, or any field in which professionals interact with elementary-aged children. An intentionally broad definition of multicultural education is used in this book. We define multicultural education to include race, culture, language, socioeconomic status, national or ethnic origin, religion, gender, special needs, social conditions, family configurations, age, geographic variation, sexual orientation, and academic abilities and achievement.

The book is comprised of seven chapters. The first chapter provides a rationale for the use of cases in examining issues of diversity. The remaining six chapters present thirty-six cases that are organized around themes. These themes include culture, academic performance and expectations, safety and prosocial behaviors, social issues, special needs, and the family. Cases are written from different perspectives and are structured differently. Some cases are intentionally open ended so that many suggestions to the situation presented can be formulated. Other cases are closed and the decisions made by the participants in the case can be evaluated by those reading it. This text differs from existing casebooks in that it includes cases written from a variety of perspectives and experience levels on a broad array of diverse characteristics. Whereas some casebooks often contain a case or two that focus on diversity, this book is entirely devoted to critically examining diversity issues within the context of elementary school education. This casebook focuses on the elementary school years (prekindergarten to fifth grade). With intensive focus on this age and grade range, we have provided a comprehensive view of the diversity issues that are present in preschools and elementary schools. Each case begins with an abstract that orients the reader to the content of the case. Additionally, some cases pose guiding questions at the beginning of the case. Each case concludes with carefully structured questions for reflection as well as a list of resources that will allow the reader to explore the issues presented in the case in greater depth.

The content of this book was developed by fifty-three authors who each are dedicated to fostering culturally responsive teaching. We hope that their work will serve as a catalyst for teachers' thinking that will ultimately impact the experiences of elementary school children. We are indebted to their efforts and hope that they merit positive outcomes in individuals who learn from this text.

ACKNOWLEDGMENTS

The idea for this text came from a series of small studies that were funded by The University of Georgia College of Education Multicultural Education Initiative. Data from this work was the genesis of our inquiry into case-based instructional material for the study of diversity. On a careful examination of the existing case-based materials available for teacher education on diversity, we found very little that could maximize the potential of the learning in which our students were involved. At the same time, we looked at the individuals with whom we work on a daily basis and recognized the powerful stories that they had related to diversity. Whether these individuals were our colleagues at The University of Georgia; our students; the incredible teachers, administrators, and school-based personnel who enable our teacher education students to have meaningful field experiences; or the students and parents whom we have known over the years, we wanted them to have an opportunity to tell their stories and share their experiences about diversity. We are grateful for their time, energy, and enthusiasm for this project. We appreciate the understanding and flexibility they showed us as we edited the content of the cases and abstracts for instructional purposes and consistency of style. We hope that their experiences and insights provide meaningful learning for all who use this book.

We are grateful for the incredible support that was provided by Stephanie Bales throughout the development of this book. She kept us on track and made the composition of this text a pleasure. So much so that her own contribution of experience is included as one of the cases in the text. We also acknowledge the help of I-Mei Ma, a doctoral student in the Department of Elementary Education at The University of Georgia, who helped us gather information for the resources provided at the end of each case. We would like to thank the helpful reviewers of the text who provided excellent comments and suggestions that served to strengthen the content of this casebook: Saundra J. McKee, Clarion University of Pennsylvania; Yolanda Watts Johnson, Marquette University; and Raymond Wong, Weber State University.

Special thanks are extended to the editorial staff at Allyn & Bacon. We would especially like to thank Traci Mueller for her enthusiasm for this project.

Stacey would like to thank her husband, John, and her daughter, Maggie, for their unending love and patience. John and Maggie make each day an incredible joy. Stacey hopes that one day Maggie will live in a world that is responsive to the unique characteristics of each child.

Beverly would like to thank her husband, Dave, and the contributors who permitted us to share their outstanding work with our readers.

Judy would like to thank her husband, Richard, and three children, Cam, DeAnn, and Becky. Judy expresses appreciation for the many students, teachers, and colleagues who have influenced her multicultural journey and commitment to case-based instruction.

Stacey Neuharth-Pritchett

Beverly D. Payne

Judith C. Reiff

REFERENCES

Campbell, D. (1996). *Choosing democracy: A practical guide to multicultural education.* Englewood Cliffs, NJ: Prentice Hall.
Diaz, C. (2001). The third millennium. In C. Diaz (Ed.), *Multicultural education for the twenty-first century* (pp. 11–22). New York: Longman.

Fox, W., & Gay, G. (1995). Integrating multicultural and curriculum principles in teacher education. *Peabody Journal of Education, 70*(3), 64–82.

Olmedo, I. M. (1997). Challenging old assumptions: Preparing teachers for inner city schools. *Teaching and Teacher Education, 13*(3), 245–258.

ABOUT THE CASE AUTHORS

Angel Abney is a doctoral student in the Department of Mathematics Education at The University of Georgia. Her research interests include gender equity in mathematics education, students' mathematical self-concepts, and predation and competition models along with other dynamic systems.

Martha Allexsaht-Snider is an associate professor and head of the Early Childhood Education Program at The University of Georgia. She received her Ph.D. from the University of California, Santa Barbara, in cross-cultural education and is a former bilingual teacher and teacher of English as a second language. Her research interests include family–school linkages in diverse contexts, equity in mathematics teaching and learning, and professional development and teacher education in multicultural and multilingual settings.

Jennifer W. Anthony received her B.S. in early childhood education from The University of Georgia (First Honor Graduate, Summa Cum Laude, with Honors). Anthony graduated with her master's in teaching additional languages in the area of teaching English to speakers of other languages from The University of Georgia in 2002. During her first two years as a kindergarten teacher, she taught an entire class of English language learners in Gainesville, Georgia. She currently teaches kindergarten in the Clarke County school district in Athens, Georgia.

Mary W. Armsworth is an associate professor in the Counseling Psychology Program in the Department of Educational Psychology at the University of Houston. She has been a member of the faculty since 1985 and has specialized in teaching graduate students in the areas of psychological trauma and victimization. Armsworth's research interests have focused on the effects of abuse on development, prevalence of traumatic events in kindergarten through twelfth-grade students, and approaches to assisting teachers and counselors in understanding the effects of trauma on academic performance. She has provided clinical services for traumatized children and adults as a licensed psychologist.

Stephanie Bales has been employed by The University of Georgia since 1984 and has been the office manager in the Department of Elementary Education since 1988. She is currently an undergraduate student, working toward her B.S. in middle grades education. She has a wonderful husband, a daughter who is a first-year college student, and a son in the eighth grade.

Jill Barber is the director of training for the Counseling and Psychological Services Department at The University of Georgia Health Center. She has been an

English teacher in an urban culturally diverse junior high school. She has conducted assessments and therapy with children referred for child abuse through a rural school district. Her research includes work on understanding the psychological sequelae of child abuse, effective training methods for changing attitudes and knowledge about HIV, and integrating feminist and multicultural perspectives in counseling.

Mark and Kathryn Barker have been registered foster parents in Alabama for five years. They have three adult children and two grandchildren. The Barkers hope that their experiences as foster parents will educate others about the obstacles foster children encounter.

Barbara Bradley is a doctoral student in the Department of Reading Education at The University of Georgia. Her interests include emergent literacy, orthographic development, and language acquisition and development. Barbara worked with young children with special needs and their families for fourteen years.

Vicki Bunke received her doctoral degree in school psychology from The University of Georgia. She is currently employed as a school psychologist in the Cobb County school district.

Paige E. Campbell is an assistant professor of early childhood education at Georgia College and State University in Milledgeville, Georgia. She lives in Athens, Georgia, with her family and four dogs, and is a soccer aficionado going on thirty years.

Susan B. Cardin has been teaching elementary school for eleven years. She has taught and worked with children from four years of age to children in the fourth grade. Completing her master's degree in early childhood education, she has been teaching in an inclusive public school program for children who are deaf and hard-of-hearing.

Jeannelle Carlisle has been teaching reading and language arts for the past fifteen years. A veteran teacher, she recently earned a master's degree in middle grades education from The University of Georgia. She is currently developing an English as a second language program for the school system in Banks County, Georgia. Carlisle frequently serves as a mentor for both new teachers and students who are placed at risk.

R. C. Carter is a social studies teacher and the Coordinated Vocational Academic Education coordinator at Winder-Barrow High School in Winder, Georgia. He earned an undergraduate history degree in 1972 at Southern Illinois University and a master of arts in teaching from Piedmont College in August of 2001.

Louis A. Castenell, Jr., has served as dean of the College of Education at The University of Georgia since 1999. Castenell also served as acting associate provost for institutional diversity for The University of Georgia. Castenell has authored or edited books on higher education leadership and received the 2002 Distinguished Alumni Award for Achievement in Higher Education from the University of Illinois.

Aaron Childers teaches technology for sixth, seventh, and eighth graders at Palmer Middle School in the Cobb County public schools in Georgia. He earned a bachelor of science degree in education from The University of Georgia.

Rachel Davis-Haley is an assistant professor in the Department of Elementary Education at The University of Georgia. Her primary research interests are in documenting the school experiences of African American adolescent females.

Lola Finn began her teaching career in 1952 teaching first through eighth grades in a one-room school house and continued until her retirement in 1994. She was an elementary school principal for seventeen years. Finn serves as an adjunct university instructor and teaches elementary teaching methods classes as well as supervising student teachers.

Yvette Q. Getch is an associate professor in the Department of Counseling and Human Development Services at The University of Georgia. Getch's primary areas of research include developing advocacy skills training materials for students who have disabilities or chronic illnesses. She has coauthored training materials for school personnel to assist in the management of asthma in early education environments.

Michelle Graham holds a master's degree in social work, a master's of science degree in therapy, and a doctoral degree in social work. Her areas of research and interest include medical social work, childhood bereavement, and social work education. She currently works for the Council on Social Work Education.

David K. Grant has worked in special education since 1992. As a Peace Corps Fellow, he earned an M.S. and Ph.D. in special education and international education from the Rossier School of Education at the University of Southern California. He taught students classified as severely emotionally and behaviorally disordered at the Sumter Youth Development Center near Americus, Georgia. He is currently working for Solano County Office of Education in northern California as an assisstive technology specialist. In addition, he is a composer who has produced a CD based on the lives of incarcerated students, "Songs from the Big House" as well as an audio book, "Out of the Blue, the Disabled Jr. Lifeguards of Mexico," based on his doctoral research in coastal Oaxaca, Mexico.

Tarek C. Grantham is an assistant professor in the Department of Educational Psychology at The University of Georgia. He teaches courses in the Gifted and Creative Education Program and his research focuses on underrepresentation and underachievement among diverse youth, particularly African Americans. Grantham serves on the Education Commission of the National Association for Gifted Children (NAGC) and is a member of the National Association for the Education of Young Children.

Claire E. Hamilton is an associate professor of early childhood education at The University of Georgia. She provides training to child care providers working with homeless children and has served on the board of the Nancy Travis House, a program providing child care resources for homeless families in Athens, Georgia, since 1994.

Jennifer Hargrove is a doctoral student in the Department of Elementary Education at The University of Georgia. Her research interests include learning through play and early literacy assessment of children preschool through age six. She lives in Athens, Georgia, and is a kindergarten teacher at Alps Road Elementary School.

Thomas P. Hébert is an associate professor of educational psychology in the College of Education at The University of Georgia. He teaches graduate courses in gifted and creative education and is a research fellow for the Torrance Center for Creative Studies. His research interests include counseling issues, underachievement in high-ability students, and problems faced by gifted young men.

Patricia M. Hentenaar graduated from Binghamton University with a B.A. in psychology and The University of Georgia with an M.S. in special education. She has worked for three school districts in Georgia and has currently held her position at Murray O. Kennedy Elementary School in Winder, Georgia, for thirteen years. She is an interrelated special education teacher and special education staffing coordinator.

Sylvia Hutchinson holds a master's degree and Ph.D. in reading education. Her areas of research and interest include children's literature, and faculty support and development in higher education. She is a professor emerita at The University of Georgia Institute of Higher Education.

Nakheung Kim is a native of Korea where he taught kindergarten for two years. He received his master's degree in curriculum and instruction from Pennsylvania State University. He is currently pursuing his doctoral degree in early childhood education at The University of Georgia. His research interests include the professional development of early childhood teachers. He is married with a three-year-old son.

Linda A. Long earned her doctoral degree in educational psychology from The University of Georgia. She has taught university courses as part of the teacher education program and conducted research focusing on achievement issues of gifted minority school children. Her specific research interests include counseling, social emotional development, achievement motivation, and family and school issues of African American students. She currently works in private practice as a psychotherapist and as a consultant with state agencies and the judicial system concerning interventions with children and families.

Linda Lord is a third-grade teacher at Murray O. Kennedy Elementary School in Barrow County, Georgia. After receiving her doctoral degree in elementary education from The University of Georgia, she returned to the public school classroom. She has eight years of teaching experience.

Rebecca Mann graduated from The University of Georgia with a B.S. degree in early childhood education. She is currently working on a graduate degree.

JoAnn Marshall holds a baccalaureate degree in English from the University of Alabama and is pursuing a master's degree in management of nonprofit organizations at The University of Georgia. In the future, she hopes to work with nonprofit organizations that serve children.

Carson McCutcheon graduated from The University of Georgia with a bachelor's degree in elementary education. She stayed on at The University of Georgia to receive her master's in early childhood education while teaching part time in a remedial education program for elementary school students. She currently teaches third grade in Augusta, Georgia.

Inore G. Mendoza is currently pursuing her undergraduate degree in nursing at the Medical College of Georgia. She is a native of the Philippines and moved to the United States when she was in elementary school.

Denise S. Mewborn is an associate professor of mathematics education at The University of Georgia. Her research addresses preservice elementary teachers' sense-making practices in the mathematics classroom and the role that teachers' mathematical content knowledge plays in the crafting of their instructional practices. She teaches mathematics methods courses for preservice and in-service elementary teachers and graduate courses in mathematics teacher education.

Stacey Neuharth-Pritchett is an associate professor of elementary education at The University of Georgia. She teaches in a teacher preparation program that specializes in teachers of prekindergarten to second grade. Her research interests include children's early academic performance in schools, transition to school issues for children in Head Start, and chronic health conditions of young children.

Sharon E. Nichols is an associate professor of science education at the University of Alabama. She is coauthor of an elementary science casebook and has recently conducted collaborative research in the Philippines under the auspices of the Spencer Small Research Grants Program.

Pat Nickell is a retired university faculty member who specialized in social science education. She has also had an extensive and rewarding career as a public schoolteacher and central office administrator.

P. Elizabeth Pate received her Ph.D. in curriculum and instruction from Texas A&M University. She is an associate professor in the Middle School Program at The University of Georgia. Her research and teaching interests focus on democratic and academic community learning.

Beverly D. Payne recently retired from The University of Georgia as a member of the elementary education faculty. For more than twenty years, she coordinated the early childhood education program. Her research interests include teacher education, with a particular focus on the role that teacher thought and affective traits play in teacher competence; and student variables that may interact in the instructional setting, in particular, test anxiety and being placed at risk.

Victoria Person is a second-grade teacher at Fowler Drive Elementary School in Athens, Georgia. She is an advocate for young children and frequently serves as a mentor for new teachers.

Matthew P. Quirk graduated in 1999 from Penn State University with a bachelor of science degree in elementary education. He is currently working on his Ph.D. in educational psychology at The University of Georgia. His research interest in early reading development has lead him to teach an experimental remedial reading program to second-grade students in the Athens, Georgia, area over the past two years.

Julia Reguero de Atiles is a faculty member with a joint appointment in the Department of Elementary Education and the Department of Child and Family Development at The University of Georgia. She is the coordinator of the Prekindergarten to Second Grade Emphasis Teacher Education Program. She was born and raised in Puerto Rico. Her research interests center on second language acquisition and teacher education issues for students whose first language is not English.

Judith C. Reiff retired from The University of Georgia in 2002 from the Department of Elementary Education. Her research interests include diversity and learning styles as they relate to instruction, and multicultural teacher education. She is the recipient of a 1998 Josiah Meigs Award for Excellence in Teaching, the highest university recognition for distinguished teaching, and a College of Education award for outstanding teaching at The University of Georgia.

Dee Russell is an associate professor of early childhood education in the John H. Lounsbury School of Education at Georgia College and State University in Milledgeville, Georgia. His interests include developing a close and open reading of Dewey, reconsidering the history of early childhood education, and collecting books and figures of Pinocchio.

Stacy Schwartz is a Ph.D. candidate in elementary education at The University of Georgia. She has taught kindergarten, second, and fourth grades as well as teacher education classes. She was awarded a University of Georgia Outstanding Teaching Assistant Award in 2001. Her research interests include social justice, literacy, and teacher–family relationships.

Theresa Silva is a fourth-grade teacher at Casay Elementary School in the province of Antique in the Philippines. She conducts action research in her classroom and has been instrumental in developing the Casay Elementary Environmental Education and Indigenous Studies Center.

Tara Terry-Childers received her doctoral degree in school psychology from The University of Georgia. She is currently employed at The Howard School as a school psychologist.

Xernona J. Thomas, MSW, served as the homeless education coordinator in a small, metropolitan school district for three years. She provided services to children and families in schools and area homeless shelters. She served on the board of the Nancy Travis House, a program providing child care resources for homeless families in Athens, Georgia. Currently, Thomas works as an assistant school principal and social worker in a rural middle school.

Deborah J. Tippins is a professor of science and early childhood education at The University of Georgia. She is the former director of research for the National Science Teachers Association and recently spent a year in the Philippines collaborating in science education research.

Julie B. Van Soelen presently teaches seventh grade near Atlanta, Georgia. Having degrees in elementary education, middle grades education, and educational leadership, she chooses to remain a teacher–leader, mentoring novices and providing professional development through Population Connection.

Thomas Van Soelen is taking a hiatus from elementary classroom teaching to teach and coordinate in the Partnership Program within the Department of Elementary Education at The University of Georgia. His research interests include teacher collaboration, learning communities, and teacher induction programs. He currently coaches a Critical Friends Group composed of novice teachers, supporting them in their struggles with teaching and learning.

Dorothy White is an associate professor in the Department of Mathematics Education. She teaches undergraduate and graduate mathematics methods courses. Her research interests center on examining effective strategies to structure classroom discourse and its implications to equity issues in mathematics education.

CHAPTER 1

USING DIVERSE CASES
A RATIONALE AND
SUGGESTED GUIDELINES

More than 90 percent of teachers in the United States are white, middle-class females from rural or suburban backgrounds who have minimal knowledge about the contexts in which children live and the characteristics of children of different racial, economic, linguistic, and familial backgrounds. Indications are that the demographic data in the teaching force do not reflect the student population in the schools (Leavell, Cowart, & Wilhelm, 1999). The postsecondary faculty who prepare teachers are predominately white males who also have had minimal experience in urban schools. Currently, students of color comprise 30 percent of the nation's school age youth, and about 40 percent of this population will be students of color by the year 2020 (Diaz, 2001; Leavell et al., 1999). Such complexity of demographics and lack of experience with individuals with diverse backgrounds creates a near crisis for teachers and teacher educators as they attempt to explore multicultural issues with monocultural students (Banks, 2001; Delpit, 1995; Sleeter, 1993).

Research overwhelmingly supports the opinion that preservice teacher education programs, in general, do not alter student attitudes and beliefs (Neuharth-Pritchett, Reiff, & Pearson, 2001). Yet evidence indicates some teacher education programs with particular features may have an impact on particular aspects of teacher development (Larkin & Sleeter, 1995; Zeichner, 1993). Multicultural teacher education programs that infuse a multicultural perspective across the curricula have been found to be effective (Artiles & McClafferty, 1998; Wiggins & Follow, 1999). However, simply a cognitive understanding about other cultures is not sufficient to be "multiculturally competent" because this competency must also be coupled with a caring and respectful attitude (Bennett, 2001). Multicultural teacher education programs must include information on the social, political, and economic realities related to schooling (Campbell, 1996; Cannella & Reiff, 1994a, 1994b). Thus, educators need to cultivate in their preservice teachers a respect for diversity and an understanding of the responsibilities that they have as members of a pluralistic democracy (Campbell, 1996; Larkin & Sleeter,

Today's complex school demographics present instructional challenges for teachers, especially when teaching students whose cultural backgrounds differ from their own.

1995). Teachers need to be educated to promote democratic principles and to create learning environments for all students regardless of the students' ethnicity, racial identity, or socioeconomic status (Grant, 1994; Sleeter & Grant, 1999).

A means for understanding diversity and promoting cultural competence is through "cultural therapy, a process of bringing one's own culture—assumptions, goals, values, beliefs, and communicative models—to a level of awareness that permits one to perceive it as a potential bias in social interaction and in the acquisition or transmission of skills and knowledge. Cultural therapy is a means of consciousness-raising to make explicit unequal power relationships in the classroom, the school, and the larger society" (Bennett, 2001, p. 198). Teachers who are able to make connections with their students are usually more aware of "how their cultural orientations and predispositions, and those of students, influence their classroom teaching" (Powell, 1997, p. 467). Social class, race, gender, religion, language, and ethnicity are integral components of everyone's cultural composition.

As researchers Neuharth-Pritchett and colleagues (2001) and Butte (1999) note, preservice and in-service students must strive to develop a complex definition of diversity. Within this text, we broadly define multicultural education to include such components as race, culture, language, socioeconomic status, na-

tional or ethnic origin, religion, gender, special needs, social conditions, fam
configurations, age, geographic variation, sexual orientation, and academic abilities and achievement. We are purposefully broadly inclusive in our definition of
diversity because in our own experience with teacher education programs we find
that multicultural education often is only discussed in terms of race or ethnicity.
Although these two elements of diversity are important to consider, so are the
many other characteristics of students that drive the context in which they are
schooled. Too often, we talk about diversity in isolated ways and neglect the complex interactions of many elements of our diverse backgrounds. Therefore,
teacher preparation programs must emphasize how these components intersect
rather than treating them in isolation as mutually exclusive characteristics. Multicultural teacher preparation programs must respond to the demographics in the
school and the nation, recognize the importance of a global connection, become
more inclusive of groups previously ignored, and provide opportunities for preservice and in-service students to become multiculturally literate and competent.

Our society was founded on democratic principles that explicitly respect
and value individual differences and equality. Schools are institutions that either
inhibit or promote the strengths of citizens in a democratic society (Banks, 1994;
Gollnick & Chinn, 1998). Therefore, teachers should be educated to promote
the principles of equality and justice by creating a learning environment for all
students, regardless of ethnic group, racial identity, or socioeconomic status
(Banks, 1994; Sleeter & Grant, 1999).

Multiple strategies are needed to infuse multicultural education, cognitive
learning, and affective understanding into coursework and teacher preparation
programs (Vaughn, 2002). One approach to multicultural education is the implementation of case-based instruction. As Wasserman (1994) noted, "effective
case method teaching allows students to grow away from a desperate quest for
right answers" (p. 611). Incorporating the use of cases or stories is a pedagogi-
cally effective approach (Kagan, 1993) to promote multicultural education in the
broad sense. Kowalski, Weaver, and Henson (1990) define a case as a description
of a real or realistic situation that incorporates the facts needed to clarify and
identify a solution to the situation presented. When teacher educators model
culturally responsive pedagogy and discuss issues of diversity through case-based
instruction, preservice and in-service teachers experience heightened awareness
and direct involvement in multicultural issues. Cases engage students in active
learning to analyze and to problem solve realistic situations in classrooms. The
cases presented in this text often do not have endings. The cases raise questions,
connect with theory, and are effective for reducing student resistance related to
diversity issues through self-awareness, discussion, and analysis (Kagan, 1990).

Teachers make numerous decisions every day about a variety of topics
without the opportunity to consult the literature or peers. Cases are especially
important in teacher education because they provide a safe environment for the
instructor and students to analyze and problem solve complex and diverse situations with other learners (Teitel, 1996). "By deconstructing their own beliefs and

their practices, students and faculty, alike, may begin the
nceptualizing schooling so that it values the uniqueness and
individuals" (Neuharth-Pritchett et al., 2001, p. 268).
    e of law has used cases since the 1880s; business since the
    psychology, medicine, and public policy for several decades
(Kagan, 1990; Tippins, Koballa, & Payne, 2002). How the cases are used in these
fields differs in relation to the field's purpose, content, and method (Merseth,
1991). In a 1986 report from the Carnegie Task Force on Teaching, *A Nation Prepared: Teachers for the Twenty-First Century*, it was recommended that teacher education programs consider incorporating cases into instruction because of their
benefits. In the past decade case-based instruction has become common in teacher
education and has been proven to be an effective strategy in the classroom (Kagan,
1993; Shulman, 1992; Silverman, Welty, & Lyon, 1996; Tippins et al., 2002).

PHILOSOPHICAL BASIS

The philosophical premise of this elementary diversity casebook is consistent
with the trend of preparing elementary education teachers to function in a constructivist learning environment. Like all learners, teachers need to construct
their own knowledge and theories of learning that are developmental and that
are based on experience, reflection, interaction with others, and exposure to effective teaching models (Lundeberg & Scheurman, 1997). Case-based pedagogy
can be supported by the portion of the knowledge base that asserts that teachers'
knowledge is (1) contextual, that is, situation specific; (2) interactive, informed,
and informing through interaction; and (3) speculative, because much of teachers'
work involves uncertainty (Clark & Lampert, 1986). Cases can provide situation-
specific circumstances that help teachers connect theory and practice in a
supportive, interactive environment (Ertmer, Newby, & MacDougall, 1996; Richardson & Ginter, 1998).
    The case-based approach is situated in the principles of constructivism; it
assumes to "intrinsically address cultural diversity" because "constructivist perspectives welcome the multiple voices that we must come to hear in teacher education in response to the cultural diversity in our society" (Cannella & Reiff,
1994a, p. 43). A constructivist view of teaching holds that knowledge is both
personal and social, and that meaning is constructed at the crossroads of knowledge, subject matter, and personal experience. Constructivism is comprised of a
number of characteristics (Kauchak & Eggen, 1998). One of these characteristics involves learners constructing their own understandings. Rather than the
student being the recipient of information and the teacher being the sole provider of content, the student must be an active participant engaged in the learning process. Case-based instruction is an excellent means by which to facilitate
this active engagement of the learner. Because students bring their own sets of
experiences to the learning environment, the variety of responses that result

from case discussions serve to expand the knowledge of the teacher and learners as well as their repertoires of strategies. In addition, the current understanding and knowledge base that a student brings to the learning environment drives the direction, breadth, and depth of the new knowledge gained. Because active learning does not take place in isolation, cases promote interaction among students with regard to problem solving complex issues about diversity. Learning occurs in the context of current understanding and is facilitated by social interaction students share their ideas with peers, both in small groups and within the total society of the classroom while working with authentic tasks, problems, and questions. Constructivist approaches using cases also serve to create meaningful or authentic learning opportunities for students. By being able to place themselves in the case situations, students may engage in critical reflection that may ultimately influence their teaching practices (Harrington, Quinn-Leering, & Hodson, 1996). Through critical reflection preservice teachers may reinvent teacher education programs although the field must focus on incremental steps toward that goal (McIntyre, 1997).

ADVANTAGES OF CASE-BASED INSTRUCTION

The use of case-based instruction in teacher education has been advanced as a meaningful way to facilitate learning and engage students (Barnett, 1998; Moje & Wade, 1997). Merseth (1991) highlighted advantages to case-based instruction. Case-based instruction helps students develop skills in critical analysis and problem solving through active listening and social exchange of ideas (Harrington, 1995). The development of these critical-analysis skills provides a foundation for teachers to become effective decision makers in practice. Cases help students reflect on the potential incongruence of theory and practice with regard to diversity issues.

Early childhood teacher education programs and public schools must capitalize on opportunities using students' formative experiences, offering support throughout their coursework and field placements, in order to assist students in their conceptualization and continued reflection on multicultural education (Neuharth-Pritchett et al., 2001). Too often, students of another culture are perceived by preservice teachers to be dysfunctional or placed at risk (Larkin & Sleeter, 1995). This perception is sometimes heightened by low expectations of students by school-based teachers and administrators, inappropriate curriculum and testing, ability grouping, and culturally irrelevant strategies. Ultimately, these factors may contribute to students' failing academically, feeling powerless, becoming unmotivated, and even becoming angry (Baruth & Manning, 1996; Kuykendall, 1992). Knowing students, especially their culture, is essential preparation for successful learning. Cases are an excellent means by which to accomplish this goal. Yet with the following caution: One example or situation does not allow for a generalization to be made to the larger diverse population.

Another advantage to case-based instruction is that students become involved in their own learning. Students develop ownership of their learning through the preparation, analysis, and discussion of the case and the resultant problem solving that stems from such involvement. The ultimate advantage is that case-based instruction promotes the creation of a community of learners. As Silverman and colleagues (1996) note, "using case-method teaching has demonstrated that new teachers go into their own classroom more ready to deal with the myriad of problems they must face if as students they have prepared seriously for case discussions by taking the time to analyze the cases and to develop solutions based on the educational theory and have taken part in case discussions with both thoughtful contributions and active listening" (p. xxiv).

Other specific advantages of case-based instruction are related to multicultural education (Allain & Pettus, 1998). One advantage is the development of the students' understanding and awareness of issues and challenges related to diversity and multicultural education. Case-based instruction provides prospective teachers with simulated experiences for the development of critical-thinking and problem-solving abilities when working with diverse groups of students. Such experiences may also help preservice and in-service teachers critique their concepts, attitudes, and skills for helping students function in a multicultural society. These skills and attitudes help teachers maximize learning opportunities for all of their current or future students.

THE STRUCTURE OF THIS TEXT

Each case in this book on diversity is preceded by an abstract briefly summarizing the case. Individual chapters employ different ending strategies. For example, some cases are presented as unresolved dilemmas; the nature of the problem may suggest many solutions. Other cases are more finalized; a situation is presented and the action by the teacher is reported. Students and instructors can evaluate the choices that the characters in the cases made. In the open approach, guiding questions (e.g., What would you do in this situation? What is the critical incident in this case?) are posed and the direction of the case's merit is left to the instructor and students.

Cases conclude with thoughtful Questions for Reflection and Discussion for individual consideration and group discussion. Instructor and students are encouraged to identify and problem solve the cases for the multiple layers of issues and challenges that center on diversity. The cases are constructed in such a way that the student is a responsible and an active learner. After reading a case several times, the students must analyze the issue(s), consider appropriate theories and diverse perspectives on the issue(s), and contemplate solutions. Then, with others, the student should engage in dialogue that collectively represents the critical thinking and analysis of their own thoughts as well as that of the group. The editors want to emphasize that we do not want to characterize the

Case-based instruction provides prospective teachers with simulated experience for the development of critical-thinking and problem-solving skills when working with diverse classrooms.

cases as "problems" but rather as challenges and diverse situations for the teacher and students to consider. Although each case describes the experiences of a particular child, a classroom, or a school, by no means should a generalization be made to all members of the group represented. The use of cases in classroom teaching often sways the teacher from didactic presentation; instead the teacher serves as a facilitator to foster understanding, to ask questions, to provide bridging statements, to sustain the flow of discussion, and to recognize students' contributions. The diversity issues within the cases in this text represent classrooms and current scenarios in classrooms, and they should be viewed as opportunities for students and teachers to gain life experiences.

GUIDELINES FOR THE USE OF CASES

In our own experiences using cases in our preservice and graduate teacher preparation programs, we have developed some guidelines for the use of cases. The

case facilitator provides the context for the cases, encourages student participation and analysis, presents relevant research and theory, and summarizes the
discussion and alternative solutions. We believe that there should be some structure to allow the facilitator to guide the learners but that there is no "one right
way" for case analyses or discussions to occur. Some additional specific suggestions for the use of cases are as follows:

1. Brainstorm with the class guidelines for group discussions that facilitate an
   accepting and democratic environment.
2. Be explicit about expectations for the preparation and discussion of each case.
3. Provide a theoretical framework and relevant research for the particular
   aspects of diversity presented in the case. This may include a minilecture
   on the background of the topical area presented in the case, which may
   take place either at the beginning or end of the case discussion.
4. Provide additional readings (such as those suggested at the end of given
   cases or other scholarly material) and expect students to research the case
   topic to augment the case discussion.
5. Vary the classroom configurations or physical space (including tables and
   chairs) to help facilitate discussion of the cases, to encourage dialogue
   among students, and to allow for the participation of all students.
6. Vary the grouping arrangement for discussion of the case. For example, develop groups with a combination of more-experienced and less-experienced
   teachers, or divide groups based on their "own" diverse characteristics (e.g.,
   grade level taught, marital status, geographic location, etc.). Provide some
   background about active listening and respect for all shared opinions among
   the students.
7. Include activities along with discussion. Some examples include role-playing
   the characters in the case to simulate and extend that which was presented
   in the case, or visual representations of the case (e.g., charts, timelines,
   pros and cons, response letters to the main character of the case). A sample
   set of questions, outline for analysis strategies for the cases, and potential
   probing questions would also be helpful for both the students and teacher.
8. Summarize and explain all the different perspectives the case represents
   that the students generated. Engage in dialogue about these perspectives.
   The facilitator should guide the discussion and encourage the conversation among the students but not dominate the analysis of the case or the
   resultant solutions to the case.
9. Bring closure to the case with the construction of realistic solutions and a
   discussion of possible consequences of each solution for the different individuals represented in the case.
10. Obtain additional feedback on the process of the case discussion and activi-
    ties. One suggestion might be a "quick-write," in which the students reveal
    the knowledge they gained, summarizing what they learned or experienced,
    both affectively and cognitively.

Most chapters conclude with resources, such as a list of scholarly readings, information on professional organizations relevant to the case, or web sites. The goal of variation in the case presentation is to maintain the interest of readers of the text as well as to promote the text as one that may be used in a number of different contexts.

SUMMARY

Focusing on the advantages previously summarized, this diversity casebook is an excellent supplement to textbooks for courses in teacher preparation, special education, social work, or other professional coursework where individuals are preparing to work with children and families. This book presents a collection of cases that explores a wide range of diversity issues. The unique contributions of this book include (1) a variety of perspectives in the stories of authors for the given chapters, (2) a wide-range continuum of diversity issues, and (3) specific tailoring of the diversity cases to the elementary school level (prekindergarten to fifth grade). The cases may stand alone, but we have organized them around related themes in six chapters, including culture, academic performance and expectations, safety and prosocial behaviors, social issues, special needs, and the family. The cases present diverse situations teachers and others have experienced with young children and in elementary classrooms. The cases were written by teacher educators, public and private school teachers, administrators, graduate students, undergraduate preservice teacher education students, student teachers, psychologists, clinicians, social workers, and parents. Thus, the cases are written from at least one perspective of the aforementioned groups. Yet alternative perspectives may be incorporated in each case depending on the experiences of the individual reader and the resultant dialogue.

We hope that this collection of cases will assist those interested in the field of education to truly understand the students with whom they work. We further hope that it will foster cultural sensitivity of those who work with our children by enabling those who use the cases to critically reflect on their beliefs and practices. By using a case approach, we hope to represent the diversity that exists in our schools and the richness that it brings.

REFERENCES

Allain, V., & Pettus, A. (1998). *Teaching diverse students: Preparing with cases.* Bloomington, IN: Phi Delta Kappa Educational Foundation.

Artiles, A. J., & McClafferty, K. (1998). Learning to teach culturally diverse learners: Charting change in preservice teachers' thinking about effective teaching. *The Elementary School Journal, 98*(3), 189–220.

Banks, J. (1994). *An introduction to multicultural education.* Boston: Allyn & Bacon.

Banks, J. (2001). Multicultural education: Goals, possibilities, and challenges. In C. Diaz (Ed.), *Multicultural education for the twenty-first century* (pp. 11–22). New York: Longman.

Barnett, C. (1998). Mathematics teaching cases as a catalyst for informed strategic inquiry. *Teaching and Teacher Education, 14*(1), 81–93.

Baruth, L., & Manning, L. (1996). *Multicultural education of children and adolescents* (2nd ed.). Needham Heights, MA: Simon & Schuster.

Bennett, C. (2001). Genres of research in multicultural education. *Review of Educational Research, 71*(2), 171–217.

Butte, G. (1999). *Multicultural education: Raising consciousness.* Belmont, CA: Wadsworth.

Campbell, D. (1996). *Choosing democracy: A practical guide to multicultural education.* Englewood Cliffs, NJ: Prentice Hall.

Canella, G. A., & Reiff, J. C. (1994a). Preparing teachers for cultural diversity: Constructivist orientations. *Action in Teacher Education, 16*(3), 37–45.

Canella, G. A., & Reiff, J. C. (1994b). Teacher preparation for diversity. *Equity and Excellence in Education, 27*(3), 28–33.

Clark, C., & Lampert, M. (1986). The study of teacher thinking: Implications for teacher education. *Journal of Teacher Education, 37*(5), 27–31.

Delpit, L. (1995). *Other people's children.* New York: The New Press.

Diaz, C. (2001). The third millennium. In C. Diaz (Ed.), *Multicultural education for the twenty-first century* (pp. 11–22). New York: Longman.

Ertmer, P. A., Newby, T. J., & MacDougall, M. (1996). Students' responses and approaches to case-based instruction: The role of reflective self-regulation. *American Educational Research Journal, 33*(3), 719–752.

Gollnick, D., & Chinn, P. (1998). *Multicultural education in a pluralistic society.* Columbus, OH: Charles Merrill.

Grant, C. A. (1994). Best practices in teacher preparation for urban schools: Lessons from the multicultural teacher education literature. *Action in Teacher Education, 16*(3), 1–18.

Harrington, H. L. (1995). Fostering reasoned decisions: Case-based pedagogy and the professional development of teachers. *Teaching and Teacher Education, 11*(3), 203–214.

Harrington, H. L., Quinn-Leering, K., & Hodson, L. (1996). Written case analyses and critical reflection. *Teaching and Teacher Education, 12*(1), 25–37.

Kagan, D. M. (1990). Ways of evaluating teacher cognition: Inferences concerning the Goldilocks principle. *Review of Educational Research, 60*(3), 19–69.

Kagan, D. M. (1993). Contexts for the use of classroom cases. *American Educational Research Journal, 30*(4), 703–723.

Kauchak, D., & Eggen, P. (1998). *Learning and teaching: Research-based methods* (3rd ed.). Boston: Allyn & Bacon.

Kowalski, T. J., Weaver, R. A., & Henson, K. T. (1990). *Case studies on teaching.* New York: Longman.

Kuykendall, C. (1992). *From rage to hope: Strategies for reclaiming Black and Hispanic students.* Bloomington, IN: National Education Service.

Larkin, J. M., & Sleeter, C. E. (1995). *Developing multicultural teacher education curricula.* Albany: State University of New York Press.

Leavell, A., Cowart, M., & Wilhelm, R. (1999). Strategies for preparing culturally responsive teachers. *Equity and Excellence in Education, 32*(1), 64–71.

Lundeberg, M. A., & Scheurman, G. (1997). Looking means seeing more: Developing pedagogical knowledge through case analysis. *Teaching and Teacher Education, 13*(8), 783–797.

McIntyre, A. (1997). Constructing an image of a white teacher. *Teachers College Record, 98*(4), 653–681.

Merseth, K. (1991). *The case for cases in teacher education.* Washington, DC: American Association for Higher Education.

Moje, E. B., & Wade, S. E. (1997). What case discussions reveal about teacher thinking. *Teaching and Teacher Education, 13*(7), 691–712.

Neuharth-Pritchett, S., Reiff, J. C., & Pearson, C. (2001). Through the eyes of preservice teachers: Implications for the multicultural journey from teacher education. *Journal of Research in Childhood Education, 15*(2), 256–279.

Powell, R. (1997). Then the beauty emerges: A longitudinal case study of culturally relevant teaching. *Teaching and Teacher Education, 13*(5), 467–484.

Richardson, W. D., & Ginter, P. M. (1998). Using living cases to teach the strategic planning process. *Journal of Education for Business, 73,* 269–273.

Schulman, J. H. (Ed.). (1992). *Case methods in teacher education.* New York: Teachers College Press.

Silverman, R., Welty, W., & Lyon, S. (1996). *Case studies for teacher problem solving* (2nd ed.). New York: McGraw Hill.

Sleeter, C. E. (1993). How white teacher construct race. In C. McCarthy & W. Crinclow (Eds.), *Race, identity, and representation in education* (pp. 157–171). New York: Routledge.

Sleeter, C. E., & Grant, C. (1999). *Making choices for multicultural education: Five approaches to race, class, and gender.* New York: Merrill.

Teitel, L. (1996). Getting down to cases. *Contemporary Education, 67*(4), 200–205.

Tippins, D., Koballa, T., & Payne, B. (2002). *Learning from cases: Unraveling the complexities of elementary science teaching.* Boston: Allyn & Bacon.

Vaughn, W. (2002). Teaching for diversity and social justice: Preservice teachers engage in assignments to promote multicultural education. *Journal of Professional Studies, 9*(2), 61–69.

Wasserman, S. (1994). Using cases to study teaching. *Phi Delta Kappan, 75*(8), 602–604, 606–608, 610–611.

Wiggins, R., & Follow, E. (1999). Development of knowledge, attitudes, and commitment to teach diverse student populations. *Journal of Teacher Education, 50*(2), 94–105.

Zeichner, K. M. (1993). Traditions of practice in U.S. preservice teacher education programs. *Teaching and Teacher Education, 9*(1), 1–13.

CHAPTER 2

CULTURE

> Multicultural education is necessary to help all of the nation's future citizens acquire the knowledge, attitudes, and skills needed to survive in the twenty-first century. Nothing less than the nation's survival is at stake. (Diaz, 2001, p. 20)

Classrooms have become more diverse resulting in teachers being responsible for children with linguistic, economic, cultural, religious, and racial commonalities as well as differences. Teachers who are culturally responsive understand knowledge as social construction, think critically about curriculum and events, challenge their students to view concepts and events from diverse perspectives, and are learners with their students about themselves and others. "Knowledge reflects the social context in which it is created and…has normative and value assumptions" (Diaz, 2001, p. 18). The following cases address realistic situations in our society that prospective teachers need to recognize, consider critically, and problem solve with others who can provide different viewpoints. The process of making decisions regarding the various cases can be adapted to the classroom when the teacher problem solves with the students' personal and societal issues. "Those of us who are committed to teaching preservice teachers about multicultural issues must find ways to enable those privileged students to explore their own beliefs, attitudes, life experiences, and privileges in order to develop new perspectives about themselves and about others who are not members of the dominant culture" (Vaughn, 2002, p. 62). Case-based instruction provides a forum for teachers and students to reflect, deconstruct, and reconstruct their attitudes and beliefs while applying theory and research to practice.

A reflective case describes the adjustments and difficulties of an international college student from Puerto Rico, specifically as it relates to linguistic differences. Julia Reguero de Atiles's experiences and thoughtful suggestions are useful to teachers at all grade levels.

An increasing number of international students are enrolling in elementary classrooms with varying linguistic and cultural differences. Teachers are searching for strategies to accommodate their individual needs. Jennifer W. Anthony details her own classroom and the strategies she uses to facilitate their in-clusion in the many school activities. Jennifer's open communication with families and her ideas for parent participation attest to her commitment to cre-ating a welcoming environment for everyone. Through the numerous activities that Jennifer describes, the families and students all feel valued and appreciated.

Another reflective case is written by Stephanie Bales who remembers her experiences growing up in a small southern town through her recollections as a high school student during integration. This case provides a framework for class members to reflect on their own life experiences, how their experiences affected them, and how they changed because of those particular experiences.

Rachel Davis-Haley and Louis A. Castenell, Jr., articulate the dilemma in a Catholic school related to two minority high academic achievers, Eboni and Carlos, and a controversial reading assignment of *The Adventures of Huckleberry Finn*. A primary question involves whether the school administrators and faculty took appropriate actions in dealing with the situation.

An international dilemma is the collision of economics and ecology. The setting for the next case by Theresa Silva, Sharon E. Nichols, and Deborah J. Tippins is the Philippines. Specifically, tension occurs when a child, Antonio, is confronted with the knowledge from his fourth-grade teacher, Perla, about the urgency to save trees to help the environment; however, Antonio's father is a farmer who cuts down trees to make a living by making and selling charcoal in order to have money to buy food. The authors of the case reminds us that the values, language, and struggles of children in poverty may conflict with the cur-riculum in the elementary school.

Thomas Van Soelen's timely case, "Domestic Discrimination," focuses on the harassment Amena, a Muslim girl, faced after September 11, 2001.

Inore G. Mendoza, a nursing candidate, describes her "Elementary Edu-cation Experience" as a student from Manila, the Philippines, entering an inner-city school in Marietta, Georgia, as a fifth grader. She honestly describes her academic and personal experiences during that year. Mendoza's family moved at the end of her fifth-grade year, and she started middle school in a suburban setting.

Thomas and Julie B. Van Soelen focus on the topic of bullying and teasing; unfortunately, this issue is becoming more prevalent and serious in the elemen-tary schools. Than, a Vietnamese American fourth grader, is ridiculed but the di-lemma becomes more complicated because of the academic consequences for Than and the other children involved.

REFERENCES

Diaz, C. (2001). The third millennium. In C. Diaz (Ed.), *Multicultural education for the twenty-first century* (pp. 11–22). New York: Longman.
Vaughn, W. (2002). Teaching for diversity and social justice: Preservice teachers engage in assign-ments to promote multicultural education. *Journal of Professional Studies, 9*(2), 61–69.

CASES

CASE 2.1

LANGUAGE
A Part of Who You Are

Julia Reguero de Atiles

Born and raised in Puerto Rico, the author considers the challenges of adapting to another language and culture at age eighteen. Limitations brought forward by lack of proficiency in English include feelings of inadequacy and isolation. Some customs and cultural differences are discussed. The role of language in life is presented as more than a form of communication. Can you identify defining moments in Julia's adaptation to another culture? What factors contributed to her success?

I vividly remember that fall. I was eighteen years old, and, like many adolescents, I was looking forward to moving away from home—far away from all the rules, regulations about dating, and curfews strictly set by my dad. It did not matter that I was moving into a dorm room and starting college in a few days. What mattered most was that I would be in Virginia and my parents would be in Puerto Rico with the rest of my family where I had grown up.

I had studied English since I was in the first grade. It was a subject, just like math, Spanish, science, and social studies at my school. I was excited about college life and not at all worried about having to speak in English or not knowing a single person on campus. Then the airport shuttle left with my parents in it and there I stood not sure of whether I could find my way back to my dorm room. I had a sinking feeling inside. I wanted to cry, but I was much too proud to let my parents see me do that as they waved good-bye.

Classrooms have become more diverse, resulting in teachers being responsible for the education of children with linguistic, economic, cultural, religious, and racial differences.

My interest and determination to do well in my new environment carried me through. I was a very stubborn adolescent and giving in was not an option. I certainly experienced many feelings of inadequacy, learned quickly that I barely knew English, and felt lonely and unable to communicate. We had to introduce ourselves during the first meeting called by our resident advisor. I did not hear a thing the other girls mentioned. I was petrified thinking about what I would say and how I would say it when it was my turn.

The girls in the rooms next to mine and across the hall were very nice and one of them had a lot of interest in Spanish. That gave me a sense of relief because I could ask her to help me with English, and I volunteered to help her with Spanish. Even with this extra practice, I hated the fact that I could not follow their conversations very well. They would ask me questions and I would be embarrassed to ask repeatedly "what?" or "say that again, please?" After many attempts to guess what they were asking, I would nod and say "yes" and smile. They would exclaim "yes!" and I would say "yes" again but had no idea whether "yes" was the right answer or not.

My friends figured out I was not understanding and stopped directing questions at me or asked very simple ones. The first few weeks were horrible. They were much more than I had bargained for in my "I can conquer it all" adolescent thinking. My daily experiences and difficulties with the English language were very lonely and, at times, very isolating.

Exam time came and I was scared to death. I studied hard. I could read and understand very well, but my class notes were not great and note taking in English was difficult for me. At times I would write myself notes in Spanish because I was still translating in my mind instead of thinking in English. I wasted a lot of time translating and missed half of the lecture information. I was scared that after all the studying I had done I would take a test and not understand what I was being asked, even when I probably knew the answer. I was terrified of misinterpreting. I felt especially inadequate when I had to ask each of my teachers whether it would be OK if I brought my Spanish–English dictionary to the exam—my security blanket. My accent must have been so strong and my English grammar so pathetic that they all agreed I could use it.

Time passed and my English skills progressed. I begged the girls in the dorm to please tell me when I said things incorrectly. After all, how was I supposed to learn if no one pointed out the mistakes? But they did not always do that. They thought it was cute that I mispronounced some words or conjugated verbs incorrectly; however, they edited my papers and offered their friendship.

I knew deep down that if I did not speak up in my limited English I would be unable to develop a social support system of friends. I would be more lonely. I started putting my embarrassment aside and spoke, or at least made an attempt to speak. I was grateful that most people tried to understand what I was saying and responded accordingly. I started to feel that I belonged there.

The semester passed. I was getting Cs and above, and I was happy with those, even though I really wanted the straight As I was accustomed to in high school. I thought that I was understanding more and more, and I was talking more and more. As my confidence increased I stopped carrying my Spanish–English dictionary with me and laughed when my dorm room friends exclaimed, "Oh no, you are losing your accent!"

It has been almost two decades since I came to the United States. I still feel apprehensive and inadequate at times. My disadvantage now is that most people think I am proficient in English. I am no longer expected to have difficulties. Yet I do!

I could tell you many stories that make me laugh now about the consequences of my misinterpretations of the English language. I did many dumb things simply because I did not understand or did not know. However, I prefer to tell you a little bit more about what I have learned through my experiences.

I made a decision to come study in the United States, and I chose to be in an English-only environment. I felt confident before coming that I would be just fine because I had studied English in school, so at least I had some knowledge of the English language. However, this is very different from the child whose parents decide to move to a country where a different language dominates. These children don't always have the determination, the confidence, or the desire to be there. It often is not their choice but the choice of their parents. At age eighteen and with the best attitude about being immersed in a foreign language, culture, and environment, I ended up feeling very lonely, scared, inadequate, and unable to communicate. Those are very terrifying feelings, even for an adult.

Imagine what it is like for a child. Many children experience separation anxiety when they enter preschool and even elementary school. There are feelings of apprehension and concern when anyone enters a new setting. Add to those feelings and fears the stress of not speaking the language, or not being able to understand what goes on around you. It has to be overwhelming! Children may be nodding and smiling, just like I did, but they probably have the same sinking feelings inside, as I did. Others may be crying and outwardly demonstrating their fears and apprehensions. They all need warmth and understanding.

I greatly value all the knowledge I have gained about the English language. It has helped me communicate, but it has also been the vehicle by which I comprehend those around me. It is a key to understanding the culture of English speakers in the United States. Words and expressions of our language depict things that are important in our culture. Sometimes there are words that cannot be translated to another language, not with the exact same meaning. Perhaps because cultures are unique.

After I married a fellow Latin American (my husband is a native of the Dominican Republic) and had children of my own, it became very important to me that my heritage, his heritage, and our cultures be passed on to our young children. Though my children were born and are being raised in the United States, we speak Spanish at home. They have typical Latino names, Ricardo Horacio and Ana Teresa (pronounced all with short vowel sounds because in Spanish there is only one sound for the vowels, matching the English short). We eat rice and beans, yuca, platano, bacalao, and so on, just like I did when I was growing up. We are Catholics, like most Latinos. We hope to pass down the values with which we grew up, embracing familism rather than total autonomy and independence. Puerto Rican and Dominican families, like many other Latino cultures, are characterized by embracing the value of familism, a set of privileges and responsibilities pertaining to members of a given family network (Heller, 1976).

Thus, in a way my children live in two worlds! The difference between their Spanish-speaking, familistic, Latino home and their English-speaking, encouraging of independence, American society in which they live requires them to be bicultural. This is important to us because so much of who we are is defined by our language and our culture. Also, we want them to be able to communicate with their relatives, grandparents, aunts, uncles, and cousins who live in Puerto Rico and the Dominican Republic (even though many of them do speak English).

Balancing our two worlds is not always easy. So much of acceptance, fitting in, and self-esteem is determined by how people in those worlds respond to us. In my experience, I have found people who believe that the development of the child's home language interferes with the child's ability to learn and develop English language skills. Consider for example the following personal experience that I had:

> When my son, Ricardo, was three years old he was attending a preschool program along with seventeen other children. He was fully bilingual (with as much language as we may expect from a three year old), but four or five of his peers spoke absolutely no English. My son did not like his teacher, resulting in a period of silence. He refused to speak to her. She would ask him questions and he would not respond to her comments or requests. She assumed that he did not understand her. The teacher questioned me one day asking, "Are you going to stay in this country?" I was puzzled by her question but replied that we were planning to remain where we were. She then proceeded to say "you should stop speaking in Spanish to your son at home so that he can learn English." I chose to reply by simply stating that I was certain that he spoke English as well as he spoke Spanish and that I was sure he was understanding her when she spoke to him.

This example highlights many issues. As I mentioned previously, language and culture are intimately related. Byrnes and Cortéz (1992) note that disregarding a child's native language is denying a part of who the child is and the cultural background the child brings to school. There exists, as well, the possible erosion of parent–child communication, should parents believe (or take the advice) that speaking to their child in their native language is not in the best interest of their child's learning. This is especially troublesome when a child's parents are not proficient in English and the child begins speaking English at home. The significant adults in a child's life (especially parents and teachers) should encourage and support the development of the native language as well as English, so that the child may become bilingual and have access to two cultures (Byrnes & Cortéz, 1992). Research has consistently illustrated that first language influence on the second language is negligible. "The acquisition of two languages need not hamper, developmentally, the acquisition of either language" (García, 1986, p. 103). Children construct the new language in much the same way in which they learned the first language (Dulay, Burt, & Krashen, 1982). Proficiency in the first language, however, does contribute to the development of the second language (NAEYC, 1996).

Through my own experiences I learned that the process of acquiring a second language takes time; it can make you feel very self-conscious, lonely, and inhibited. I learned that through the acquisition of another language one may learn and gain understanding of the individual and culture who use it. Thus, I learned that my own native language was more than simply a form of communicating; it was rather an integral part of who I am, my heritage, and my culture. I have also learned through my studies that development of one language does not have negative implications on the development of another language. By respecting an individual's home language, one respects and acknowledges the diversity within all of us. Language is culture. As members of this society, it is our responsibility to be empathetic of those who are trying to learn our language. Furthermore, it is our job to celebrate our language differences.

QUESTIONS FOR REFLECTION AND DISCUSSION

1. Have you ever been misunderstood because the person with whom you were speaking had a very different point of view from your own? How did you feel? What problems emerged? How would you feel if you suddenly had to live in an environment where your language was not spoken? How would you cope? Can you think of how you would have felt when you were a child?

2. If you have traveled to a place where your native language was not spoken, what helped you understand the people and the environment around you? On what assistance did you rely? As a teacher, what strategies can you use to communicate with your students excluding or minimizing the role of verbal or written English? What are some of the assumptions that teachers have about children whose first language is not the mainstream language? In your experience, how have the teachers you have worked with responded and reacted to language issues in the classroom?

REFERENCES

Byrnes, D. A., & Cortéz, D. (1992). Language diversity in the classroom. In D. A. Byrnes & G. Kiger (Eds.), *Common bonds: Anti-bias teaching in a diverse society* (pp. 71–85). Wheaton, MD: Association for Childhood Education International.

Dulay, H., Burt, M., & Krashen, S. (1982). *Language two*. New York: Oxford University Press.

Garčía, E. E. (1986). Bilingual development and the education of bilingual children during early childhood. *American Journal of Education, 95*(1), 96–119.

Heller, P. L. (1976). Familism scale: Revalidation and revision. *Journal of Marriage and the Family, 38*(3), 423–429.

National Association for the Education of Young Children. (1996). NAEYC position statement: Responding to linguistic and cultural diversity—Recommendations for effective early childhood education. *Young Children, 5*(12), 4–12.

WORLD WIDE WEB RESOURCES

Teachers of English to Speakers of Other Languages (www.tesol.org)

The National Clearinghouse for English Language Acquisition and Language Instruction Educational Programs (www.ncbe.gwu.edu)

Eric Clearinghouse on Language and Linguistics (www.cal.org/ericcll/)

CASE 2.2

TEACHING ENGLISH AS A SECOND LANGUAGE
A Kindergarten Teacher's Perspective

Jennifer W. Anthony

This case presents a study of a kindergarten class of Mexican American children and their families. Each of the fourteen students is an English language learner, and each speaks Spanish as the primary or home language. The students vary greatly in their levels of Spanish and English language proficiency, just as they do in their development of skills in other areas. The author is their classroom teacher, responsible for their school learning experiences in reading, language arts, mathematics, science, and social studies. As a first-year teacher, the writing is based on first-semester reflections from a teaching journal kept on a nearly daily basis while teaching. Compare and contrast the various appropriate strategies Jennifer uses with her kindergarten class. Consider why these activities and strategies are developmentally appropriate for a diverse class of kindergarteners.

MEETING STUDENTS AND FAMILIES

During preplanning, I spent some time reviewing my new class list, along with student registration papers. Students whose primary or home language is not English register at a special center in our school system. This center is designed to meet the needs of English language learners and their families. The valuable information gained from these registration meetings is passed on to school administrators and classroom teachers. Paperwork includes family information, home language, length of time in the United States, previous school experiences, a student writing sample, a language assessment battery score, and eligibility status for English to speakers of other languages (ESOL) services.

On review of this class information, I became aware of my students' and their parents' nationalities and home languages. I used the class information to contact the students and families by mail and telephone to personally invite them to the upcoming open house at our school. Because the majority of parents indicated fluency in Spanish and only some indicated proficiency in English, I mailed a parent letter written in Spanish about the open house. I also included an invitation note just for the students. The day before the open house, I contacted someone in each child's family by phone to encourage attendance at the meeting. I was excited to make a positive introduction to the mothers, the fathers, and, in some cases, the uncles and the brothers of the students in my class.

At the open house, all students attended with at least one family member. I communicated with most parents in Spanish and smiled a lot. Almost all of the school paperwork is presented in English and Spanish, so parents may understand all of the many forms. I checked out the school's digital camera to take the children's pictures. The display screen on the camera provided immediate gratification for the students after I took their pictures. These pictures helped me match faces and names before the first day of school. I also used them to label student places on the students' "Look What We Did" bulletin board and to make calendar helper sticks.

PLANNING THE FIRST DAYS
OF KINDERGARTEN

While planning the first day of school, I referred to several professional resources (see the resources at the end of this case) and my notes from a previous experience on the first day of school in my mentor teacher's classroom. I made a daily schedule for the first day that I knew would need to be flexible. I was anxious to begin communicating with and getting to know my students. The first day plan emphasized learning and practicing important school routines.

During preplanning, I met with my mentor teacher, my paraprofessional, and the teacher with whom I am teamed. Together, we shared the resources provided by a paraprofessional. These initial meetings provided opportunities to plan meaningful collaborative activities and projects between my kindergarten class and my mentor's first-grade class and also between the other two kindergarten classes. Both of these other two classes have a more mixed racial and linguistic population than does my class, so I was excited about the social learning opportunities that would likely stem from differences in language proficiencies and background experiences among the children.

Two collaborative activities planned for the first weeks of school between the neighboring first-grade class and my class focused on the outdoor garden beside our classrooms. First, two native Spanish speaking "tour guides" from the first-grade class would take my students on a tour of the garden, explaining their work in creating the garden the past spring. The other project would extend several weeks. From a terrific resource on the World Wide Web (Journey North, www.learner.org/jnorth/), we learned about a monarch butterfly migration project involving students in Canada, the United States, and Mexico. My mentor and I planned to have a shared bilingual literature experience once a week with our two classes. We planned to read a selection (related in some way to current topics of study) in English and Spanish and possibly provide a literature extension activity in which the two classes could interact together.

My team kindergarten teacher, our paraprofessional, and I discussed having interactive experiences once a week to encourage social development between the two groups of students and also to reinforce language arts objectives for the week. We planned a time for these "Fun Friday" activities in our class schedules so we would remember our ideas during busy planning times.

THE CHILDREN ARRIVE FOR THE FIRST DAYS OF KINDERGARTEN

After working with and getting to know the children for two days, I was pleased with their adjustment as a group to school. The children responded well to modeling of appropriate behaviors and simple verbal commands in English. Some of the children were comfortable speaking English to me, although most of the children used Spanish to communicate. Individual differences in developmental abilities across domain areas were apparent from the first days of school. Some students wrote legible letters quickly, and some children had no previous experience holding a writing utensil or scissors. Everything about school seemed so new to the children—walking in a straight line, keeping their hands in their laps, and other procedures. We practiced and discussed everything from flushing the toilet to taking care of books. The students were very attentive and interested in learning the new routines of life in kindergarten.

Although most of the learning during the first days of school centered on procedures, the students also participated in creating several critical elements of their classroom environment. The first day, the students helped make a class name chart, organized alphabetically by the first letter of each student's first name (McCarrier, Pinnell, & Fountas, 2000). The students also created a list of important rules to follow in our classroom. Another mainstay was the class birthday graph (Bolenbaugh, 2000). These three organizers produced by students and displayed in the classroom are referred to throughout the school year.

EFFECTIVE TEACHING METHODS
FOR THE FIRST WEEKS OF SCHOOL

The most meaningful learning experiences the children have in my classroom are often shared among all members of the class. These shared activities are naturally extended through various language experiences. One of my favorite tools to use with the children is photography. Capturing various learning activities in photographs provides wonderful motivation for continued learning experiences and language development with the topic of study.

Using the digital camera the second week of school, I recorded three important shared learning experiences. Then, these photos were scanned, arranged with simple text, and displayed. After being displayed, these photo pages became the first class-made book for the classroom library.

When the shape of the week was the circle, the children went on a circle hunt in the classroom. Along with taking individual photos of students with their circles, I recorded student names and a brief description of their found circles on our easel chart. Other uses of photography involved trips to the garden outside our classroom. After reading *The Sunflower That Went Flop* by Joy Cowley (1982), we found two sunflowers that went flop to cut and bring inside for study at our science center. Later, while studying colors, we went back to the garden to look for colors. The students were given a paint sample strip and matched their strips to colors of living and nonliving things in the garden. Labeled by color words, these photographs of the children holding their paint strip next to the color object in the garden made a wonderful text to be shared during independent reading time.

At the end of the second week of school, I reflected on various thematic activities the students had participated in while studying their first letter, shape, and color. The cooking activities, science experiments, and language experiences were wonderful, but I could see that planning and carrying out activities would not completely fulfill my job in helping each of my students reach his or her potential. In only two weeks, I recognized a need for many of my students to have opportunities for reinforcement and enrichment of the concepts I had been introducing, practicing, and reviewing. I began thinking about the challenge to provide meaningful and individually appropriate learning experiences, and what context or contexts would best accommodate these experiences.

A MEMORABLE ENCOUNTER WITH NATURE

The butterfly project my class and the neighboring first-grade class did the first month of school provided students with motivating tasks and hands-on experiences with nature. First, the students created paper butterflies to be sent to Mexico as part of a symbolic monarch migration sponsored by Journey North, hoping that butterflies would return to us in the spring from Mexico, following the migration pattern of the monarch butterfly. The most exciting part of the project was observing the growth of real monarchs from caterpillars to chrysalises to butterflies for two weeks in our science center. After watching the beautiful monarchs emerge from their chrysalises, our class released three butterflies into the school garden, watching each of them take flight for the first time.

This learning experience provided a common means for practicing language because we all observed the growth and release of the butterflies at school. Through reading fiction and nonfiction literature, viewing sightings of real monarch migrations to Mexico on the Internet, and making personal journal responses (drawing and labeling), students experienced a variety of multidisciplinary tasks related to one topic of interest. After the butterflies were released, the students met with me individually and in pairs to view photos of the classroom metamorphosis. Students told the story of our monarchs (most in English, some in Spanish) to me at the computer, while I recorded their words for a very special class book.

The concluding journal entries the children produced impressed me; some of the children labeled their monarch drawings by referring to the literature I had made available to them. Children whom I initially believed were far from writing their names were suddenly labeling their work with a legible first and last name. Along with giving the entire class a meaningful topic to discuss and share excitement about, the extended period of the butterfly experience and the firsthand observation of the monarchs created a curious wonder and appreciation for nature in each of us.

MEANINGFUL LEARNING
IN UNIQUE SETTINGS

The routines of kindergarten life are critical components to a student's comfort and success in school, but opportunities must be taken to extend student learning experiences outside of normal daily routines. Teachers and students should be flexible and open to a variety of contexts for meaningful learning. Interactive experiences with students in other classrooms, regular story time guests from the outside community, and field trips are examples of opening the classroom doors to new and different situations.

A weekly treat for my students is visiting and working with students in neighboring classrooms. My kindergarteners visit the neighboring first-grade students for a bilingual story time and follow-up activity. One popular reading was Eric Carle's *The Very Hungry Caterpillar* in English (1969) and Spanish (1994).

When studying apples and the letter *a*, my students and their peers in the neighboring kindergarten class had an apple tasting party and made a graph depicting individual and class favorite kinds of apples. Another collaborative activity emphasizing number sense involved the students making edible dominoes out of graham crackers, chocolate chips, and frosting.

At the end of November, my class participated in activities designed to introduce different kinds of bulbs to students in four different kindergarten and first-grade classrooms. After learning about onions, garlic, and tulips and tasting onion rings and garlic toast, the students planted tulip bulbs in front of our school that would later bloom, announcing the first day of spring (another Journey North project). These interactive experiences offered my students unique social learning opportunities that I could not facilitate if I closed my door to collaborative activities.

Another means of opening the classroom doors is inviting adults outside of the school to be a part of our classroom as story time guests. My class has two regular story time readers, making our daily story time a special treat at least once a week. Each volunteer speaks to the children in her native language. One of the volunteers communicates and reads to the children in English, and the other volunteer communicates and reads to the children in Spanish. The children adore both volunteers and express their gratitude by being interested and attentive to them and the literature they share.

Field trips offer my kindergarten class a special opportunity to recognize that enjoyable learning exists outside of school grounds. Field trips should be exciting and memorable for the class. Enrichment activities abound before and after students experience a trip into the community. For these reasons, perfect attendance is certainly an important goal for any field trip. In my class, field trips are not privileges held over students' heads for behavior management; field trips are critical learning adventures intended to be experienced by all members of the class.

Pictures taken during our first field trip to a pumpkin patch capture the emotions surrounding the entire journey. Printed, scanned, and/or developed photos offer endless opportunities for language enrichment activities. Students can sequence, label, write about, and practice vocabulary using photos from a class field trip. Scanning student journal response drawings made immediately after the trip onto pages with printed trip photos help students make even more connections to this shared learning experience. Adding student text to pages for titles, captions, and descriptions makes the class field trip book a unique addition to the classroom library.

MAKING STORIES COME TO LIFE

Storytelling and wordless picture books interest my young English language learners and help diversify the types of literature I share with them daily. In my professional development as a teacher, storytelling has always interested me, and after attending a storytelling workshop and investing in storytelling resource books with a colleague, I decided it was time to give storytelling a real try in my classroom. Initially, I questioned the appropriateness of storytelling for my students because almost all of the story comprehension depends on verbal delivery, listening skills, and understanding English. I knew that the wonderful illustrations in picture books serve as excellent scaffolds for my language-learning students. Yet I never want to limit my expectations of my students because of their language backgrounds.

The power of storytelling lies in personal connection with the audience (Isbell & Raines, 2000). Making and keeping eye contact with my students when I am telling a story makes me aware of how they listen much more than when I make sporadic eye contact while reading a book. After my first storytelling lesson, I made a mental note to *always* keep high expectations for my students. Their attentiveness and verbal participation during the story, along with their accurate retelling through dramatizing the story, revealed their verbal comprehension abilities to be much more developed than I initially perceived.

Another tool for bringing stories to life is the wordless picture book. During our weekly study of letter *f*, I shared David Wiesner's *Tuesday* (1991), an almost wordless picture book full of flying frogs. I shared the book with the children without interjecting much the first time and let them share their immediate reactions as they studied the unique illustrations. Then, we went back through each page or scene of the book and wrote our version of the story on chart paper. This interactive writing activity was similar to what I have done with the pictures of the children for class books. After listening to the children share their thoughts and descriptions of the pictures freely with the group, I scaffolded their responses into complete sentences for a cohesive story. The students wrote together by sharing their ideas with the group and then read their story together with me from the chart paper. This literature experience became such a special one that I typed the class story retelling onto a page for each child to keep along with his or her own copy of *Tuesday*.

INTEGRATING SCIENCE
INTO WEEKLY ACTIVITIES

My kindergarten students are natural scientists, full of wonder and curiosity for their surrounding environment. Following a letter-of-the-week schedule, we have at least one planned activity devoted to science objectives each week. We add these activities to a list of "ABC Science Experiments." These experiments, other related science activities, and an open science center provide real situations for students to practice language, while simultaneously reinforcing important science skills

ADAPTING THE DAILY SCHEDULE TO MEET
IMPORTANT LEARNING OBJECTIVES

During an hour devoted to language arts instruction each day, I use the first half hour to introduce and review chants and songs with familiar language patterns. We also complete a picture chart for each letter, using picture cards of objects beginning with the letter of the week. Students illustrate words that are not already found on picture cards. The picture charts, chants, and songs are bound separately in alphabetical order and available for whole group, small-group, and individual use. The students also enjoy shared writing of the daily message and playing letter drill games during this time.

The rest of the hour is used for small-group emergent reading activities. I plan these activities from the school reading series materials (Macmillan/ McGraw-Hill, 1995). My paraprofessional is present in my classroom for this segment, and we both work with a group of seven students to practice listening, speaking, reading, and writing skills. As the classroom teacher, I decide which language activities are most appropriate and purposeful for my students and the schedule by which these activities will be completed.

After completing individual assessments of progress for letter recognition and dictation skills in October, I divided my students into various small groups for an afternoon segment of skill centers. Students who were showing excellent progress were paired with individuals who were showing some progress of grasping letter recognition and dictation skills. The students who were excelling most worked with their partners as a kind of language model. Both students in the pair were given an individually appropriate task and materials to complete the task. For example, when given letter cards, the model student asked his or her partner to name the letter. Then, the model student named the letter again, made the letter sound, and said a word that began with that letter. Students not yet exhibiting progress in letter recognition or dictation skills when assessed work in two small groups with my paraprofessional and me to practice language skills. Along with using this short segment to reinforce language skills, offering a variety of practice materials allowed additional reinforcement of math concepts.

ASSESSMENT OF STUDENT PROGRESS

At the beginning of kindergarten, I perform a preassessment of basic skills for each student. When considering the developmental abilities of English language learners, it is important to remember the difference between not yet exhibiting conceptual knowledge in English and not yet exhibiting conceptual knowledge in one's native language. Transferring conceptual knowledge from one language to another is different from understanding a concept for the first time in any language. Teachers must observe carefully and make conscious efforts to understand what knowledge, experience, and skills English language learners have. It is especially difficult when required assessments (for example, standardized instruments) can only be administered in English. Instead of measuring a variety of concepts as intended, these instruments often measure only English language comprehension.

For all reports of student progress, I carefully document student achievement, making sure progress toward specific objectives is described in measurable terms. Parents and teachers should share a consistent understanding of student performance in various learning domains. Weekly reports, progress reports, and report cards should be clearly presented to parents. Consistent expectations for learning and behavior between home and school are a goal, and reports of student performance are valued as more than simply papers to be signed. I make sure reports and comments are clear and presented in the parents' fluent language, and I also make notes to explain parts of the reports that may not be clear to parents. As an educator, it is easy to forget that the outside world does not function using our jargon of "benchmarks" and "learning objectives," so I try to review important documents such as these reports for clarity before sending them home.

Teachers should work closely with administration to address the needs of English language learners regarding assessment. Important guidelines regarding required monitoring of student progress exist and must be understood by the educators of these students. ESOL professionals and administrators at elementary school and system levels should be used as resources for teachers of English language learners when issues of assessment are being considered.

OPENING LINES OF COMMUNICATION
WITH STUDENTS' FAMILIES

I welcome the opportunity to work with families with different linguistic and cultural backgrounds than my own. I value parent input and want all parents of students in my classroom to feel comfortable sharing information, concerns, and ideas about their children and the school experience with me. To encourage open communication with families, I use several methods. All communication, written and verbal, is delivered in the language the parents request at the beginning of the school year. The majority of written communication is delivered in bilingual form, encouraging English language learning for the entire family.

At our open house, I introduce parents to my system of parent–teacher communication in a brief handout of classroom procedures. Students take home parent communication folders each Tuesday and return folders with signed reports and papers Wednesday. I consider this school–home–school process an important measure of student responsibility, and I express high expectations to my students about taking care of and returning folders each week. My class has an excellent record of returning Tuesday folders with signed papers, and I praise and reward them for this behavior.

Each child's Tuesday folder is divided into two parts: sign and return, and keep at home. Included in each Tuesday folder is an individualized weekly report of student performance. I write comments to each child's parents on this report regarding pertinent issues of progress and classroom work. Parents sign, write responsive comments, and return this report each week. These reports are filed along with other parent correspondence for each child. The Tuesday folder serves as a means of transporting progress reports, report cards, homework, completed student work, school newsletters, permission forms, and so on. I also include weekly classroom newsletters for parents to keep at home. Newsletters emphasize topics of study, relevant home activities for enrichment and rein-forcement of school concepts, and important dates for parents.

Parents of students in my class have a critical voice in their children's school experience. I carefully read, listen to, and consider each of their comments, con-cerns, and questions about their child's experience in my classroom. At the begin-ning of the school year, I did not assign regular homework. The students were adjusting to kindergarten, and written homework assignments would have been inappropriate for them. After two months in school, a parent made a written re-quest that I begin assigning homework for the students to practice skills that we were learning at school. I thanked this parent for her interest and idea, and I began designing weekly reinforcement activities for the children to complete at home.

I try to take advantage of parent conferences and other informal meetings with parents to encourage a reciprocal relationship between parents and myself. Parents indicate possible times for a conference on a paper sent home in the Tuesday folder. I organize the chosen times on a master schedule, send another notice home with the conference time, and the parent sends back a note con-firming the date and time for the conference.

At parent conferences, I have student work portfolios and journals available for viewing. Class-made books featuring student photos, writing, and art are also on display. I explain local and state assessments of student performance. I review pertinent information from weekly reports and progress reports that parents have already signed and returned. I discuss with parents individual issues of concern that I may have about their child. I point out areas of strengths and challenges I see for their child at school. I ask parents to share any questions, comments, or con-cerns that they may have about their child's experience in my classroom.

I was pleased to have 100 percent attendance at parent conferences. I worked to accommodate parent schedules and transportation needs by resched-uling several conferences. Having the planned meeting to discuss each student's performance at school and how it relates to academic and behavioral expecta-tions found in various assessment forms is important to me as a teacher. I also welcome the chance to learn more about my students and their home lives. It would be ideal not to have to spend so much of the conference time "telling" parents about school evaluations and other issues; it would be ideal to learn more from them. It is ironic for me to do most of the talking when I have only known students for two months, and the parents have raised their children for five or six years. For this reason, I do not depend on parent conferences alone for communicating with parents about their children.

CREATING A WELCOMING ENVIRONMENT
FOR PARENT PARTICIPATION

I value parent participation and support in the school experience, and I hold an open-ended definition of parent involvement. Parent involvement does not look the same in various classrooms. Expecting all parents to understand the traditional roles of "room mother" is inappropriate for the diverse population of students and families that we serve today. Many educators have a misguided perception of parent involvement of families from diverse cultural and linguistic backgrounds. It is believed by some educators and community members that certain groups of parents are not involved or supportive of their children's education. Certainly, all parents from any one background do not take a proactive role in their child's education, but to stereotype particular groups of parents as uninvolved is inappropriate and unacceptable behavior for professional educators. As a teacher of English language learners, I advocate for these students and their families. I expect their support and offer my support to them in return.

In my classroom, I handle classroom parent involvement myself, without turning over duties to well-intentioned volunteers. The parents of students in my classroom have requested that I communicate with them personally about classroom needs, such as holiday parties and celebrations. Receiving instructions and duties from unfamiliar sources can be confusing and, at times, threatening to parents.

In my professional development, I have devoted personal study to issues of celebrations and traditions in the classroom environment (see the resources at the end of this case). I strive to include parents and families in the planning of meaningful events around special days of the year. For Thanksgiving, parents were invited to enjoy a special turkey dinner with their children in the classroom. All students enjoyed this treat regardless of whether their parents attended because eating together in the classroom was a special event.

I began planning early for a special December event, but I was unsure of what this event would be. After Thanksgiving, I sent a survey to parents in place of the regular newsletter in the Tuesday folder. First, I asked the parents to share any comments, ideas, questions, or concerns they had about their child's school experience thus far. Then, I asked the parents to share what holidays they celebrated in their homes and ideas about how they celebrate or would like to see holidays celebrated in the classroom. I was pleased with the honesty of responses from the families of my students.

From parent responses and also from informal conversations with the children, I learned that all of my students celebrated Christmas at home. Many of the families celebrate with the same symbols with which I am familiar. After learning this, I integrated a class Christmas tree into several lessons. I was most excited about the parents' descriptions of their traditional celebrations that were unique to their Mexican American culture. From these descriptions, I began visualizing a Christmas celebration for the children and their families at school.

I contacted two mothers who had volunteered earlier in the school year to help with special classroom events. These mothers planned the necessary components of a traditional celebration for the class. Then, I sent home this information for other parents to volunteer to contribute different items for the event. I confirmed this information in a follow-up letter and left the entire success of the celebration in the hands of the parents. The party was a huge success. The food, music, games, and treats provided by families were traditional and familiar to the children and their families. I could not have attempted such a celebration on my own because I do not own the traditions. Instead, this occasion was a time for the children and their families to shine and a time for me to sit back and learn more about them.

BEING AWARE OF SPECIAL CIRCUMSTANCES AND CHALLENGES

As a teacher of English language learners, I am aware of issues unique in many ways to the population of students and families I serve. Challenges I am constantly aware of include issues of assessment and evaluation, perceptions of parent involvement, and the need to individualize classroom instruction for student progress toward specific learning objectives. I stay in touch with the Migrant Education Program for helpful information for students whose families qualify for the program's services. I accept the challenges this population presents regarding transient enrollment and transfer of students. I work on system committees that are constantly striving to improve the educational experience for English language learners. I recognize and embrace the important role I play in the success these students and their families experience in my classroom and in our larger system of education.

QUESTIONS FOR REFLECTION AND DISCUSSION

1. What teaching methods have you learned or practiced that would be appropriate for use in a classroom of young English language learners?

2. How would you open lines of communication with parents and families of students in your classroom?

3. How would you create a welcoming environment for parent and family participation in your classroom?

4. What benefits and challenges do you recognize in working in a classroom of English language learners?

5. How can you deal with these challenges as a profess
   sources can you use for support when faced with such

6. In what ways do you think this first-year teacher w
   English language learners and their families?

7. How could this first-year teacher have been more successful?

REFERENCES

Bolenbaugh, S. (2000). Activity-based developmental learning in a collaborative first-grade class-room. *Young Children, 55*(4), 30–32.

Carle, E. (1969). *The very hungry caterpillar.* New York: Philomel.

Carle, E. (1994). *La oruga muy hambrienta* (A. E. Marcuse, Trans.). New York: Philomel.

Cowley, J. (1982). *The sunflower that went flop.* San Diego: The Wright Group.

Isbell, R., & Raines, S. C. (2000). *Tell it again! 2: Easy-to-tell stories with activities for young children.* Beltsville, MD: Gryphon House.

Macmillan/McGraw-Hill. (1995). *Beginning to read, write, and listen.* New York: Macmillan/McGraw-Hill School Division.

McCarrier, A., Pinnell, G. S., & Fountas, I. C. (2000). *Interactive writing: How language and literacy come together, K–2.* Portsmouth, NH: Heinemann.

Wiesner, D. (1991). *Tuesday.* New York: Scholastic.

RESOURCES

Bisson, J. (1997). *Celebrate! An anti-bias guide to enjoying holidays in early childhood programs.* St. Paul, MN: Redleaf Press.

Kindersley, A. (1997). *Celebrations! Festivals, carnivals, and feast days from around the world.* Photographed by B. Kindersley. New York: DK Publishing, Inc.

Peregoy, S. F., & Boyle, O. F. (1997). *Reading, writing, and learning in ESL: A resource book for K–12 teachers.* New York: Longman.

WORLD WIDE WEB RESOURCES

Author & Illustrator Links (www.libraryland.com/authors.htm)
Berit's Best Sites for Children (www.beritsbest.com/)
Journey North (www.learner.org/jnorth/)
Kay Vandergrift's Children Literature Page (www.scils.rutgers.edu/special/kay/childlit.html)
National Association for the Education of Young Children (www.naeyc.org/)
National Clearinghouse for Bilingual Education (www.ncbe.gwu.edu)

CASE 2.3

HAVE TIMES REALLY CHANGED?

Stephanie Bales

This case deals with segregation experiences of the author who grew up in a small rural county in a southern state. The case concludes with how the author's views have changed and how those views continue to shape what she will bring to her classroom. As you read this case, reflect on your own life and school experiences related to segregation and integration.

My story begins in 1968—the year I entered school as a first grader. I grew up in a small rural county in a southern state. White people lived in one area of the town, and Black people lived in a different area of town. At that time, there were only White children in school with me. I don't remember thinking about children of other colors—interesting now, knowing that the population of my town was 60 percent Black and 40 percent White.

Schools in our county at the time were divided not only along racial lines but also by grade, including primary (grades 1 to 3), elementary (grades 4 and 5), junior high (grades 6 to 8), and high school (grades 9 to 12). There were Black principals at the Black schools and White principals at the White schools.

School changed in 1970 when our school system was integrated. Some of the "upper-crust society folks" were opposed to integration and in 1970 a private, all-White school was opened. I was in the third grade at the time, but I don't remember it being much different for me. The biggest difference came the following year when I entered fourth grade. I was assigned to a school across town, a previously Black school. There was no air conditioning and I remember the smell. Some students said, "The smell was the Blacks, because Black people always smell." I don't remember much else about the fourth grade, but what I do remember is that my entire class became this really close-knit group of people. We were able to look beyond the color of our skin.

I believe we got along well because we were too young to have any preconceived notions or prejudices about people who did not look the same. Consequently, we adapted to our new lifestyle with very few problems. Even though we went through many transition periods, looking back now, our problems came from outside sources—older people, including our parents and their attitudes. I think much of that resulted from growing up in a small southern town in the late 1960s where people's attitudes were somewhat resistant to change. They have the "well, that is the way it has always been" mentality—a cycle that feeds on itself and is often hard to change. For many it was hard to adjust to the idea of no more separate schools for Whites and Blacks, that it would simply be school.

Numerous articles appeared in the local paper at that time regarding the integration of schools. Most of the articles remained upbeat and encouraging, but looking back at this time as an adult, I have to wonder how much of that was really how it was viewed. I do remember older people in the town talking of the riots that took place at the high school as integration was taking place. When I looked up the history of my town at this time in the local newspaper, however, I was unable to locate a single article that made reference to a riot.

The local newspaper, however, did report on the "planned" boycott that took place toward the end of that first year of integration in response to a list of grievances that had been presented to the school board by Black representatives. The school board encouraged the leaders in attendance to do everything possible to keep disturbance out of the public schools and encourage all children to go to school for the purpose of getting an education. I think that perhaps the issue hit too close to home, and the townspeople saw the best way to deal with it was not to deal with it at all.

Several men of the clergy wrote letters to the editor of the local paper reminding people of the fact that in God's eyes there are no color lines as well as praising local school officials for their willingness to be the laboratories where this social experiment could take place. Other articles referred to the fact that all we, as children, had seen was self-contained opportunities and that we had not recognized that the resources of the earth are not limitless. The writers of these articles suggested that we had been placed together, and, like it or not, the sensible approach was to try to work together to best use and conserve our common resources.

Looking back on my hometown, I realize the separation of races remained after the school system was initially integrated. Blacks and Whites had separate recreational playgrounds with their own pools around the city that were used in the summer. I remember every summer that the Black children would come to the White pool once—and every year the White children would get out of the pool for the entire time the Black children were there. It seems quite ridiculous now, but those children didn't know how to respond to the situation. The only thing they knew was that it should be separate.

Over the years, I don't remember race being an issue for my classmates or me. It was after graduation from high school that I saw the issue creep up on us—in my view, somewhat unexpectedly. When we had our ten-year class reunion, we were told by members of the Black community that they did not want to have a reunion with the Whites. Those of us on the planning committee were shocked. We did not know how to respond or what to do. Consequently, two separate reunions were held. As we began planning for our twenty-year reunion, we were determined that this scenario would not repeat itself—and it did not. We had a wonderful time, and we remembered as a class—as a family—all the wonderful times growing up and how pleasant it was. One class member summed it up nicely: Driving home after the reunion, I was struck by the thought that, although I may not have become intimate friends with all of you, just living, studying, and breathing next to you day after day for twelve years created a bond. I mean, after all, we endured the angst-filled teenage years together. It's as if we survived a war together! We all have our own lives now, but we have each other in common.

Have times really changed? Now as a parent, I can see that many modern social situations could be viewed in the same light as integration, for example, divorce, teenage parents of young children, and separation by social class. For me, I not only dealt with the issue of race but also grew up in a "different type" of family. My parents divorced when I was two years old, but I don't remember thinking about not having my dad around until early in my middle school years when I began to spend nights at the homes of my friends. Even though I don't remember my friends making me feel uncomfortable or asking about my father, I certainly remember feeling left out, alone, and confused.

Those same feelings will exist for many of my students as they deal with issues such as coming to a new school, realizing that they may not fit into the school structure already in place, experiencing the divorce of their parents as well as many other current social issues. History reminds us that we should learn from our past. Yet I would propose that the dividing lines among people are stronger and more entrenched than ever. There is a tiered system for many aspects of our lives. Consider a student's access to money and how that divides us. Consider that some students have concerned adults in their lives, whereas others do not. Consider that some children come to school hungry, whereas others eat only every other day. Those aspects of who we are may not be as visible as the color of our skin, but they deeply divide us into segments and have a direct influence on how successful we are. Now as I prepare to become a teacher, my hope is that I will be able to share with students my own personal experiences and help them to realize that self-worth does not come from those around us or material things but from within. We are special when we allow others, and ourselves, to be unique and to not try to fit into the preconceived mold that society places on us. I am certain that I will use my own experiences to continue to reflect on my own feelings—feelings that change with maturity and allow me to look at my own situations from different perspectives as knowledge is gained.

My love of teaching, as well as my own experiences, hopefully will allow me to guide and to nurture others in dealing with feelings of rejection and worthlessness, and in situations that are perceived as different from what is "normal." We are all alike, yet different, and that is what makes us take a minute, step back, and look at situations from all perspectives. Then, from a different angle, we can recognize that we are in control of how we respond to others in our lives.

QUESTIONS FOR REFLECTION AND DISCUSSION

1. What are some ways to bring students into a conversation regarding the history of segregation?

2. What issues still exist regarding segregation (e.g., race, gender, socioeconomic status)?

3. Are we still instilling feelings of segregation in our own classrooms? In what ways? How can these feelings and actions be countered?

RESOURCES

Bridges, R., & Lundell, M. (Eds.). (2000). *Through my eyes.* New York: Scholastic Press.
Raffel, J. A. (1998). *Historical dictionary of school segregation and desegregation: The American experience.* Westport, CT: Greenwood.
Thurman, H. (1997). *The luminous darkness: A personal interpretation of segregation and the ground of hope.* Richmond, IN: Friends United Press.

WORLD WIDE WEB RESOURCES

Anti-Defamation League (www.adl.org/tools_teachers/lesson_racial_segregation.html)
Coalition to Defend Affirmative Action and Integration and Fight for Equality by Any Means Necessary (www.bamn.com/)

Encyclopedia Britanica Online: Civil Rights Movement (http://search2.eb.com/blackhistory/
    micro/129/80.html)
Southern Poverty Law Center (www.splcenter.org)

CASE 2.4

WHAT ONE CATHOLIC SCHOOL LEARNED FROM MARK TWAIN'S *THE ADVENTURES OF HUCKLEBERRY FINN!*

Rachel Davis-Haley
Louis A. Castenell, Jr.

St. Joseph the Worker is a Catholic school in the midwestern United States serving 550 students enrolled in grades kindergarten through fifth. The student population is racially mixed, but the classes are grouped homogeneously according to ability levels of the students. This case examines an incident that occurred in a fifth-grade reading class and poses questions to the reader regarding the responsibility of the school's administration and faculty. Additionally, you will be asked to examine the role that parents play in their children's education. You will also be asked to determine whether the school is operating from a multicultural perspective and whether the school took appropriate actions. Do you believe a multicultural ceiling effect exists for minority children? Why or why not?

St. Joseph the Worker Catholic School, known for its focus on creating a student-centered inclusive environment, is located in a large midwestern urban municipality we will call Liberal-land (pseudonym). The city, home to 1.2 million residents, enjoys an ethnically diverse population. Forty-two percent of its residents are people of color and 58 percent are of European descent (Caucasian American). The yearly median income of Liberal-land's citizens is $22,000. The city has an unemployment rate of 8.1 percent. In the past decade, Liberal-land has enjoyed several economic spurts and is home to major league basketball, football, and baseball teams. Liberal-land also has had its share of race problems. About a month ago, a White police officer in an all-Black neighborhood shot a fourth unarmed African American man to death. Rioting led to a state-imposed curfew for all of Liberal-land's citizens.

St. Joseph the Worker serves approximately 550 students enrolled in kindergarten through fifth grade. There are two classes per grade level with approximately thirty to thirty-five students in each class. The class size is typical for Catholic schools serving urban environments. The ethnic composition of the student population at St. Joseph the Worker is also diverse, consisting of 40 percent

African American, 55 percent Caucasian American, and 5 percent other (including Asian American, Hispanic American, and other ethnic groups). The school is divided equally by gender. The median income of the parents of St. Joseph the Worker's students is approximately $40,000. Students come from a variety of economic and sociocultural backgrounds. Many students live in the neighborhood in which the school is located. This neighborhood consists primarily of working- and middle-class Caucasian American families. Students also travel from low-socioeconomic African American and Hispanic American neighborhoods and middle-class African American neighborhoods. However, the majority of St. Joseph the Worker's students are from African American and Caucasian American working- and middle-class families.

The school's philosophy is one that adopts practices, policies, and beliefs of Roman Catholicism posited in Martin's (1996) *Cultural Diversity in Catholic Schools: Challenges and Opportunities for Catholic Educators.* In his text, Martin asserts that the challenge of Roman Catholic education is to design meaningful education for all students. The curriculum of St. Joseph the Worker aims to provide success for all students, not only those who accommodate themselves to a single way of learning. There is also evidence that reveals that Catholic schools are more successful at educating minority students than their public counterparts (York, 1996). On entering the school, students are given placement tests. The results of these tests determine whether students are placed in advanced or grade-level classes. The grade-level classes tend to be more heterogeneously mixed. Once students are placed, movement from the grade-level class to the advanced class and vice versa occurs through recommendation by the teacher. The classes offered at St. Joseph the Worker are standard. Students take reading, language arts, science, social studies, religion, mathematics, art, and physical education each week.

St. Joseph the Worker also offers a wide variety of extracurricular activities. Students may participate in the student government, inter-Catholic league touch football, basketball, volleyball, softball, hockey, and track and field. Students also have the opportunity to participate in speech and debate clubs, a math club, and a writing club, which are all sponsored by faculty and parent volunteers. The faculty of St. Joseph the Worker are Roman Catholic. There are equal numbers of lay and ordained teachers. St. Joseph the Worker is known in the archdiocese for Liberal-land for its annual Cultural Fest. Each year, the parents, students, and faculty of St. Joseph the Worker have a festival to honor different cultures. The school's cafeteria is transformed into a cultural center with each class volunteering to sponsor a booth. Each class selects a country and agrees to create a context where visitors might experience what it is like to visit the chosen country. At each booth, a visitor might receive demographic information about the country, sample food from that country, see pictures of people in their native dress, and hear music from the chosen country. The classes also provide a short written description of each country, including information such as the country's flora, weather, population, per capita income, and occupations.

Eboni and Carlos, two African American students who attend St. Joseph the Worker, sat down one day to share their experiences as minority students in a fifth-grade Roman Catholic environment. Additionally, Eboni shared her sometimes painful experiences of being female and being in advanced classes.

Academically, Eboni and Carlos were high academic achievers and were two of five African American students placed in the school's advanced fifth-grade class. Both students shared that they were supported by their teachers, and, when asked if they felt free to respond in the academic environment and whether their teachers actively assisted them, answered the questions. Eboni responded, "Yes, for the most part, my personality made me ask questions when I didn't understand something. Some teachers may have wanted to move on, but I felt like a lot of the questions I asked were similar to ones that other students had asked. A lot of money was being paid for my education and I was going to take the time to get all of the concepts. Most of my teachers were very responsive to my questions." Carlos also agreed that the teachers were responsive and reported that he felt comfortable going to them for help when necessary.

Eboni also shared that she was an outgoing student. She did not mind confronting people on issues in which she strongly believed; she also shared that she thought it was her responsibility to *represent:* She felt that there were few African Americans in the advanced classes and if the few in those classes did not participate, then they would be invisible. She believed strongly that she had much to contribute and that she had the right to be heard. Therefore, Eboni chose visibility. She participated in many extracurricular activities and was very active in the student government association. Eboni described herself as an initiator. Carlos, however, responded that he wasn't interested in the same things as Eboni. He participated in the science club because he liked science and thought that the people in the club were nice. He also reported that he made good grades and would defend his position if threatened.

When asked if St. Joseph the Worker was a place where these students thought that diversity was welcomed, they were hesitant but responded yes. Both Eboni and Carlos agreed that they believed the school's administration wanted to make sure that students learned about their cultures, but the administration was unsure of how to go about making this a reality. Eboni and Carlos thought the administration (teachers, counselor, and principal) was open and responsive to diversity, but left the responsibility of disseminating information about diversity to the students. In other words, the African American and Hispanic American students were responsible for teaching the Caucasian American students about diversity.

When asked whether the students talked about non-White cultures in class and read text containing African Americans or texts written by African Americans, Eboni responded, "Yes we did, especially when we would read books that have the word nigger, nigger, nigger…on every other page. When we read *The Adventures of Huckleberry Finn* by Mark Twain [first published in 1885 in the United States], it caused a big controversy. We were in reading class and we were reading out loud—every other page would say nigger, nigger. The craziest thing was that the teacher wasn't shocked. He said he wasn't shocked because it was a traditional book and everybody read it. He couldn't understand why I did not want to read a book that said 'nigger! nigger! nigger!' I told him that if we continued to read this book, then I was going to tell my parents that it offended me and that they would also be offended. I reminded my teacher that he did not want to deal with my parents. He didn't understand!" Eboni further shared that the teacher, an ordained brother, made things even worse. Brother Johnny (a pseudonym) responded to Eboni's outrage and threats by putting the responsibility back on Eboni, Carlos, and the other African American students in this particular reading class.

Brother Johnny instructed the African American students to devise a project in which the students could deal with the controversy created by reading *The Adventures of Huckleberry Finn*. The African American students would earn extra credit for their work, but the project had to be completely developed by them. After meeting, the students decided to develop and administer a survey to the two fifth-grade classes, and have some discussion in each class about the findings of the survey. The students' parents helped their children develop the surveys. Carlos stated, "Yes, we did the surveys then we talked to people about their opinions of the book. I remember some of the people being really disturbed about some of the comments and some people basically conveyed an attitude of 'we don't care.' It seemed like the teacher thought it was a good idea to do something creative with a controversial issue." Eboni added, "I think his intention was not to deal with the issue himself. If he gave it to us then we would not do anything with it…but I don't think he realized how much we would do. The project started out with directions to get some newspaper and magazine articles and read about it, do some art on how it made us feel. We decided to take it to another level by doing a survey, relaying how we personally felt about it. When the class started debating and really telling how we felt about the use of the word and the stuff that came out of using the 'N' word and the book…we added a little bit…and I know Brother Johnny wasn't expecting it."

When asked if the students got to talk about issues of race in any other class, Carlos responded, "Not really. I think some classes had the chance to talk about race issues, but the teachers were not willing to promote that…there was this one teacher who was really good, but he skimmed over slavery. And again, the civil rights movement was only mentioned briefly. As good as the teacher was, he should have gone into it deeper."

The students were responsible for the discussion about diversity that happened at St. Joseph the Worker. Although the students reported that the administration was supportive of the idea of inclusion, they were disappointed that they were responsible for creating the activities and bringing awareness to the faculty and staff. The staff was not aware of the inappropriateness and offensiveness of some of the passages in *The Adventures of Huckleberry Finn*. An interview with one of the parents also revealed the parent's perception of an administration that was interested in diversity but unqualified and unwilling to seek help when making diversity a reality at the school.

St. Joseph the Worker teachers and administrators were involved in a dangerous process when interacting with their non-White students. That is, the faculty openly engaged in a process of making all of their students disengage from their racial identity. They practiced a discourse of "racelessness." This would explain why Brother Johnny did not think that the word *nigger* would offend Eboni. This would also explain why some of the students displayed an "I don't care" attitude when they discussed the surveys with Carlos. In an interview with one of the parents of the participants, it was revealed that the administration of the school was not open to ideas even from parents of their minority students. The parent shared that the school's closed-door policy was disconcerting, especially to educated African American parents who themselves were significantly more educated than the faculty and staff, and believed that they had much to contribute to the school. This parent found it strange that when African American families did call on the school to offer their experiences and expertise, the administration of St. Joseph the Worker responded that they would somehow involve them, but this never happened in practice. He further shared that they (a group of parents) called St. Joseph the Worker to offer assistance to the school's faculty on education issues (one parent was the dean of the college of education in the city where the school was located). St. Joseph the Worker never responded or took the parents up on their offers. One parent was troubled because he knew that the administration and faculty at the school were not qualified to deal with the issues of diversity that confronted the students. The parent shared that the school's staff and administration were afraid to admit not knowing and afraid to give up issues of control.

There also existed an intimidation factor—when Black educated parents met outside school, they generalized that they were too educated, too assertive, and deduced that they intimidated St. Joseph the Worker's administration. These Black parents displaced the comfort level of the school's faculty and administration. One parent shared that at the school there was the unintended effect of cultural and intellectual genocide—if the mission of Roman Catholic schools is to promote academic excellence in a Christian environment, how do you reconcile the school's practices? The school personnel's refusal to learn how to teach diverse students in a manner different from the traditional educational presentations did not cause teachers and administrators disequilibrium. It appears that the school justified not accepting the parents' interventions by claiming that they were servicing minority students by their mere admission into a school like St. Joseph the Worker. The teachers were not aware of individual learning styles. They taught one way and expected the students to conform to their way. Even with a college of education offering seminars in the city, the school was unwilling to accept offers and unwilling to change.

Given Eboni's and Carlos's raw talent, they were underachievers—they had parents who were educated, committed and involved, parents who were aware that their children were not achieving to their fullest potential. For instance,

African American and Hispanic American students at St. Joseph the Worker were being advised and counseled to attend second-class middle schools, whereas some of the Caucasian American students were being counseled and encouraged to go to the better middle schools in the city. There were established relationships with certain high schools, but the counselors did not forge new relationships with the more competitive middle schools and they did not encourage African American and Hispanic American students to attend the more competitive institutions. The administration and faculty of the school promoted multiculturalism, with a ceiling effect. The high-achieving Black students were not pushed to their fullest potential. So, in that respect, the talented Black students enrolled were underachievers because of the ceiling effect.

In a final conversation with one of the parents, this parent remarked that he found it extremely funny and ironic that St. Joseph the Worker was now taking credit for Eboni's and Carlos's successes. The school was unwilling to accept the fact that Eboni and Carlos would have been successful anywhere because of their talents and strong family support.

QUESTIONS FOR REFLECTION AND DISCUSSION

1. State the problem(s) of this case.

2. What issues are involved in identifying the problem(s) of this case?

3. In assigning the students to create a project to deal with the controversy created by *The Adventures of Huckleberry Finn*, was the teacher acting in his best judgment?

4. From the teacher's perspective, *The Adventures of Huckleberry Finn* is a classic; if its language might offend one group of students, do you not read the book? As a teacher, how do you deal with this dilemma?

5. How would you respond if you were Brother Johnny?

6. The African American parents seemed to believe that they intimidated the faculty and administration of St. Joseph the Worker. If you had the opportunity to address the parents of the African American students, what would you say to them? How would you help them to work with the teachers and not be interpreted as intimidating to the faculty and administration?

7. How could you use the African American parents as resources?

8. If you were the teacher, would you approach a mentor teacher or another teacher to deal with this teaching dilemma?

9. Should the principal step in and act as instructional leader, taking over in this instance?

10. Should the advisory board be consulted? What do you believe their response would be?

REFERENCES

Martin, S. (1996). *Cultural diversity in Catholic schools: Challenges and opportunities for Catholic educators.* Washington, DC: The National Catholic Education Association.

York, D. E. (1996). The academic achievement of African Americans in Catholic schools: A review of the literature. In J. J. Irvine and M. Foster (Eds.), *Growing up African American in Catholic schools* (pp. 11–46). New York: Teachers College Press.

RESOURCES

The American Association of University Women. (1992). *How schools shortchange girls: The AAUW report.* New York: Marlowe and Company.

Banner, J., & Cannin, H. (1997). The personal qualities of teaching: What teachers do cannot be distinguished from who they are. *Change, 29*(6), 39–42.

Ford, D. Y. (1993). Support for the achievement ideology and determinants of underachievement as perceived by gifted, above average and average Black students. *Journal of the Education of the Gifted, 16*(3), 280–298.

Sadker, M., & Sadker, D. (1994). *Failing at fairness: How schools cheat girls.* New York: Touchstone Books.

Stavely, L. M. (1974). *Three to get ready: The education of a White family on inner city schools.* Madison: The University of Wisconsin Press.

Tatum, B. D. (1997). *Why are all the Black kids sitting together in the cafeteria? And other conversations about race.* New York: Basic Books.

Twain, M. (1885). *The Adventures of Huckleberry Finn.* New York: Charles L. Webster and Company.

CASE 2.5

WHERE HAVE ALL THE IPIL-IPIL TREES GONE? SCIENCE EDUCATION THROUGH THE POLITICS OF POVERTY

Theresa Silva

Sharon E. Nichols

Deborah J. Tippins

The culture of poverty is reflected in the science education experiences of young children throughout the world. In some cases, poverty is intergenerational, existing across several generations. In other cases, poverty is situational, an artifact of temporary situations. In either case, children living in poverty enter the science classroom carrying with them a set of values, beliefs, languages, and struggles that contrast sharply with the typical science curriculum. In this case, Perla, a fourth-grade teacher in the rural barangay community of the Philippines wrestles with the lack of fit between the home lives of her students and what she is teaching in science. Perla is a composite of many elementary teachers living and working in rural areas of the Philippines. As you study this case, write down other examples of politics and poverty for discussion.

Historically, the question of young children's success in science has been framed as a question of availability of resources, access to the community of science, and provision of culturally relevant pedagogy. Teachers across many diverse contexts echo the common sentiment that "if only we had enough up-to-date textbooks, hands-on equipment, and materials reflecting the natural resources of

Teachers search for effective strategies to respond to the special challenges of teaching children who live in poverty.

our own communities, then all children would experience success in school science." For children living and learning in poverty, however, success in school science is elusive and far more complex. Far too often their life experiences and ways of knowing, doing, and communicating are devalued from a standpoint of what constitutes legitimate science. For teachers, worldwide, finding connections between the lives of children in poverty and school science is a daunting task.

My name is Perla Salizar and I teach fourth grade in the barangay school of Casay in the Philippines. I grew up in this barangay with my six brothers and two sisters. My father and brothers were fishermen and my mother was a housewife who washed clothes, cleaned the house, and cooked food for the family. As the eldest daughter of the family, it was my responsibility to get a college education. Thus, after completing tenth grade, my final year of high school, I left the quiet life of Casay for the city to attend West Visayas State University teacher's college. I'll never forget how it felt, at the age of sixteen, to make the twenty kilometer walk with my father to San Joaquin, where I would catch the jeepney bus for the city. Along the way we crossed several streams that fanned out into the ocean, and I knew that I would miss the fresh fish of Casay. Nevertheless, I worked hard to obtain a teaching certificate in elementary science and health. I knew my family depended on me to provide a stable source of income that would see them through the unpredictable seasons of typhoon and drought.

It is now nearly twenty years later and I have six children of my own. We live in a two-room cement house next door to the nipa house where I was born. Over the years it has gradually become more difficult to make a living from fishing and rice farming here in Casay—there are fewer fish as large fishing vessels encroach on the traditional fishing grounds of our barangay. Likewise, diminishing soil quality and unpredictable weather have created increasing challenges for rice farmers. As new roads and bridges are built more people are leaving our barangay for the city or abroad where they obtain higher paying jobs. My husband used to fish but now does odd jobs throughout the barangay. Some days he fixes fences, gathers firewood, or makes bamboo tables and chairs. Often, at the end of the school day, I may find him at the tubaan, sharing stories with friends over a glass of tuba, a fermented drink made from coconut sap.

My teaching day begins in the early hours of the morning. I rise at 4:00 A.M. to feed the pig and wash the clothes while my husband ties up the goat and carabao. After bathing, I prepare a breakfast of rice and fish for my family and pack lunches of rice placed in plastic lunch boxes. In the earlier days, we packed our lunches of rice in banana leaves. At 7:00 A.M., I shout to my mother in the next house to inform her that the two youngest children are still asleep and that we are leaving for school and she has to look after them. My two eldest have gone ahead to join classmates at the high school. As I walk with my two other children to school, I begin to think about my class activities for the day.

There are fifty students in my fourth grade classroom, so my lessons must be carefully prepared ahead of time. I stayed at school until 5:00 P.M. last night, drawing pictures for my next science lesson. I have given a lot of thought to today's lesson on deforestation and soil erosion. This is an important topic for the people of this barangay. Our school sits on a bluff overlooking the Sulu Sea, and the school yard is eroding rapidly along the shore. As more and more ipil-ipil trees are being harvested for charcoal and fuel, erosion is quickly becoming an environmental concern of the barangay.

By 7:45 most of my students have arrived for the day. They arrive on foot, walking long distances from their homes along the road, beside the seashore, or near the mountains. Some arrive barefooted. Others have gathered fruits along the way that they will eat for snacks. As the last few students trickle in, I begin today's science lesson.

Perla: Good morning class. Our science lesson for today is about the importance of trees in our environment. I'll show you two pictures. Look at the pictures very closely. Who can describe what they see in this first picture?

Anita: I see big trees and small trees in the picture.

Perla: What else do you see?

Mario: The leaves of the trees are green. There are many trees. There are starapple, coconut, guava, ipil-ipil, mango, and tamarind trees.

Perla: Now let's take a look at the other picture. What can you say about this picture?

Paul: The trees are cut in the picture. Maybe some farmers cut the trees. I cannot see any more trees in the picture.

Jen: I feel very sad when I look at the picture because there are no trees to play under. We cannot have a contest to see who can climb the trees first.

Anita: There are no trees so we cannot make any dresses from the leaves.

Perla: What do you think will happen if all the trees are cut?

Mario: It will be very hot with no shade. There will be no homes for the birds.

Anita: There will be more land and space to plant more rice and corn.

Antonio: But when the rain comes the soil from the farms will be carried away by the water.

Perla: Why do you think this?

Antonio: Because there are no more tree roots to hold the water. Too much water will wash away the soil. We will have many floods.

Perla: So what shall we do to prevent floods?

Class (in unison): We plant more trees. We will not cut down the trees.

Perla: That ends our lesson for today. On Monday we will perform a science activity to look at the effects of cutting trees on our soil.

The following day was Saturday and so there was no school. Antonio went with his father to make charcoal from the ipil-ipil trees on the neighbor's farm. When they arrived at the farm, Antonio was amazed to find that all the trees had been cut. He helped his father gather the logs and pile them in a pit. They made a fire to burn the logs. When most of the logs were burned, they covered the pile with soil so that only smoke could escape. Antonio knew that they would return in a few days to remove the soil, gather the remaining charcoal, and place it in sacks. As Antonio helped his father, he thought about what he had learned in yesterday's science lesson. Antonio, being a very curious boy, addressed his father:

Antonio: Father, why did you cut all those trees? My teacher says it is not good to cut all those trees because if you cut the trees the soil will be washed away.

Father: Well, we have to cut down the trees in order to make charcoal. We must sell this charcoal in order to have money to buy our food. This is the way we earn our living.

Antonio was confused. He wondered who was right—his teacher or his father? He went to sleep that evening with questions on his mind. The questions bothered him throughout the weekend. He planned to ask his teacher about them early Monday morning.

Antonio arrived at school early Monday morning, eagerly waiting for me to arrive. As I entered the room, he said

Antonio: Good morning Ma'am.

Perla: Why are you so very early today Antonio? [Antonio was hesitant to speak up so Perla continued.] What's bothering you Antonio? Why do you look so puzzled?

Antonio: Ma'am, you were saying that it is bad to cut down all the trees. But my father said we have to cut the trees to make charcoal so that we will have money for food. Is my father doing the right thing?

I thought to myself, "What will I tell this boy?" As a teacher, I seemed at a loss: I cannot simply say that Antonio's father is wrong and I am right. There must be a better way of explaining these things to Antonio so that he won't be confused. This is a dilemma for which I have no immediate solution.

QUESTIONS FOR REFLECTION AND DISCUSSION

1. How should Perla respond to Antonio's question? Is there a "right" or "wrong" answer in this case? If you were Perla, what would you say to Antonio? What might be some possible implications of your response?

2. Indirect forms of communication are often valued in many cultures. What are some indirect methods of communication or activities that Perla might use to educate Antonio's father about environmental problems associated with deforestation? How effective would it be if Perla simply were to tell Antonio that his family should not cut down trees?

3. How should Perla handle the emotional and value-laden aspect of environmental science topics in the classroom, especially those issues that directly impact the economic livelihood of community members?

4. Confronted with a similar situation, how would you help Antonio negotiate between the world of school science and the hard reality of poverty?

5. What are some activities that Perla might use both in and outside her classroom to help students understand the complex relationship between deforestation and soil erosion? How could Perla involve students in authentic inquiry into environmental issues in the community?

RESOURCE

Payne, R. K. (1998). *A framework for understanding poverty* (Rev. ed.). Highlands, TX: RFT Publishing.

WORLD WIDE WEB RESOURCES

National Center for Children in Poverty (http://cpmcnet.Columbia.edu/dept/nccp)
National Law Center on Homelessness and Poverty (www.nlchp.org)
National Science Teachers Association (www.nsta.org)
United Nations Cyberschool Bus—Poverty Curriculum (www0.un.org/cyberschoolbus/poverty
    2000/index.asp)

The authors would like to express their appreciation to the Spencer Foundation for their research support.

CASE 2.6

DOMESTIC DISCRIMINATION
Thomas Van Soelen

Amena contends with reactions from her fourth-grade classmates and their hostility toward her after the events of September 11. The case also presents interesting questions about the roles of teachers, parents, and schools during times of national disasters. Have you experienced discrimination? In what context? How did you feel in that situation? What was your reaction? Do you think you ever discriminated against someone?

September 11, 2001, was certainly a tragic day in U.S. history. Arguably, at no other time in recent memory has the United States felt so vulnerable on its own shores. An unfortunate outcome of this tragedy has been recourse by U.S. citizens of religious and ethnic discrimination in the workplace, public arenas, and schools.

Like most elementary school administrators, Sever Elementary principal Marcia Roberts chose not to air the widespread television footage of the air disasters in New York City, Washington, DC, and Pennsylvania. The larger school district to which she was accountable sent very clear and stipulated e-mail messages that none of the 120,000 students it served would find out about the tragedy at school on that fateful day.

The school day had already begun in this East Coast city, so it was easy to control the flow of information because students did not know what had happened prior to boarding the buses for school. That worked for September 11—not for September 12 and thereafter.

Amena arrived home on September 11 and found her mother, Marhat, crying at the kitchen table. Her sister Amira was also seated at the table with a stone-cold expression on her face, staring off into space.

"Mami, what is it? What is wrong?" Marhat lifted her head, adjusted her hijab around her face, and sat Amena down for the news about her uncle who worked in Trade Tower 2.

"We don't know yet, dear, but your uncle Nash may have been involved in a very bad accident." As the last word barely escaped her lips, Marhat's head again fell to the table, engulfed by her own sobs.

The phone had been ringing nonstop all night; the constant calls were from family members in New York, Seattle, and Pakistan keeping abreast of the situation. Amena was already in bed that evening when the phone rang again; however, this call was different. It was suddenly very noisy downstairs and she heard someone bounding up the stairs, skipping every other stair.

Amira burst into the room and shouted, "Amena, get up! Nash is safe!" As the two girls danced around the room and jumped on the bed, Marhat soon came up to join in their revelry.

"All right, girls," Marhat finally said. "Time to get to bed. It will be a great day tomorrow!" Even though Marhat had lived in the United States for twenty-one years, she could not accurately predict how their lives would change.

It started at the bus stop in the morning. Amena noticed that the mothers of her friends were holding the shoulders of their children, prohibiting them from participating in their normal morning routine of talking, sharing, and being noisy. It persisted on the short bus ride to Sever. Amena felt her hijab move occasionally around her head but when she would turn around the boys behind her were always doing something else. It continued in the classroom with more overt acts that left Amena feeling uncomfortable and scared.

Walking into her classroom was always a highlight of Amena's day. Her teacher, Mrs. Ross, made it a point to physically station herself at the doorway so she could "properly welcome you to school" with a hug and an affirming phrase. As Amena drew closer to her third-grade classroom on September 12, she immediately noticed the absence of Mrs. Ross. In fact, several other teachers were streaming in and out of the classroom, many of their faces streaked with tears. Donning uncharacteristically frizzy hair, Mrs. Ross was at her desk with her head in her hands. Other teachers were rubbing her back, offering her coffee, shooing away her students, and encouraging them to "get to work." Amena wasn't sure what that meant, but she was sure that part of it included staying away from Mrs. Ross's desk.

Eventually, Amena's teacher regained her composure and her colleagues left the room. As she stood up, Amena noticed that Mrs. Ross's face was blotchy and red and the beautiful colors that usually surrounded her eyes were curiously absent.

As Mrs. Ross encouraged children to "clump" near the Calendar Math bulletin board, she was clutching a picture from her desk. Slowly, painstakingly, and considering every word, Mrs. Ross explained that Mr. Ross left on a business trip yesterday and was flying to New York. As the gasps subsided among the children, Laura said, "But that's good, right? No planes going *to* New York crashed. Right?"

"Honey, you're absolutely right. The only problem is that I haven't heard from him yet. You see, his meeting was supposed to be at one of the Trade Towers." As she fought back tears, Mrs. Ross clutched the photograph tighter and looked up to see twenty-two pairs of sympathetic eyes. Contrary to the district's freshly constructed policy about the events of September 11, Mrs. Ross opened up a conversation among the children and asked if anyone wanted to talk about what happened yesterday.

Charles watched television with his dad until midnight. Nadine's mother knew someone who was missing in New York. Antonio shared that his uncle lived in New Jersey but had overslept and missed his train. Justine's comment took all of the listeners by surprise: "Are there going to be more crashes?" Mrs. Ross paused before answering. The pause was long enough to evoke a response from Bob who had, not by coincidence, sat behind Amena on the bus that morning.

Bob jumped up and tautly pointed at Amena, stating, "*She* did it. *They* did it. They are the ones who crashed the planes!" More gasps rippled through the class. Charles responded, "You can't say that! They don't know that for sure!" As the conversations overlapped and grew louder, Mrs. Ross, overcome by her own grief, began sobbing again which prompted Bob to sit down and the others to be quiet.

Mrs. Roberts, the principal, happened to enter the room at that juncture and brought one of the building's substitute teachers to relieve Mrs. Ross of her fourth-grade class. As the students turned to the back of the room and watched Mrs. Ross leave, one pair of eyes still faced forward. Amena blinked definitively and tried to make sense of what had just happened. *She* wasn't on a plane yesterday. *Her family* didn't do anything wrong. What had Bob meant?

Time on the playground was usually quite unsupervised. Teachers were outside but spent most of their time sitting at a picnic table, chatting, and grading papers. They called this time TDPE: teacher directed physical education. All Amena knew was that they were outside and weren't watching.

Especially today the teachers seemed engrossed in their conversations and oblivious to the playground antics. Amena and her friends were walking out to the field to engage in their usual game of Red Rover. She noticed that several boys walking the opposite direction were looking at her with ugly faces. She couldn't be sure, but it sounded like two of them told the girls to "go home!" When they were almost in their favorite spot, one of Amena's friends noticed that Bob and a group of his friends were following them out to the field. When the girls stopped walking, Bob kept walking and collided shoulders with Amena, who was on the end of the string of girls.

"Hey!" Amena cried, grabbing her shoulder. "That hurt!"

"Good!" cried Bob with raging eyes. "Maybe you'll go home. You don't belong here."

As the boys ran away toward the school building, Amena rubbed her sore shoulder and felt the comforting rubs on her back, courtesy of her friends.

The rest of the day was marred by her experiences on the playground, the classroom, and even the bus stop. Amena could not concentrate on the layers of the rain forest or the "trick" of multiplying double-digit numbers. She kept replaying the events that brought her to this point and kept asking herself what she had done wrong.

Unfortunately, Amena had one more negative environment to cope with before she could enjoy the haven of her own home. On the bus ride home, students were agitated, talking loudly and laughing, even shooting a spitwad or two. Amena had carefully chosen a seat far away from Bob. In her quest to leave him near the front of the bus, she forgot that Bill, one of Bob's brothers, always sits in the back of the bus.

The bus was at a stop sign when Bill suddenly stood up and pointed, in a fashion markedly familiar, and shouted, "You're the terrorist!" Responses varied among members in the back of the bus. Some laughed because they thought it was funny or because they were uncomfortable. Others gasped in fear or dismay. The younger students near the front of the bus stretched their bodies tall and turned their heads to see what image they would now associate with "terrorist."

Bill had not expected a reaction from Amena. In his previous interactions with her and Amira, Bill had found them both to be very quiet girls, easily dominated. However, Amena turned and spoke with a fierceness that her voice rarely exhibited: "I am not!"

"Yes, you are," Bill retorted. "You have black skin and dark hair and wear those things just like those people."

Unprovoked by any patriotism that day, Amena responded, "This is my country. I live here."

"Well, this may be your country, but you're still bad." Bill closed the door on the conversation as the bus driver reminded him to sit down for the third and final time.

Marhat was waiting at the bus stop today. Amena ran from the bus, her hijab and long hair flowing behind her. As she got closer to her mother, Marhat noticed Amena's flushed face and red eyes and opened her arms. Amena fell into her mother's embrace, holding tight and sobbing.

A bouquet of flowers were on the counter at Amena's home. "Who are these for?" she asked her mother.

"Amira's school gave them to her today. They wanted to let her know that they appreciate her and are thinking about her." Marhat responded.

"I don't want to go to school anymore. They think I'm bad!" stated Amena as she flung down her backpack and ran up the stairs, skipping every other stair.

Amena emerged from her room close to mealtime. She stopped a few steps short of the main floor when she heard Noor, Marhat's best friend, in the kitchen. "It was an awful experience," Noor was saying. "My classes today were antagonistic! A security guard insisted on walking me out to my car." Noor was a student at the local university. "You'd think that a place of educated people…" her voice trailed off. "One man even told me that if I would just take my hijab—I think he called it a 'Muslim thing'—off, I would be fine. He even had the audacity to say that I was *asking for it* by wearing it. 'What am I asking for?' I asked him. He couldn't even say it, but I knew what he meant. At the end of class, I told him that if I had to die in my scarf, I would, but it's not coming off." Noor's intense words were disconcerting to Amena. Usually Noor did not talk this way.

The next morning, Marhat woke up Amena with a kiss on the forehead and tousle of her hair. "I have a tummyache," Amena informed her mother.

"I thought you might," replied Marhat. "Let's you get ready for school, and I'll make a breakfast that will take care of that tummy."

Amena sat near the front of the bus with the kindergartners today, September 13. She scrunched low in her seat and held her hijab close to her body, stroking its soft, silky fabric. As she neared the classroom door, she spotted Mrs. Ross's friendly face! Amid reminders from the fifth-grade safety patrols not to run, she reached her teacher. "How's Mr. Ross?" she asked, breathless.

"He's safe, Amena. Isn't that good news?" informed Mrs. Ross.

Yes, that's good news, thought Amena. Good news for you.

QUESTIONS FOR REFLECTION AND DISCUSSION

1. How do teachers negotiate mandates from school districts?

2. How do teachers' personal experiences affect classrooms?

3. How does the building of a community come into play in times of tragedy? How can teachers build an effective community?

4. In multiethnic and multicultural classrooms, how do teachers respect and respond to individual children's varying experiences?

5. How can these situations be opportunities for home–school connections?

WORLD WIDE WEB RESOURCES

National Association of Arab Americans: Helping Children Cope (www.adc.org/index.php?id=253)
Arab World and Islamic Resources: 540 pages of lesson plans, essays, classroom exercises, and information on every aspect of Arab culture and Islam (www.telegraphave.com)
Council on Islamic Education (www.cie.org)
National Association of Arab Americans: Reteaching the Teachers Campaign (www.adc.org/index.php?284)

CASE 2.7

AN ELEMENTARY EDUCATION EXPERIENCE OF ADJUSTMENT AND TRANSITION
Inore G. Mendoza

The following case provides a description of elementary education experiences as a student from Manila, the Philippines, enters an inner-city school and a year later a suburban school, and the readjustment problems that occurred with those transitions. Before you read this case, think and reflect about the most difficult time(s) you had in adjusting to school. What were those situations and how did you feel?

In the summer of 1991, my family moved from Manila, the Philippines, to Marietta, Georgia. Through the eyes of an eleven year old, everything about the United States was large, intimidating, and confusing. My family lived in a modest apartment that my mother shared with another Filipino nurse. Although in retrospect the place seemed rather small for a family of four and a roommate, I think we did quite well at the time. Then again, I was only eleven years old and my brother was only five. My brother and I saw snow for the first time during our first winter in Georgia while living in that apartment. I remember my brother and I were waiting at the school bus stop wearing big fluffy winter coats that made us look five times larger than we really were.

From those apartments at Woodlake Drive, we were bussed to Pine Forest Elementary School where I began fifth grade and my brother began kindergarten. The school was located in the inner-city Marietta area just across the street from the high school. Nearby were neighborhoods where many immigrants lived, so the school environment was very diverse. My principal was African American and the two fifth-grade teachers were white, one male and one female. I encountered about the same number of African American and white faculty in the school. As for my fellow students, I remember befriending a Puerto Rican boy, Hindu twins, several Mexican children, African Americans, and Caucasians all in the same classrooms. To me we were simply a bunch of kids going to school frowning on schoolwork and enjoying recess.

Being in a new country, I became even more withdrawn than my normal shy self. Although I had grown up learning English both at home and at school, I was overwhelmed by how fast people spoke and by all the different accents. If I didn't understand something, I thought it safer to agree and try to do just as I was told. For example, I remember an incident when Ms. Thornton, our homeroom teacher, asked us to "put up" the spelling papers we had just graded. I thought she wanted to collect them, so I proceeded to raise my paper in the air to be collected. When I saw my classmates placing the papers back in their folders, I immediately retracted my raised hand and shuffled the piece of paper in my bag hoping nobody noticed my mistake. I felt embarrassed even though I don't think anyone really noticed. Only as I learned through different experiences did I fully grasp the range of meaning given to the phrase "put up."

I remember Ms. Thornton as a very patient and kind teacher who had several children from other countries in her class. She spoke with a distinct southern accent that was easy to comprehend. Sometimes I think she made a special effort to enunciate and speak slowly in order to be understood clearly, especially when we went over spelling and vocabulary. She conducted her classes in a pretty steady pace. I do not seem to remember any difficulty understanding any task assigned to me. I sometimes thought the basic core curriculum was easier than I expected. I found American history pretty interesting because I had never been exposed to it before. I distinctly remember enjoying researching a report on Crazy Horse, a famous Native American warrior. Throughout the year, Ms. Thornton made herself available to any student who needed extra help with schoolwork. She was also very keen and a stern disciplinarian; unruly boys and giggly girls had to think twice before doing anything she might detect.

I tried to do my best in school despite having some trouble with the language. It seemed simple enough to just follow the rules as best I could and not get in trouble. My parents also instilled in me that, as someone who was "different," I had to double my efforts in order to seem at par with everyone else. I think Ms. Thornton noticed that I was trying as hard as I could and made a special effort to help me out when needed. I remember one afternoon when I didn't do too well on a spelling test, she asked me to stay after class to review. I spelled the words out loud instead of taking a written test and did better. In fact, I even was selected to compete in the school spelling bee, which I won.

Generally, I didn't have problems keeping up with my schoolwork, but getting used to the difference in the way things worked in the United States took a little more effort. First, I noticed that the class rules and decorum were a lot different from what I was used to at the Philippine schools. Back home students were conditioned from kindergarten to sit attentively while the teacher lectured and to stand when addressed by the teacher. We were even obligated to stand when the instructor entered and left the class. In the United States, I was disappointed to notice that my fifth-grade classmates slouched over the desks and some even took naps during class. Also, in the United States, the students were allowed to remain in their seats when answering questions. The first time I was asked to address the teacher from my desk, I stood out of habit. I kept practicing this until my teacher asked me why I kept standing when she called on me. At the time I could not express that it was just how I learned to do things. Ms. Thornton went on to explain how this practice was a sign of respect for the teacher. However, after being put on the spot like that, I learned never to stand again.

Also in the Philippines we were encouraged to compete with one another in answering the teacher's question. So, when questions were asked, I was more than eager to raise my hand as quickly as I could and give the right answer. I didn't realize that a person that does this was labeled a "goody-goody" and "teacher's pet." I didn't discover until much later that being "smart" was a socially unacceptable thing. I could not be satisfied slouching in my seat, however, looking bored. For example, U.S. students recite the Pledge of Allegiance every morning after the announcements. In the Philippines we had to sing the National Anthem in a weekly assembly, but we didn't have to pay homage to our country every single day. Only after studying U.S. history thoroughly did I understand the real meaning and purpose of this pledge. Other than the routine classroom activities, I think I faired pretty well in adjusting to this new environment.

I did not seem to have trouble making friends in any of my classes. Because there were only two fifth-grade classes, I pretty much knew everyone, especially when the classes were mixed during physical education, art, and computer classes. Because many of us had different backgrounds, everyone seemed very tolerant and understanding about different cultures. Of course, there were some students that got "picked on" just as in any grade school. The guys hated the girls, and vice versa. Peer crowds were starting to form, and they usually ended up divided along racial lines, Latinos and African Americans, specifically. Overall, however, it was a pretty friendly environment for someone who kept mostly to herself. The scenario almost seemed too much like the idea of America that was presented on that show, *Sesame Street*, of which I was an avid watcher. Of course in the real world there was no Big Bird or Oscar the Grouch.

Most of the things I learned about U.S. culture during the early months of our Georgia residence, I learned by observing how others behaved and interacted. My classmates would teach me certain slang words and give some fashion tips. Lunchtime was the best time to watch and learn about all sorts of fun things. We could talk about anything we wanted for an entire period. I was greatly entertained by a certain Puerto Rican boy who spoke in a most animated manner with fluctuating intonations and wild hand gestures that were meant to enhance the stories he told. I also listened intently to what the girls talked about, mainly boys, television, and magazines. Overall, I had a healthy elementary school experience despite the many changes I had to adjust to during my first year in the United States.

Although my fifth-grade year went relatively smoothly, I had much still to learn regarding the social culture within the U.S. school system. Toward the latter end of the fifth grade, my family moved from the inner-city Marietta area to a house in a more suburban setting. I began middle school there and discovered the entire school dynamic was completely different, especially in terms of racial proportions. By the time I attended middle school, I discovered most friendships rooted in elementary school had long been solidified among my classmates. I was a stranger once again. As I grew and continued to mature in this new atmosphere, I learned that the United States is not like Sesame Street at all.

QUESTIONS FOR REFLECTION AND DISCUSSION

1. How much has Inore's teacher prepared the class for Inore's arrival?
2. Do you agree with the teacher's action of exploring Inore's standing-up behavior?
3. What are some strategies that schools could use to help facilitate smooth transitions for children who have recently immigrated to the United States?

WORLD WIDE WEB RESOURCES

Immigration and Naturalization Service: Teacher and Student Resources (www.ins.usdoj.gov/graphics/aboutins/history/teacher/)
Proteacher: Immigration to American Lesson Plans for Elementary Teachers (K–6) (www.proteacher.com/090154.shmtl)
The National Immigration Forum (www.immigrationforum.org/)

CASE 2.8

THE TEASING OF THAN

Thomas Van Soelen

Julie B. Van Soelen

Than is having great difficulty in his fourth-grade classroom. By initiating a parent–teacher conference, his teachers find out what is troubling Than and his family. The teachers attempt to intervene, yet Than is still frustrated with school. Consider the causes and possible ways to prevent and resolve the situation.

Discrimination originates in unsuspecting ways from surprising sources. Adult environments are not the only arenas that demonstrate inequity. Maltreatment of fellow students does not always boil down to members of a majority group inflating themselves via issues of race, ethnicity, or socioeconomic class.

Than is a Vietnamese American student at Horace Mann Elementary in a northwestern state. He is part of a fourth-grade departmentalized setting in which he has four different teachers for the four academic subjects during the day. The school has six homerooms per grade level. Nestled in a suburban cul-de-sac, Horace Mann is not considered diverse: 83 percent of its students are white, 10 percent African American, and the remaining a mixture of ethnicities.

Recently having moved from California, Than came to the area with his mother to join his extended family. After repeated business failures, a restaurant venture was the new business of choice for his family.

Horace Mann is Than's second school in the county. He transferred from an elementary school in the same geographic cluster after the first semester. His teachers were unaware of the reason for the transfer until the first parent conference with Than's mother.

After a rough academic start at Horace Mann, Than's teachers called home to schedule a parent conference with Than's mother. Repeated messages left with an unidentified male voice yielded no response from Than's mother. The teachers sent notes home in Than's backpack with firm instructions to return them. After the fourth note, a response was returned that agreed to an after-school conference.

On a rainy Thursday afternoon, the teachers met a few minutes before Than's mother was due to arrive in order to make a list of their concerns: very little academic progress, moodiness, and an inability to see the board. They did not realize that the main issue of conversation at this conference would not be any of those on their list.

A weary, shy, and timid parent entered the conference with Than following closely behind. After a one-sided discussion of academic issues with very little input from Than's mother, Mrs. Sherman initiated a discussion about Than's inability to see the board.

"Have you ever noticed Than having difficulty seeing things?" asked Mrs. Sherman.

"No," replied Than's mother.

"Than, can you read the board right now?" Mrs. Sherman continued.

Than looked up at the board and feebly attempted to read the assignments that were listed for the various classes. After squinting considerably, he gave up.

"It doesn't matter, anyway," responded Than's mother. "We don't have money for glasses right now."

"That's alright," chimed in Miss Walker. "We have a program here called CARE (concerned adults resource exchange) that will pay for the eye exam for Than." After several words of encouragement, Than's mother agreed to the eye exam.

"Finally, we need to talk about something else regarding Than," began Mr. Finchel. "Some days he participates in class and responds to questions. Other days he is not engaged and seems very distant. More importantly, there are days where his emotions seem to be on a roller coaster changing from one minute to the next. All of us are concerned."

Without a moment of hesitation, Than's mother responded, "I am not shocked. He is teased so much here." Expecting more details, the teachers waited and watched Than's mother critically eye her son, who, with his head in his hands, was crying.

"They say his teeth are weird...They say he looks weird...They say he is too short," listed Than's mother without a break between sentences. "That's why we are here. At his last school, he couldn't take it anymore. Every day, every class, it never stopped."

"Than, can you tell us more about these times?" asked Mrs. Kirchner.

Than's head sunk lower into his hands and quiet whimpering sounds emanated from his throat. As the teachers continued to probe, Than's despair in the conference was escalating with little concern exhibited by his mother, so the teachers closed the conference. The teachers decided to observe Than carefully in the coming days because no names were offered by him as sources of the teasing.

One week later, Than arrived at Horace Mann with new black glasses that were slightly too large for his small frame. His effort appeared strong and he seemed to have a desire to perform better academically. Soon after the glasses arrived, however, the teachers noticed the same lack of follow-through that led to the first parent conference. Each of Than's teachers attempted to talk to Than about what was causing this change in his behavior. Each time, Than responded with a bowed head and a silent response. Knowing no other recourse, Than was referred to the counselor for a conference.

Dr. Williams met with Than and conferenced with his teachers after school. Than spoke very little in the conference with Dr. Williams and would not tell her the names of the teasing students. "Some people are victims everywhere," said Dr. Williams, updating his teachers. "Other kids can spot victims and simply move in and rip them up. Until Than learns how *not* to be a victim, the teasing will continue."

The teachers were unsettled regarding the words of the counselor. Before they had a chance to respond as a group, a critical situation took place on the way to lunch. Miss Walker overheard comments from a small group of girls who were intentionally loud enough for Than and others to hear.

"Ooh, Than, who's your friend in the mall last night? He mighty fine!" commented Latoya.

"Mmmm, mmmm, he sure was. Why he friends with you?" questioned Keisha.

"Uh-huh, maybe he lend you money to get those glasses from goodwill?" laughed Chantel.

As the three African American girls giggled uncontrollably and continued to make derogatory comments about Than's appearance, Miss Walker saw Than's diminutive body shrink even more. It was difficult for other students to see him remove his glasses and slip them inside his oversized coat. The glasses were never worn again. The teachers would not know until much later that the glasses did indeed come from charity.

The teachers and the counselor held conferences with the three girls, separately. All three denied harassing Than and responded to the perceived accusations by sulking and not participating in the classroom. Conferences with the parents of the girls yielded no additional help. Than left school the next Friday and never returned.

QUESTIONS FOR REFLECTION AND DISCUSSION

1. How do teachers create nurturing environments for students that have experienced ridicule in the past?

2. What do you think about Dr. Williams phrase, "Some people are victims everywhere?"

3. What could be the next step for Than's intervention?

4. How would this story have changed if Than wasn't Vietnamese American? If the three girls weren't African American?

5. How can classroom teachers develop trusting relationships with students where sensitive issues can be brought to light?

WORLD WIDE WEB RESOURCES

Youth Challenge Online: Teaching Human Rights and Responsibilities (www.hreoc.gov.au/youth challenge/index.html)

National Institute for Urban School Improvement on the Nexus of Race, Disability, and Over-representation (www.edc.org/urban/)

Peace Academy: An Internet Resource. Specific resources for K–12 Educators (www.nowar.no/peaceacademy/causesofwar5.html)

CHAPTER 3

ACADEMIC PERFORMANCE AND EXPECTATIONS

In this chapter we look at the negative impact of two common practices in education—low or inappropriate teacher expectations and grade retention—on children's academic achievement. Just as teaching is a holistic, complex activity, so is learning. It is not always possible to determine why learning does or does not take place. Research evidence suggests, however, that student learning can be improved when teachers and students set their sights high. The expectations teachers have for their students and the assumptions they make about their potential have a tangible effect on student achievement. An extensive body of research beginning with *Pygmalion in the Classroom* (Rosenthal & Jacobson, 1968) clearly establishes that teacher expectations do play a significant role in determining how well and how much students learn. Students tend to internalize the beliefs teachers have about their abilities. When teachers believe in students, students believe in themselves. In other words, students tend to give to teachers as much or as little as teachers expect of them. Schools that set high expectations for all students and provide the support necessary to achieve those expectations have high rates of academic success (Brook, Nomura, & Cohen, 1989; Slavin, Karweit, & Madden, 1989). Despite evidence to the contrary, many teachers continue to cling to the belief that some students cannot learn, and so they hold low expectations for them. These low expectations then get expressed in watered down and fragmented curriculum, often for students of color who are also poor (Moll, 1988; Nieto, 1992; Oakes, 1985). Teachers with high expectations for all students, however, effectively translate their beliefs into academically demanding curriculum. The first case, "Hallway Math Again," by Dorothy White illustrates graphically the power of teacher expectations on student behavior and academic achievement. Patrick, a third grader, begins the year eager to learn mathematics; however, by the end of the school year, Patrick's interest and achievement in mathematics have plummeted and his behavior problems have escalated until they are out of control.

It is easy to see that children who are disabled, poor, unable to speak English, or abused may have problems in school, but we don't normally think of children who are gifted and talented as being at risk. Nevertheless, children who are bored by work that is too simple or are treated by teachers as though they are not bright and talented may begin to daydream or to become disruptive; students who are taunted by classmates for being "eggheads" or "nerds" may begin to fail on purpose; and children whose parents press them to be "the best" may develop unhealthy levels of perfectionism. Indeed, research has shown that gifted students are often in danger of underachievement, low self-esteem, and social and behavioral problems. Although estimates of the number of gifted students who are underachieving is difficult to measure, the U.S. Commission on Excellence in Education (1983) estimated 50 percent; and Ford (1995) found that 46 percent of gifted Black students were underachieving. Added to these problems is the issue of underrepresentation of children of color in gifted programs. Some of these minority groups of gifted learners may be underrepresented by as much as 30 to 70 percent, with an average of 50 percent (Ross, 1993).

In the second case, "When a Gifted Student Underachieves: A Dilemma for Teachers, Parents, and Counselors," Thomas Hérbert describes a talented, urban fifth grader's underachievement. Dylan's experiences illustrate the need to examine our educational and counseling practices for gifted underachievers and to design personalized school environments for talent development.

Next, Denise S. Mewborn and Angel Abney provide a thoughtful case on how gender issues in classrooms may promote or inhibit children's achievement in a mathematics classroom. Both children's responses and the teacher's interactions with children provide the basis for critically analyzing gender issues in classrooms.

In the fourth case, "Schooling Gifted Black Children: Issues for Parents and Teachers," Tarek C. Grantham and Linda A. Long present a number of concerns and experiences that a Black family with two gifted children have when making transitions between school districts. Issues of giftedness, professionalism, equality, expectations, and how these areas impact the decisions of Black parents, schools with gifted programs, and teachers of gifted Black students are addressed.

Another research finding that has significant implications for thousands of students each year is that of grade retention. The debate over grade retention has been going on since the 1970s with the pendulum swinging back and forth as the public and educators try to determine whether retention or grade failure is the proper response to low student performance. A review of the current literature, however, reveals a very consistent theme regarding the effects of grade retention. For most children retention has a negative effect on student achievement, classroom behavior, social adjustment, attitude toward school, and school attendance, and results in high dropout rates, especially for poor and minority students (U.S. Department of Education, 1999). Research conducted on kindergarten retention yields three similar findings (Shepard & Smith, 1989): (1) kindergarten retention does nothing to boost subsequent academic achievement; (2) regardless of what the extra year may be called, there is a social stigma for children who attend an extra year; and (3) retention actually fosters inappropriate academic demands in first grade. In the final case, "To Retain or Not to Retain?" Matthew P. Quirk describes a kindergarten teacher's struggle with the decision of whether to advance one of her female students to the first grade.

REFERENCES

Brook, J., Nomura, C., & Cohen, P. (1989). A network of influences on adolescent drug involvement: Neighborhood, school, peer, and family. *Genetic, Social, and General Psychology Monographs, 111*(1), 303–321.

Ford, D. Y. (1995). *A study of achievement and underachievement among gifted, potentially gifted, and average African-American students.* Storrs, CT: National Research Center on the Gifted and Talent. (ERIC Document Reproduction Service No. ED429394)

Moll, L. C. (1988). Some key issues in teaching Latino students. *Language Arts, 65*(5), 465–472.

Nieto, S. (1992). *Affirming diversity: The sociopolitical context of multicultural education.* White Plains, NY: Longman.

Oakes, J. (1985). *Keeping track: How schools structure inequality.* New Haven, CT: Yale University Press.

Rosenthal, R., & Jacobson, L. (1968). *Pygmalian in the classroom: Teachers' expectations and pupils' intellectual development.* New York: Holt, Rinehart & Winston.

Ross, P. (1993). *National excellence: A case for developing America's talent.* Washington, DC: Office of Educational Research and Improvement (ED), Programs for the Improvement of Practice.

Shephard, L. A., & Smith, M. L. (1989). Academic and emotional effects of kindergarten retention in one school district. In L. A. Shephard & M. L. Smith, (Eds.), *Flunking grades: Research and policies on retention* (pp. 79–107). Philadelphia, PA: The Falmer Press.

Slavin, R., Karweit, N., & Madden, N. (1989). *Effective programs for students at risk.* Boston: Allyn & Bacon.

U.S. Commission on Excellence in Education. (1983). *A nation at risk: The imperative for educational reform.* Washington, DC: U.S. Government Printing Office.

U.S. Department of Education. (1999). Taking responsibility for ending social promotion: A guide for educators and local officials [on-line]. Available at www.csteep.bc.edu/ctestweb/retention/retention2.html. Retrieved March 28, 2002.

CASES

CASE 3.1

HALLWAY MATH AGAIN?

Dorothy White

This case presents the experiences of Patrick, a third grader in Ms. Miller's mathematics class. Patrick started the school year eager to learn. However, during the year his feelings of isolation lead him to misbehave. As a result of his behavior,

The expectations teachers have for their students and the assumptions they make about their potential impacts the students' achievement.

> *Patrick was often sent by Ms. Miller to work on his mathematics assignment in the hallway thereby physically and intellectually isolating him from the classroom. By the end of the school year, Patrick thinks he has found a way to avoid being sent to the hallway.*

There are several ways that children perceive themselves to be isolated in the classroom. One form of isolation is *physical isolation*, where a child is physically removed or set apart from the rest of the class. Another form of isolation is *intellectual isolation*. In this form, children are disengaged from classroom activities and discussions and are often made to feel separated from the rest of the class. As teachers, it is important to detect when and why children are isolated in the classroom and to discover ways to ensure that all children consider themselves a part of the learning environment.

Patrick was a third grader in Ms. Miller's mathematics class. At the beginning of the year, Patrick liked school and was eager to start third grade. He was especially looking forward to his math class because he did well in his second-grade math class. In Ms. Miller's classroom, desks are arranged into clusters of four.

Patrick was glad he was assigned to sit in a cluster in the front of the class because he was close to the chalk board and the teacher could see how hard he worked and how smart he was. Patrick sat at a cluster with Asa, Mary, and Yvonne.

Patrick was usually one of the first children to raise his hand when Ms. Miller asked a question. He liked to answer questions and to show his work but was rarely selected to answer. Instead, Ms. Miller almost always called on Asa, Mary, Ryan, Danny, or Myshea to answer her questions. These five children were soon known as the "smart kids," and Patrick and the rest of the class were expected to listen to them and to learn. Patrick did not understand why he was not included as one of the smart kids like he was in second grade. He tried raising his hand politely and when that did not work he would wave his hand and say "Me, me, pick me!" but Ms. Miller still did not pick him. Patrick began to feel like he was invisible in his mathematics class and often voiced his frustration when other people were selected instead of him with, "Man! He always gets to answer!"

After the morning review, the class usually worked in groups to solve problems on a worksheet. Patrick did not like to work with his group. He did not feel like he was a part of the group. Asa and Mary would do most of the work and he and Yvonne would have to sit and watch. Yvonne would often get called away from class to work with the resource teacher so Patrick was left to watch Asa and Mary work. When he would offer his suggestions, Asa and Mary would say how they had a better way and would dismiss Patrick's ideas. Patrick's frustration with his group would sometimes result in him standing up and shouting. It was during these times that Ms. Miller would notice that he was not working well with his peers:

Ms. Miller: Patrick, that's very, very impolite. Come on turn around, and join your group.

Patrick: Can I go to another desk?

Ms. Miller: There is no other desk, we're full. You can do this, pull your desk away and work by yourself. Shouting tells us you want to be by yourself. [Ms. Miller looks at the rest of the group.] Don't discuss anything with him, OK?

Patrick began to hate his math class, especially the group work. He did not want to tattle on Asa and Mary, he just wanted to work with some other children in the class that would listen to him and let him share in the work. He wanted to find a group where he felt like he belonged. So Patrick began to walk away from his group and to drift to other groups. Ms. Miller would often find him wandering.

Ms. Miller: Patrick, why are you walking around?

Patrick: I don't know what to do.

Ms. Miller: Well, what group could you join? [Ms. Miller looks around the room at all the groups.] Why don't you join Danny's group over there? See what you can do with them. I'll be right back to see what you did. I'm just trying to get to everybody.

Unfortunately, Ms. Miller rarely went back to check on Patrick. Patrick would sit and watch the "new" group and still not know what he was to do. He did not want to ask Ms. Miller or the students next to him because he did not want to seem dumb. He knew he was not one of the "smart" kids, but he was not dumb either! So Patrick usually worked alone, signed his name, and turned in his paper to Ms. Miller.

By the second month of school, Patrick rarely volunteered to answer questions. He, and most of the twenty-four students in his class, knew that Ms. Miller was only going to call on the five "smart" kids to answer her questions so he didn't bother to volunteer anymore. At first, he would sit quietly and wait for Ms. Miller to pass out the daily materials and worksheets. Then he began to doodle or search through his desk. He did not think Ms. Miller was talking to him, so he tried to find other things to do.

Ms. Miller: Patrick are you watching?

Patrick: I can't find my pencil.

Ms. Miller: I need your attention. If you're not going to pay attention, you have to go stand by the door.

Patrick: OK.

Patrick started the school year as a B student, but was slowly becoming borderline failing. He became easily distracted, refused to work with others, and was often made to sit or to stand in the back of the class where he worked alone. Although Patrick did not understand everything and often felt intellectually isolated when he was made to stand in the back of the class, he was physically in the class and could hear enough to remain involved in some of the activities. Ms. Miller would remark, "Patrick needs to maybe take some time out. Just have him sit aside at a table. He's got a good thinking head, but he does have trouble getting down to work at times."

By the middle of the year, Patrick's feelings of isolation did not change, and he started to act out. Ms. Miller's initial approach of having Patrick work alone or stand in the back of the room worked for a while but soon had no effect on Patrick's behavior. Patrick became angry and would have outbursts in the class where he would throw things, fight, or curse at other students. As a result, he was often sent to the hallway to complete his assignments.

On one particular day, Patrick and Yvonne had been exchanging nasty words all morning. Ms. Miller had not noticed the two until Patrick's outburst:

Ms. Miller: Let's get this problem started. All right 560 students from your school are going to Wolf Tent Farm Park this week.

Patrick: SHUT UP, YOU BITCH, I HATE YOU!!

Ms. Miller: Alright heads down! Patrick you're leaving. Go!

Patrick: No, no, no! [Patrick stomps his feet.]

Ms. Miller: Patrick, come on. Take this. [Passes him the worksheet of problems and escorts him to the door.]

Patrick: No! [Leaves room and sits by the wall in hallway.]

Ms. Miller: Alright how am I to solve this? Five hundred sixty students...

Patrick did not have many friends in his math class. Most of his classmates knew that he "acted out" and did not want to get in trouble with him. Although Patrick was not the only student in Ms. Miller's class that did not stay on task, he was often singled out for his behavior. Notice the following exchange with Patrick and Fernando.

Patrick: Ms. Miller, Fernando is bothering me.

Ms. Miller: Pardon?

Patrick: Fernando is bothering me.

Ms. Miller: Fernando will you get your chair and sit down. You're not to be.... [Ms. Miller walks away and checks on another group of children who are working. Five minutes later, Patrick and Fernando are pushing each other. Ms. Miller calls across the room as she walks over to where Patrick and Fernando are located.]

Ms. Miller: Patrick you need to leave the room now. I can't take it anymore. Patrick, Patrick, go. You have to go. Get up, get up.

Patrick: One more chance?

Ms. Miller: No.

Patrick: One more?

Ms. Miller: No.

Patrick: What about Fernando?

Ms. Miller: I don't know what it is with you and Fernando, but you pick on him everyday.

Patrick: I don't pick on him.

Ms. Miller: Here. [Passes Patrick his worksheet as he leaves to work in the hallway.]

In the hallway, Patrick tried to complete his work but found it difficult because he did not understand what he was supposed to do. Most times, he would guess or draw pictures. When he was sent to stand in the back of the class, he could at least hear what was going on. But in the hallway, he was really alone. Outside, he was physically and intellectually isolated from his class. Patrick did not like that feeling at all. Moreover, Patrick's parents were very disappointed in him.

By the end of the school year, after several hallway episodes, Patrick had learned how to avoid being sent to the hallway:

Ms. Miller: Boys and girls, I need, need your attention this way.... [Rings bell for the attention of the class.].... Good Paul.... How's Patrick doing? I haven't heard a peep out of him, very good.

Russell: Patrick is underneath the table.

Ms. Miller: Russell, you're to watch the board, you know. Just ignore him. He's not bothering anyone. Alright I gave you some paper so you can just write as I write. [The lesson continues.]

QUESTIONS FOR REFLECTION AND DISCUSSION

1. In what ways did Patrick feel isolated in his mathematics class?

2. How did Ms. Miller's interactions with the "smart kids" contribute to Patrick's feelings of isolation?

3. How did being sent to the hallway help or hinder Patrick's behavior?

4. How could Ms. Miller have structured her mathematics lessons so that all students felt actively involved?

RESOURCES

Corwin, R. B., Storeygard, J., & Price, L. S. (1996). *Talking mathematics: Supporting children's voices.* Portsmouth, NH: Heinemann.

National Council of Teachers of Mathematics. (2000). *Principles and standards for school mathematics.* Reston, VA: Author.

National Council of Teachers of Mathematics. (1991). *Professional standards for teaching mathematics.* Reston, VA: Author.

Schifter, D. (Ed.). (1996). *What's happening in math class? Envisioning new practices through teacher narratives* (Vol. 1). New York: Teachers College Press.

Schifter, D. (Ed.), (1996). *What's happening in math class? Reconstructing professional identities* (Vol. 2). New York: Teachers College Press.

WORLD WIDE WEB RESOURCES

National Council of Teachers of Mathematics (www.nctm.org)

CASE 3.2

WHEN A GIFTED STUDENT UNDERACHIEVES
A Dilemma for Teachers, Parents, and Counselors

Thomas P. Hébert

Nothing is more frustrating to educators and parents than a bright child who doesn't participate in school. In this account of Dylan McCarthy, a talented urban youngster, the author describes a fifth grader's underachievement. In doing so, the story unfolds as Dylan's disinterest in school concerns his teachers, parents, and school counselor. Dylan's experience illustrates a need to examine our educational and counseling practices for gifted underachievers and to design personalized school environments for talent development.

Dylan McCarthy stepped out of the subway station and began walking along one of Boston's busiest streets. As he maneuvered his way along the crowded sidewalk, he appeared to carry the weight of the world on his shoulders. The sandy haired, freckled faced fifth grader stopped to browse through every magazine stand along Washington Avenue, surveyed the latest comic books, and checked out the most recent edition of *Sports Illustrated*. He knew he was just killing time. He didn't care if he would be late for baseball practice, and he knew the conversation he was planning on having with Coach Gradowski was not going to be fun. He could just see his coach's face turning beet red and could hear the dreaded holler. But Dylan was determined to stick with his plan. As he approached Kennedy Park, he checked his duffel bag once more. Inside the bag was the Little League uniform he planned to turn in to his coach. He checked to make sure he hadn't forgotten anything. Arriving at the field, he heard Coach Gradowski's gruff voice call out, "Well, it's about time you got here, McCarthy! You're late. That's gonna be 20 extra laps around the park for you today. You know the rules. When am I ever gonna get it through that thick head of yours? Huh? Tell me, big guy!"

"Hey Coach, I need to talk to you about something."

"I haven't got time to listen to your problems today, McCarthy. I've got a baseball team to run. Some of these guys want to play ball, remember? So get out on that field, and let me see you work on throwin' that ball with a little speed. Hurry! Get out there!"

Dylan took a deep breath, and with all the courage he could summon, he blurted, "Coach, you don't understand. I want to quit the team. I'm here today to turn in my uniform. I don't want to play any more."

"What do you mean? You don't want to play? What are you? Some kinda pansy? You're my star shortstop. What do you expect me to do without a short-stop? You know Sullivan can't fill your shoes. Now get out there and practice!"

As Dylan reached into his duffel bag and pulled out his uniform, the expression on his coach's face changed. He realized the young boy meant what he said. He really was here to quit.

Dylan walked over to the back of the coach's van and left his uniform on the back seat. Coach stood there shaking his head. As Dylan attempted to say goodbye, Mr. Gradowski cut him off, muttering, "You're gonna regret this one day, McCarthy. Trust me, you're gonna be sorry."

Dylan McCarthy was not feeling sorry. He knew he did not want to continue playing baseball. He had lost his interest in the team. He didn't care if the coach thought he was a pansy. He had practiced his speech over and over in his head for weeks. Although he figured he would feel so relieved when it was over, Dylan didn't feel that way at all. Instead, he felt another wave of dread wash over him. He now had to figure out what he was going to say to his parents when

Coach Gradowski called his dad. He could just hear his dad carry on about his never sticking to a commitment. He still had a couple of hours before his family expected him home for dinner, so he planned to walk home a roundabout way. He turned down Quincy Avenue and decided to spend some time in his favorite museum. Mrs. Capitanio, his art teacher, had mentioned on Tuesday that the museum was featuring a special exhibit on cartooning. She seemed really excited about the work that was being displayed, and she encouraged the students to talk to their parents about taking them to see the new show. Dylan decided this would be a great way to kill some more time before he had to face the "I'm so disappointed in you" speech from his dad.

It was a quiet Friday afternoon, the perfect ending to a hectic week at Kingswood Elementary School. Barbara King was seated at her desk grading her fifth graders' papers when Laura Capitanio came rushing into her classroom holding a small canvas. The art teacher was obviously excited as she waved Dylan McCarthy's work and placed it on the desk before her.

"Barb, will you look at this? This kid is incredible! Dylan never ceases to amaze me with his talent. I've been teaching art for fifteen years, and I've never met a student with such a natural gift. I introduced the fifth graders to Salvador Dali this month and for the past three weeks Dylan has been working on surrealism. Look at the imagery in this painting. It's amazing."

As Barbara admired the young boy's painting, she, too, was impressed with his artistic ability. She smiled as Laura carried on about Dylan's artistic talent and his ability to "see the world through the eyes of an artist." Laura explained to Barbara that she was struggling with a dilemma. She wanted to recommend Dylan for the city's magnet program in fine arts for next year, but this would mean that Dylan would no longer be involved in her art program. Having talented youngsters like Dylan McCarthy kept Laura Capitanio professionally invigorated as she exclaimed, "It's kids like Dylan who keep me believing that I can make a difference."

Laura decided she wanted to share Dylan's painting with the staff in the front office, so she grabbed the painting from Barb's desk and dashed out of the room, leaving Barbara with her thoughts. Barbara was pleased to see Dylan's painting; however, she had mixed feelings that afternoon. She'd been worried about Dylan for awhile. She couldn't help but wonder why Dylan would immerse himself in surrealism so passionately. She reflected on an article she had read recently about troubled young adolescent boys hiding from their personal problems through their artwork, and she remembered how the author had indicated that Dali's surrealism proved to be an escape for many youngsters. This seemed consistent with what she'd noticed lately about Dylan.

As she reached for her grade book, she thought about Dylan's recent lack of progress in her fifth-grade class. She also thought about the conversation she had earlier in the week with the school's enrichment teacher, Kathy Johnston. Kathy had shared her concerns about Dylan's lack of motivation in the gifted program. Kathy had been working with Dylan since he was identified for the program in first grade, with an IQ score of 135, creativity test scores in the ninety-eighth percentiles, and strong teacher recommendations. She pointed out that this was the first year Dylan had chosen not to pursue an independent study project during research time in the resource room. In the past, Dylan had been so enthusiastic about his individual research projects on dinosaurs, World War II, and marine biology, and he had always been a competitor on the elementary school's Quiz Bowl team. This year was different, and Kathy Johnston was perplexed. She mentioned to Barbara she had decided that Dylan was simply experiencing nothing more than a late "fourth-grade slump."

Barbara King was not convinced that Dylan's behavior was merely a slump. She thought back to her lunchroom duty several days ago when she had watched Dylan eating his lunch alone in a corner of the school cafeteria. In the sea of boisterous young adolescents, he had appeared more detached than ever. As Barbara supervised the lunchroom, she had noticed Dylan closely watching the antics of a group of youngsters at the next table. The young men involved in rowdy conversation had a reputation at Kingswood for their roguish behavior. Teachers in the faculty lounge had commented on the likelihood that these boys would some day become a middle school gang. Barbara had worried as she watched Dylan becoming intrigued with the behavior of the disreputable students. Now as Barbara reviewed her class grade book, she felt guilty. She had been meaning to call Dylan's parents to talk about his plummeting grades and the recent change in his behavior, but she dreaded making that call and had been putting it off for several weeks.

Elaine and John McCarthy had been good friends of Barbara's during their years together at Boston College. Barb and Elaine had majored in elementary education together. She knew that Elaine was teaching in a parochial school in the city, and John had been employed in the city planner's office. Barb thought back to their college days during the late sixties and smiled to herself. She reflected on her own idealism at that time and the passion she, Elaine, and John had for a number of causes. Elaine and John had been significant personalities at Boston College, taking on an overwhelming load of extracurricular activities and providing leadership on a number of important campaigns involving students' rights. These two well-established professionals continued their involvement in important causes; they were well known for their work as urban social activists. Barb had taught their older daughter Meghan a number of years ago and had marveled at how wonderful a student she was. Having excelled academically, socially, and athletically, Meghan had a magical way of turning everything she touched into gold. In fact, Barbara had just read in the *Boston Globe* how Meghan had been awarded a Rhodes Scholarship and would be studying in Oxford in the fall. As she read the article she wondered how Dylan had coped with having such a tough act to follow.

Although she dreaded making that phone call to her old friends, she knew it was something she had to do. As she reviewed Dylan's grades, she noted that his language arts average had dropped from an A to a C. He had not turned in any social studies homework for two weeks and had failed his most recent test. His grades in science were also dropping. She thought back to a conversation in the teachers lounge several days ago with Mr. O'Reilly, Dylan's math teacher. Steve O'Reilly had referred to Dylan as a "kid with an attitude." Apparently, his progress in math might also be a problem. She wondered if any of Dylan's other teachers had contacted his parents. She decided to include Kathy Johnston, Dylan's enrichment teacher, in her plan. She would call the McCarthy's and arrange a parent–teacher conference. Having Kathy at the meeting might help Barbara deliver the troublesome message to Dylan's parents.

Barbara poured coffee for John and Elaine as they waited for Kathy Johnston to arrive in Barb's classroom. Elaine initiated the conversation with her concerns for her son.

"I'm so grateful to you for calling us, Barbara. We've been noticing a number of changes in Dylan at home lately and wondered if the same was true in school. John has been upset with him for dropping out of Little League."

John interrupted, "He seems to have so few interests these days. All he does after school is lie on his bed and read one Brian Jacques novel after another. We can't get him outside. This is the same kid who was the star shortstop on his team. The kid is a natural athlete, and now we don't even hear anything about sports or the guys he used to hang out with. We don't know who his friends are these days. When we ask him about it, he just shrugs his shoulders. I don't know what to think."

Elaine became teary-eyed as she spoke, "He so different from his sister Meghan. We've always been able to communicate so openly with our daughter. She's always been so easygoing. I guess boys are just different. He seems so moody all the time."

Kathy Johnston arrived in the classroom and apologized for being late. The McCarthy's were happy to see her again. They knew her quite well because she had been working with Dylan since first grade, and they felt assured that she had his best interests at heart. Kathy shared with John and Elaine that Dylan had not begun an independent study project, and she was wondering if they might have an explanation for this. Both parents assured Kathy that the enrichment program she facilitated had been the highlight of Dylan's elementary school experiences for years. They were puzzled but John expressed his frustration saying, "That's consistent with what we are seeing. He doesn't have any interests these days and he's simply not making a commitment to anything."

Elaine became more emotional as she spoke and described what Dylan had been like as a younger child. "Dylan has always been such a sensitive child. I'll always remember the night we stayed up until the wee hours of the morning attempting to comfort him after he watched the movie *E.T.* He was such an emotional mess after that movie. We thought he'd never fall asleep."

John interjected, "Yes, this little guy wouldn't be able to fall asleep because he was worrying about bald eagles becoming extinct! After awhile, we hesitated about allowing him to watch *National Geographic* specials on television. We never knew what might happen as a result."

With more emotion in Elaine's voice, she commented, "And when his first-grade teacher had the class involved in a project raising money for a soup kitchen, we dealt with night after night of assurances that his efforts would definitely make a difference for the homeless people in Boston. He was convinced we could deliver pillows and blankets to all of them throughout the city! Even though he has this deep sensitivity and intelligence, he simply doesn't seem to care about anything these days. I just don't understand."

Barbara hesitated before she continued. "I need to let you know where Dylan stands academically in a number of his subjects. First of all, I want you to know that Laura Capitanio, the art teacher, thinks the world of Dylan. She was in here only a few days ago so excited about a beautiful painting Dylan had finished in her art room. She thinks he's one of the most gifted artists she's ever seen. I did check with Steve O'Reilly and I know there are problems in math. Steve couldn't be here this afternoon, but he left Dylan's math test grades with me. Steve claims that Dylan hasn't turned in any math homework lately, and he failed his most recent test."

Barbara could tell this news was not what Elaine and John McCarthy wanted to hear, but she continued, "I'm not seeing any social studies homework from Dylan, and his grades in language arts and science are also spiraling downward. Right now he has a C average in language arts and a D in social studies and science."

"This is totally out of control!" John McCarthy blurted. "Wait until I get home. This kid is in deep trouble!"

Barbara King remained calm as she spoke, "Now John, keep in mind, lots of kids go through stages like this. Dylan may be trying to tell us something. We have to listen closely. Several days ago in language arts class, I asked the students to work on writing simple cinquain poems and I was surprised with the response I got from Dylan. I found his poem rather troubling. Here, I want the two of you to take a look at this."

Barbara placed the poem on the table before them. She read:

Fifth Grade
A place to vegetate
Boring, frustrating, wasting
Free my spirit—send me away
Failure

When they were finished reading the poem, Kathy Johnston spoke softly, "I've changed my mind. What I thought was simply a slump is more serious than I thought. Poor little guy, I've known Dylan for years, and I hate to see this happening to him. Elaine, John, do you think we should have Dylan chat with our school counselor? Rob Costello is a great guy. He's really got a great way of working with our kids. The students here really gravitate to him. He's like a big burly teddy bear, but we've seen him make a difference for a lot of kids. Maybe Dylan would let us know what's troubling him through a little work with Rob. What do you think?"

Elaine McCarthy sighed and leaned back in her chair. Her worried look registered her concern for her son. John McCarthy placed his arm around his wife's shoulders, looked down at the table and spoke softly, "Yes, I do think we'd better get Dylan working with this Rob guy as soon as we can."

Rob Costello had been a school counselor at Kingswood Elementary for eight years. He really enjoyed his work, but he often admitted that he rarely saw a gifted student in his office, and this frustrated him. He often shared with the teachers that one of his greatest joys was counseling gifted children. He was intrigued with how they viewed the world differently, marveled at their creative ways of expressing themselves, and admired their sensitive and empathic qualities. Rob was looking forward to meeting Dylan McCarthy. He'd done his homework in preparing for his first session, having talked with all of Dylan's teachers and the McCarthy's.

When Dylan arrived, Rob noticed that Dylan naturally seemed quite nervous. After chatting casually for a few minutes, he turned to a collection of board games in his office and suggested a game of chess. Dylan shrugged his shoulders, smiled softly, and agreed to a game. As Dylan eyed the chess board closely and began to plan his strategy, Rob slowly began his questions for his young client.

"So tell me, how are things going in fifth grade these days?"

Again Dylan shrugged his shoulders and mumbled, "OK, I guess."

"Tell me, what's your favorite subject this year?"

"Art."

"Art class, huh? Tell me about it."

"Mrs. Capitanio's class is cool. I really like her. She let's us work on awesome stuff."

As Rob Costello continued the conversation with Dylan, he realized the report the Kingswood teachers had presented to him concerning Dylan seemed very consistent with what he was seeing that day in his office. Rob thought to himself, "This gifted little guy has lots of layers I'll have to unravel before I get to the heart of his issues. I just wonder how I'll get through."

"So tell me about math class these days."

With that prompt, Dylan appeared even more reluctant and said nothing.

Rob spoke again, "I would think a really sharp guy like you would really enjoy math."

As he carried out his next move on the chessboard, he began to divulge his thoughts, "I have a problem with my teacher."

When Rob encouraged him to continue, Dylan described his feelings about Steve O'Reilly, "I don't like him as a person. I just don't respect him at all."

Rob questioned him further, asking, "Can you tell me more about that?"

Dylan appeared uncomfortable but nevertheless he continued, "He's one of those teachers that picks on kids. Kids like Montoya Marshall. Just because he's different, I guess. Montoya is a little crazy. All the kids in fifth grade know that, but Mr. O'Reilly treats him like an outcast."

Rob noted the emotion that came across Dylan's face as he spoke. He probed further by asking, "An outcast? Tell me about that."

"I think he had to go to the principal's office three times this week. He's always in trouble. Mr. O'Reilly kicks him out of class every day. He doesn't try to do anything to help him! He just yells at him and says things like, 'If you're gonna just sit there and be stupid, then sit there and be stupid!' He says those things in front of the whole class."

Rob commented, "It seems like Mr. O'Reilly's behavior really bothers you."

Dylan responded, "Yeah, it does. He just doesn't treat kids with respect."

As he continued to discuss the insensitivity of the math teacher, Dylan explained that if he didn't respect the teacher, there was no way he could motivate himself to work for the man. He finished his comments with an emphatic, "I think he's a real jerk."

Rob Costello realized he had made an early breakthrough. He continued, "So, tell me. What's homework like in math these days? Is it really tough?"

Dylan made a strategic move on the chessboard, placing Rob's king in check once again. As he enjoyed the exasperated look on Rob Costello's face, he smiled and proceeded to explain, "No, it's not tough at all. Math is my best subject."

Rob continued, "Are you turning in your math?"

Dylan smiled slightly and explained, "I have a personal philosophy on homework. If you know how to do it, why bother to do the homework? It's when you don't know how to do the work that you should have to sit down and figure it out, right?"

Rob smiled in return and didn't reply. He looked at Dylan to continue.

"If I've proven in class that I know the stuff, why do I have to continue to prove that I know it by doing twenty more problems at home? I just don't see the logic in that."

Rob Costello stifled a laugh as Dylan continued to grumble about the unfairness of fifth grade. He knew that he was going to really enjoy getting to know Dylan even better. He decided that Dylan McCarthy was a sharp customer, and he would expect some more very interesting conversations with him before the two of them were able to resolve Dylan's situation. Rob knew he was in for an interesting ride with Dylan, but he was looking forward to the journey.

QUESTIONS FOR REFLECTION AND DISCUSSION

1. What would you identify as the most pressing situation with which Dylan is dealing?

2. What would you propose as possible solutions to Dylan's situation?

3. What might be positive consequences of the solutions? What might be negative consequences of the solutions?

4. What wisdom does Dylan bring to the situation? How would you personally respond to the situation described?

5. What does your response to the situation reveal about your views on underachievement in gifted students?

6. What does your response to the situation reveal about your educational philosophy?

RESOURCES

Galbraith, J. (1999). *The gifted kids' survival guide.* Minneapolis, MN: Free Spirit.

Neihart, M., Reis, S. M., Robinson, N. M., & Moon, S. M. (Eds.). (2002). *The social and emotional development of gifted children: What do we know?* Waco, TX: Prufrock Press.

Rathvon, N. (1996). *The unmotivated child: Helping your underachiever become a successful student.* New York: Simon & Schuster.

Rimm, S. (1995). *Why bright kids get poor grades, and what you can do about it.* New York: Three Rivers Press.

Schmitz, C., & Galbraith, J. (1985). *Managing the social and emotional needs of the gifted: A teacher's survival guide.* Minneapolis, MN: Free Spirit.

CASE 3.3

LIFTING THE VEIL ON GENDER ISSUES

Denise S. Mewborn

Angel Abney

Ms. Gonzalez, a fifth-grade mathematics teacher, is conducting a lesson in which students are experimenting with three-dimensional geometric shapes and their nets (a two-dimensional version of the shape). Spatial visualization is an area of the curriculum in which girls have historically scored lower than boys on standardized tests in this school. Throughout the lesson Ms. Gonzalez treats the boys and girls in her classroom differently in subtle ways of which she is likely unaware. At times, however, Ms. Gonzalez makes deliberate decisions about how to respond to situations based on gender equity issues.

Ms. Gonzalez's fifth-grade students were working with three-dimensional solids in their geometry unit. The students had been given some three-dimensional solids such as cubes, tetrahedrons, and dodecahedrons and some samples of "nets" that could fold up to form these solids. The students' task was to determine which nets would make particular solids. (See Figure 3.1.)

The students were working in groups and had been allowed to choose their own teammates. Ms. Gonzalez noticed that most of the groups were single gender. Only one group contained both boys and girls. She circulated around the room to listen to students' conversations and to offer encouragement.

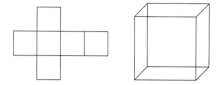

FIGURE 3.1   Net for a cube and a cube

"This is hard. I don't get it. These things are hard. I can't figure out which piece is going to go where when you fold it up," complained Rachel.

"That's OK. This is really hard. Just keep trying," offered Ms. Gonzalez. Next, she joined a group of four boys, and they were disagreeing about how to proceed.

"Gentlemen, what seems to be the problem? Why don't you take turns selecting a shape and a net to see if they match? Phillip, which one are you working on?" asked Ms. Gonzalez.

Phillip showed her the octahedron, with eight triangular faces, and the set of nets they were trying to match to the octahedron. Some of the nets the boys were considering had more than eight faces.

"What are you looking at when you try to decide if a net might match your octahedron?" asked Ms. Gonzalez.

"We're only looking at the ones with triangles for faces," answered Eric.

"Why?" asked Ms. Gonzalez.

"Because the octahedron has triangular faces, so it can't be a net that's made out of squares or pentagons," responded Eric.

"Good reasoning. Is there anything else that would be important to consider?" prompted Ms. Gonzalez.

After thinking for a minute, Joel said he didn't think there was. Ms. Gonzalez selected two nets from Phillip's pile.

"What do these two nets have in common?" Ms. Gonzalez asked.

"Ummm, they are made of triangles," answered Joel.

"Anything else?" probed Ms. Gonzalez.

"Not really. Not that I see," Joel responded.

"OK, so what's different about them?" asked Ms. Gonzalez.

"The triangles are in different spots, so when you fold them up, they're going to make different shapes," suggested Eric.

"Anything else?" she asked.

"Well, yeah. This one has eight triangles and this one has twenty. Oh! I get it! I can't use this one to make an octahedron because it has too many faces! So I shouldn't even be looking at it right now. This one either…it only has four faces. OK, I think we can do this!" shouted Joel.

"Great job! That was some excellent thinking, gentlemen! I'll leave you to work on this," said Ms. Gonzalez as she walked over to join another group of girls.

"You girls are doing a very nice job of keeping your work space neat. I like the way you have sorted all of your shapes into piles. Which shape are you working on now?"

Jodi volunteered. "We're stuck. We can't figure out if this net will make a cube or not. We keep getting all confused because we can't see where the faces will end up on the cube."

"Yeah, we've tried a couple of times, but we just can't see where the faces will go," added Sarah.

"This is confusing, isn't it? Here, let's try to make it easier for you. Let's try numbering the faces of the cube and the squares on the net and see if we can figure out where they match up," offered Ms. Gonzalez as she picked up the cube. "Janet, you write on the net while I write on the cube. Let's make this face the bottom. Mark the bottom on your net. OK, now, this square is the next face because it is adjacent to the bottom. I'm going to mark this with a 2. Janet, mark yours with a 2. No, not that one. Mark the one on the *other* side. Good. Now, let's make the next one 3. Janet, put a 3 on this square right here. Good job." Ms. Gonzalez continued in this manner until all six faces of the cube and all six squares on the net had been marked. "So, girls, do you see that this net matches perfectly with this cube?" The girls all nodded. "Good. Now see if you can do another one," suggested Ms. Gonzalez as she walked away.

Following their small-group work, Ms. Gonzalez called the class back together for a whole group discussion about how they solved the problems. She asked for volunteers to share their thinking strategies. She noted with dismay that approximately ten boys raised their hands, whereas only three girls raised theirs. Before she could call on a student to respond, Robert blurted out a comment. Although she knew she shouldn't acknowledge Robert's response because he wasn't following classroom rules about raised hands, his comment was very insightful and hit on something she wanted to discuss with the students. So, she almost subconsciously decided to pursue his comment. For several minutes she engaged Robert in an explanation of his idea, asking probing questions to get him to more clearly articulate his points. She occasionally called on other students during her dialogue with Robert to be sure that they were understanding what he was saying. However, she realized that most of her questions were directed to boys. So, after she finished with Robert's idea, she decided to call on a girl. However, no girls volunteered to answer her question. They left her with no choice but to call on a girl who had not raised her hand. "Debbie, I don't think I've heard from you today. What do you think about this problem—will this net make a cube?"

Debbie seemed reluctant to answer and simply shrugged her shoulders. Ms. Gonzalez prompted her. "Take a guess. Do you think it will work?"

"We didn't do that one in my group. I don't know if it will work," explained Debbie.

"That's OK. Just tell me what you think. Will it work? Or won't it?" pushed Ms. Gonzalez.

"Ummmmm, I don't know. I guess it will," replied Debbie, reluctantly.

"Well, let's check. Come up here and fold this net. Let's see what happens." Debbie crept to the front of the room, took the paper net from Ms. Gonzalez, and began to fold it along its edges. After a few seconds she handed it back to her teacher and said almost inaudibly, "It won't work." She immediately headed for her seat.

"Whoa. Wait a minute, Debbie. Come back up here. Tell everyone what you just told me," said Ms. Gonzalez.

"It doesn't work," said Debbie in a whisper.

"Louder, please," prompted Ms. Gonzalez.

"It doesn't work," Debbie said again.

"And why not?" pushed the teacher.

"Ummm...because the...ummm...it just doesn't. It doesn't make a cube," responded Debbie.

Sensing that Debbie was embarrassed, Ms. Gonzalez decided to let her return to her seat.

After a lengthy sharing session, Ms. Gonzalez asked the students how this activity might be related to something that people do in their jobs in the real world. After some thoughtful silence, Arianna said, "This reminds me of what my mom does. She has to look at drawings of buildings that are flat like our nets. But she has to imagine what they are going to look like when they are really built so she can be sure there won't be any problems with them."

"Interesting. What kind of job does your mother have?" asked Ms. Gonzalez.

"She's a civil engineer. They work on buildings and bridges and things like that," answered Arianna.

"Moms can't be engineers. Only dads can do that! Maybe your mom is the secretary for the engineer," blurted Theodore.

"No! My mom is really an engineer!" retorted Arianna.

Ms. Gonzalez interrupted quickly. "Do you remember when we had parents come talk to us about careers? Do you remember how we discussed the fact that everyone can do any job if they have the right education and training? Recall that we had a man who was a nurse and a woman who was in the army come talk to us. They told us that you can be a doctor or a pilot or a teacher or a photographer or anything else, as long as you stay in school and work hard to achieve your goals. Now, let's get ready for recess."

QUESTIONS FOR REFLECTION AND DISCUSSION

1. How are students praised for their academic work and who is praised for their nonacademic work? Do boys and girls get the same kind of praise?

2. Which students are given hints to assist them with solving the problem on their own and which students are given the solution?

3. What are the advantages and disadvantages of allowing students to choose their own groups? What are the advantages and disadvantages of allowing students to work in single-sex groups? Does the age of the students matter?

4. In what ways does this teacher convey that she believes that boys are naturally better at spatial reasoning than girls? How might teachers become more aware of the messages they send students?

5. What might a teacher do when some students consistently do not raise their hands to participate in class discussions? Consider asking some of your students who do not participate why they do not volunteer.

6. How might this teacher have handled Theodore's comment about women not being engineers?

RESOURCES

American Association of University Women. (1991). *Shortchanging girls, shortchanging America.* Washington, DC: Author.

American Association of University Women. (1992). *The AAUW report: How schools shortchange girls.* Washington, DC: Author.

American Association of University Women. (1995). *Growing smart: What's working for girls in school.* Washington, DC: Author.

American Association of University Women. (1998). *Gender gaps: Where schools still fail our children.* Washington, DC: Author.

American Association of University Women. (2001). *Beyond the "gender wars": A conversation about girls, boys, and education.* Washington, DC: Author.

Bernstein, L., Winkler, A., & Zierdt-Warshaw, L. (1996). *Multicultural women of science: Three centuries of contributions with hands-on experiments and activities for thirty-seven weeks.* Maywood, NJ: Peoples Publishing Group.

Chapman, A. (1997). *A great balancing act: Equitable education for boys and girls.* Washington, DC: National Association of Independent Schools.

Sanders, J., Koch, J., & Urso, J. (1997). *Gender equity right from the start: Instructional activities for teacher educators in mathematics, science, and technology.* Mahwah, NJ: Erlbaum.

Sadker, M., & Sadker, D. (1994). *Failing at fairness: How America's schools cheat girls.* New York: Scribner.

CASE 3.4

SCHOOLING GIFTED BLACK CHILDREN
Issues for Parents and Teachers

Tarek C. Grantham

Linda A. Long

This case presents a number of concerns and experiences that Black parents have when making transitions between school districts. These are concerns that teachers must address when advising and providing quality educational experiences for gifted Black youth. The realities that a Black family (Sandra and Jamar) faces are illustrated through a dialogue with an elementary school teacher and friend

(Penny), as well as family members. Sandra and Jamar have obtained background information on the new school district, and also sought professional and personal insights into the perceptions and expectations that educators and family members have of Black children and their experiences in the Cornell County School District. You are challenged to explore and address issues regarding giftedness, professionalism, equality, expectations, and how these areas may impact the decisions of Black parents, schools with gifted programs, and teachers of gifted Black students.

Sandra: Hello Penny! This is Sandra Austin.

Penny: Sandra. Sandra from the student government association?

Sandra: Yes, can you believe it? I know it's been a long time, hasn't it?

Penny: Yes it has. What a pleasant surprise! What have you been up to?

Sandra: Well, my husband and I are considering relocation to your area. He recently graduated and received a job offer from Electronics International in Verlington. We have wanted to move to the area for a long time, hearing about all of the good job opportunities there. We've learned that many of our friends have found the Southwest a nice place to live and raise a family.

Penny: Wow, a new job! I knew that Jamar wanted to go back to graduate school to complete his degree, but I wasn't sure where he was in the process. I didn't know that you were considering Verlington.

Sandra: Yep. A lot has happened since we last talked. We have another addition to the family, Cameron, who is five years old, and, of course, you know Nicholas, now eight years old. We are truly blessed with healthy children who are good and really enjoy learning. This fall, Cameron will be starting kindergarten and Nicholas will be in the fourth grade. This brings me to one of the things I wanted to talk with you about. You are still teaching at the elementary level, right?

Penny: Yes, at Mary Bower Elementary.

Sandra: Good, then maybe you can help us make some decisions about housing and schools.

Penny: I'll try.

Sandra: We have to make decisions within the next two weeks regarding where we will live and to which school we will send our kids. Jamar has done some research on the different areas in the Verlington area and we wanted to get your opinion of Cornell County.

Penny: That's my district.

Sandra: No kidding. I didn't know that. I thought you lived and worked in Gardner County.

Penny: Shawn and I do still live in Gardner, but I recently changed jobs, and now I work in Cornell County.

Sandra: Many people who have moved to that area say that Cornell is a good place to be. I was wondering about the school district's academic climate, demographics, and achievement rates.

Penny: What do you mean?

Sandra: Well, as you can imagine, knowing us and our concern for our kids, Jamar and I have had some challenging times with the school district where Nicholas was enrolled. Very few Black males were in the gifted program at the elementary level, and none had skipped a grade level before. We want to enroll Nicholas and Cameron in schools that have a track record for doing a good job of recognizing and nurturing the talents of Black children, particularly Black males. We know that it is important that parents be involved in schooling their children, as we have been. But we have experienced teachers and administrators who don't know how to deal with Black children and fail to respect their parents' level of concern.

Penny: Being new to this district, I must be honest, I don't know a great deal about the pros and cons of each school, but my understanding is that the Cornell school district is committed to its diverse student body and is doing a good job with the kids, better than some of the districts in the metropolitan area. Last year was my first year, and, when I started with the district, I was hired to re-vamp the gifted program. I had been teaching for five months, and it was evident that, besides the administrators (those who hired me to establish a gifted program for students), there was no one in the district who really wanted a program for gifted students at all. Some of the elementary faculty and administrators made it clear that they thought gifted programs were wrong, claiming that they were elit-ist and undemocratic. Strong feelings regarding the need for equity in the school community have been expressed, particularly by Black parents. The previous teacher of the gifted at my current school, Lisa, endured a great deal of stress. One parent was quoted in the newspaper saying, "Out of all the Black kids in the second grade, you can only find two that are gifted? Come on!" Many parents and concerned teachers believe that the gifted program enrollment criteria allow only certain individuals to participate. They also believe that these programs cre-ate special groups. We are working hard to change the negative perceptions that exist regarding the gifted program and how we serve Black students.

Sandra: This was, in part, our concern with the school district we're leaving. We were able to work out reasonable arrangements for Nicholas by al-lowing him to skip a grade. That enabled him to receive opportunities for his abilities and talents as a gifted child. But it sure was a struggle! As we are think-ing about Cameron coming along, and Nicholas as he gets older, we feel we want to make a more informed choice about their schooling and where we live.

Penny: I understand that the previous teacher in my school worked alone and had not cultivated any friends for the programs. It is my understand-ing that she developed a pullout program that grouped students for a full day once a week. She took them on field trips that were the envy of all students in the schools and demanded special equipment for her resource room that she insisted no other child be allowed to use. She did not meet with any of the parents or other teachers and did not feel she had time to be involved in school-sponsored events, including faculty professional and social meetings. Because she was only part time, she was not required to attend. I am sure that you wouldn't have approved of that, Sandra, after you were on that governing board for the gifted program advocacy group. She left after only four months, and the program at all levels fizzled toward the end of the semester. None of faculty felt a loss. Shortly thereafter I came on board.

    Sandra: Sounds like there are some great chances for moving forward now that you are on board. Thanks for your honest perspective. I will be talking with you again very soon!

JAMAR'S SEARCH FROM THE SCHOOL DISTRICT'S WEB SITE

Jamar discovered that the Cornell County school district has a local school report card and systemwide demographic data for newcomers and residents to review. Tables 3.1 through 3.4 outline what he found. The percentage listed by each entry indicates that percent that the given cell presents of the total.

TABLE 3.1   Districtwide Enrollment: Ethnicity and Gender

	MALE		FEMALE		TOTAL	
Caucasian	1,292	18%	1,376	20%	2,668	38%
Black	1,780	25	1,888	27	3,668	52
Hispanic	220	3	196	3	416	6
Asian	164	1	168	2	332	4
Total	3,456	48%	3,628	52%	7,084	100%

*Some numbers do not total to 100% due to rounding

TABLE 3.2   Districtwide Lunch Program Enrollment: Ethnicity and Program

	FREE		REDUCED		TOTAL	
Caucasian	133	3%	400	10%	533	13%
Black	1,467	36	1,761	43	3,228	79
Hispanic	62	2	125	3	187	5
Asian	3	<1	113	3	116	3
Total	1,665	41%	2,399	59%	4,064	100%

TABLE 3.3   **Distribution of Students Identified as Gifted: Ethnicity and Gender**

	MALE		FEMALE		TOTAL	
Caucasian	387	39%	347	35%	734	74%
Black	29	3	109	11	138	14
Hispanic	10	1	10	1	20	2
Asian	50	5	50	5	100	10
Total	476	48%	516	52%	992	100%

TABLE 3.4   **Distribution of Gifted Students in Lunch Program: Ethnicity and Gender**

	FREE		REDUCED		TOTAL	
Caucasian	11	6%	21	12%	32	18%
Black	57	32	71	40	128	72
Hispanic	7	4	7	4	14	8
Asian	2	1	2	1	4	2
Total	77	43%	101	57%	178	100%

LOOKING BACK

As they make their transition, Sandra and her husband Jamar want what is best for their children, and prefer not to have to grapple with teachers and administrators to have their children's academic abilities and social needs respected and addressed. Sandra and Jamar have children who demonstrate multiple intelligences, and like their parents, really like math and science. Jamar participated in the gifted program throughout his entire academic career. Nicholas achieved the highest score on the school's standardized math test in the first grade. He also scored in the top 5 percent of his class on the science portion of the test during his third-grade year. This surprised Ms. Hansen, Nicholas's kindergarten teacher, who did not recommend Nicholas for gifted program screening. Ms. Hansen was a teacher with twenty-five years of experience who was voted teacher of the year in 1996. She felt that he did not deserve to be in the gifted program because she perceived him to be a jokester, one who had a "bad" attitude in class. Ms. Hansen's comments in Nicholas's student cumulative folder indicated "he often asked questions" of her that were "out of context and disruptive." Interestingly, another teacher, one who had training in gifted education, commented that Nicholas's participation in class was "always beyond the scope of what was being talked about in class" and "his unmatched humor promoted insightful angles through which he and his peers could understand and analyze concepts." Sandra recalled Ms. Hansen mentioning to her that, even from her time as a student in that same elementary school where she now teaches, oftentimes boys, like Nicholas, sat in the back of the classroom, failed to pay attention, did not want to learn, and tried to make fun of teachers by asking off-the-wall questions. Although eight of the "back-of-the-classroom" boys were referred for special education services by Ms. Hansen during Nicholas's kindergarten year, including Nicholas, three of the boys were later identified as gifted during their second-grade year.

LOOKING FORWARD TO THE FUTURE IN CORNELL COUNTY

Jamar asked about Sandra's conversation with Penny. Sandra commented that it was good talking with her and suggested that it would probably be good to talk with Jamar's family to see how they like school in Cornell County.

Jamar: Hello Linzey [Jamar's niece], it's good to hear your voice.

Linzey: Yours too.

Jamar: As you know, Sandra and I are thinking about moving to the area and wanted to get an idea of how you are doing in school. We were trying to understand the different levels at the elementary and middle school level.

Linzey: Well, I have been in the B level track since elementary school. I think there are three levels, special ed, regular, and STAR...of course the only reason I know about STAR is because Markel is in it.

Jamar: How did you like your classes and teachers?

Linzey: I liked most of my classes and teachers, especially this year. My English teacher—Mrs. Brown, one of my Black teachers—told me that I was

TABLE 3.5 Year-End Report on Ms. Hansen's Kindergarten Class (Requested by Sandra and Jamar Austin)

			SCREENING RECOMMENDATION		OFFICE REFERRALS FOR	
	Male	*Female*	*Gifted*	*Special Ed*	*Conduct*	*Attitude*
Caucasian	1	2	3	0	4	1
Black	12	9	1	10	30	15
Hispanic	1	1	0	0	2	0
Asian	0	1	1	0	0	0
Total	14	13	5	10	36	16

smart. She told me that Black students have to work twice as hard to get half as far as White students. This kinda shocked me when she said that. And the kicker, she said this in front of me and some other students in the class; there was no Whites in my regular level class, you know…. That girl that got put out of the STAR classes looked at me funny. She a trip; heard she didn't like being a STAR and ain't want to be in there. Even though I might not be as smart as some of them White people in the STAR classes, I think I could be getting better grades.

Jamar: Why do you say that?

Linzey: This year, my test scores were high—in the ninety-fifth percentile and stuff in the real subjects. But my grades ain't very good. I usually makes Bs and sometimes As when the class is really interesting or good. When I show my mom stuff like report cards and standardized test letters, she don't halfway understand. She just so happy that I ain't making no Ds and Fs, you know.

Jamar: You know she's proud of you.

Linzey: Yeah, she's really proud of me. This year in English, I got all As. Mrs. Brown was a hard teacher, and she taught a whole lot about Black stuff. It was really good learning about Ebonics. Mrs. Brown said she's not worried about me because she knows that I'm smart.

Jamar: Are you looking forward to next year?

Linzey: Don't say that yet. Now it's still summer and not time to start school yet. Mrs. Brown recommended me for the STAR program for the sixth grade, and it has classes in English, math, science, and civics. I was really happy about her recommendation, but I didn't tell any of my friends. I want to be in the classes, but I ain't sure about the work and them kids in the classes. Ain't a whole lot of Black people in those classes.

INSIGHTS FROM MARKEL'S EXPERIENCE, JAMAR'S NEPHEW

Markel is a seventh grader who has been in the STAR program since the fourth grade. In the first grade, teachers recommended Markel be tested for special education services because of his "maladaptive" behavior. His parents agreed that he should be tested against Jamar's protests, and, fortunately, the results from his psychological evaluation did not support placement for special education services. Later, with the encouragement from Jamar and Sandra, Markel's parents requested that he be considered for the STAR program because he scored in the ninety-second percentile overall on all sections of the school-administered standardized achievement tests during his third-grade year. The cutoff for the STAR program was the ninetieth percentile. Jamar spoke with Markel on the phone after talking with Linzey.

Markel: I don't want to be in the STAR program any more. I am tired of learning about the same White people and the same things. I want to learn about other people and other countries. The White people are just trying to advance other White people and leave Blacks behind and ignorant. I bet in the classes where there are a lot of Blacks they get to learn more about their heritage than in the STAR program, especially in civics! No one in my classes cares. In English, for example, every time I write a paper and want to talk about Blacks or issues related to Blacks, I feel like I have to do everything by myself. When we do group edits on work, the students usually don't want to work with me because they think I am going to call them racist or something. I don't know why they think this because we get along fairly well. The teacher is another story. He always gives me Bs on my papers, even after I have addressed his concerns from several rough drafts. I know I am not dumb, but he makes me feel that way. Why do I have to suffer in this and other STAR classes, getting Bs and Cs while the other Black students seem to be having fun in their classes, making As and Bs?

Jamar: Hang in there Markel. I know you can do it. I have always believed in you and know that you have what it takes to make it. Don't let them get to you.

QUESTIONS FOR REFLECTION AND DISCUSSION

1. What are typical behaviors of gifted elementary-aged children?
2. What are some of the assumptions that undergird how Ms. Hansen thinks about giftedness or gifted students?
3. What are indicators that a school's gifted program is identifying and serving students in a fair way? In an unfair way?
4. Describe the role you will take (have taken) in addressing injustices in gifted programs.
5. How do you think Penny handled herself in conversation with Sandra?
6. How can teachers be sensitive to the parental concerns of gifted Black children?
7. What are some perceived stereotypical attitudes or behaviors of Black children that are perpetuated by society? By elementary schools? By elementary schoolteachers? By Black children?

RESOURCES

Colangelo, N., & Davis, G. A. (Eds.). (1991). *Handbook of gifted education.* Boston: Allyn & Bacon.
Ford, D. Y. (1996). *Reversing underachievement among gifted Black students: Promising practices and programs.* New York: Teachers College Press.
Hale-Benson, J. (1986). *Black children: Their roots, culture, and learning styles* (2nd ed.). Baltimore, MD: Johns Hopkins University Press.
McAdoo, H. (1988). *Black families.* Newbury Park: Sage.

CASE 3.5

TO RETAIN OR NOT TO RETAIN?
Matthew P. Quirk

Ms. Johnson is a relatively new kindergarten teacher with three years of experience. In her brief tenure as a teacher, she has struggled with many decisions. The one decision that she cannot seem to reconcile or negotiate is that of retaining students who are falling behind yet who do not qualify for assistance through special education. Currently, one of her students, Julie, is struggling to complete the required material to advance to first grade. As the school year comes to a close, Ms. Johnson explores her options with her colleagues and Julie's parents.

It is the middle of May and the classroom is full of excitement. All of Ms. Johnson's students are anticipating the summer break and are looking forward to becoming "big first graders." All of the students will be promoted to first grade except for Julie, who may be retained in kindergarten for another year. At the end of kindergarten, Julie has not yet met the school's requirements for passing kindergarten. Ms. Johnson is struggling with the decision of whether to retain Julie and wonders if an extra year of kindergarten will be more beneficial for Julie than advancing her to first grade without the potential of acquiring extra supports to assist in the transition.

Ms. Johnson and her colleagues have developed strategies to help Julie with the areas in which she struggles most—letter recognition and basic math. Her work habits are poorly developed; she fails to complete assignments and has difficulty following directions. This is not unusual for the kindergarten students in Ms. Johnson's class at the beginning of the year but, because it is now May and these problems persist for Julie, Ms. Johnson is weighing these issues when considering Julie's promotion.

Both the school psychologist and special education director have observed Julie in the classroom at Ms. Johnson's request, and agree that Julie is not exhibiting the typical behaviors and abilities that most students need to move on to the first grade. They agree that she is a borderline student but want to leave the retention decision up to Ms. Johnson because she has had the most contact with Julie during the school year. In the past month, Julie has made some progress getting her assignments turned in and has done better following directions, but she is still behind the rest of the class.

Ms. Johnson called Julie's parents in for a conference to allow them to get involved in this important decision-making process. Because they both work full time, they are only able to meet on a Saturday morning, so Ms. Johnson agrees to meet with them the following Saturday at 9:00 A.M.

Ms. Johnson: Thank you for making time to come in this morning to discuss Julie's progress in my class. We have already talked about the possibility that Julie may need an extra year in kindergarten. As we discussed, we decided to

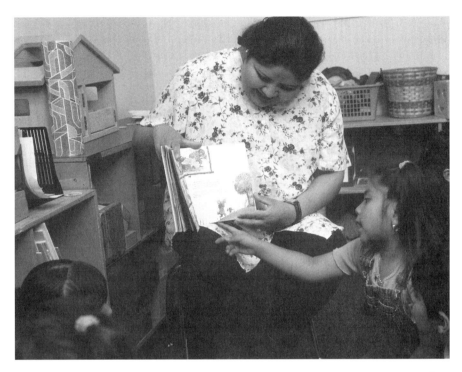

Schools that set high expectations for all students and provide the support necessary to achieve their expectations have high rates of academic success.

give her some time to see if she could make some additional progress to move on to first grade. She has been making some progress in my class and I wanted to ask you if you are trying some strategies at home?

Mother: We have been working hard to get her to follow directions at home because I know that is one of the problems we had discussed in our last conference. She has been doing everything that we ask her to do; how is she doing here at school?

Ms. Johnson: Julie is doing much better following directions lately, but she is still struggling with some of the academics that she needs to move on to the first grade.

Father: We have been helping her do her homework at night when we have time; she seems to be doing OK with our help. Please, is there anything else that we can do to help her get to first grade? I don't understand how she could be failing kindergarten. Every time we ask her what she is doing at school she tells us that she is playing and making friends.

Ms. Johnson: We do play and make friends; however, there are certain things in reading and math that she needs to be able to do for her to move to first grade. The first-grade teachers have a curriculum to follow, and if my students come into the class unprepared, it makes it difficult for them to keep up and they quickly get further and further behind.

The meeting continued and Julie's parents were obviously confused and upset as to how their child could possibly be failing kindergarten. However, the meeting served its purpose, making Julie's parents aware that the time for this decision was approaching and that there was a possibility that their daughter might be retained. Ms. Johnson is consumed with the decision, weighing the pros and cons and ultimately deciding.

Her discussion with the school psychologist revealed a lot of issues that were difficult to weigh. If Ms. Johnson retained Julie, there was the possibility that Julie would come back next year more developmentally ready to handle the tasks in kindergarten. If that were the case, retaining her would be the right decision. In the past three years, the four students that Ms. Johnson retained were young boys who simply weren't ready for school. She truly believed that the retention decision benefited the boys. Unfortunately, Julie's birthday was in December and she would turn seven during the following school year.

To be eligible for special education services for children with learning disabilities, Julie would need to show a distinct gap between her ability and her achievement. If she were moved to first grade, the class lesson material would be more difficult, and there might be a better chance that the school psychologist could identify a discrepancy. Ms. Johnson knew that many times school psychologists are reluctant to place kindergarten students in special education because they are so young and are still rapidly developing. Ms. Johnson thought if every effort is made to help a child and the student is still struggling the school psychologist is more likely to get the student special needed services.

All of these paths seemed like they could work for Julie, but none of them stood out as the right one. This decision will have a major impact on Julie's future and it weighed heavily on Ms. Johnson's mind. There had to be someone else Ms. Johnson could talk to who might be able to help her with this decision, so she decided to consult one of the first-grade teachers.

Her good friend, Mr. Henry, is a first-grade teacher and he agreed to meet with her one day after school. Unlike some of the other first-grade teachers, Mr. Henry spends a lot of time in the beginning of the year transitioning the children into first grade. He has found that by spending a few weeks reviewing some of the kindergarten concepts he allows his students to get comfortable. In the past, when a student was on the borderline and the kindergarten teacher decided to promote the student to the first grade, the child was placed in Mr. Henry's class.

Ms. Johnson explains Julie's situation to Mr. Henry. He agrees that it is a difficult decision to make and that either way Julie could benefit. Ms. Johnson shows him some examples of Julie's work and asks if he thinks that she would advance in a class like his.

Mr. Henry: I have had students at this level go both ways in the past. I had a boy last year who had work very similar to this and who was at the head of the class by the end of the year. He really needed the time in the summer to catch up with his peers developmentally.

Ms. Johnson: Julie does not have a late birthday, but I have seen some progress in the past month that may indicate she could develop over the summer. The district policy only permits one grade retention in elementary school. This has been an issue for me when I think about retaining Julie.

Ms. Johnson continued to struggle with her thoughts. If Julie were to make progress over the summer would it be better to pass her? If she does continue to struggle, would it be better to have her repeat first grade rather than kindergarten? There is a lot more academic material that she could benefit from in first grade than there is in the beginning of kindergarten. Even though she is not yet ready for first grade, Julie does not really need to repeat the beginning of kindergarten. As Ms. Johnson walked to her car at the end of the school day, she shook her head, lost in her thoughts.

QUESTIONS FOR REFLECTION AND DISCUSSION

1. What are the strengths in the approach that Ms. Johnson is taking with regard to Julie's retention?

2. What are the expectations that children may have before they reach school that would promote success in kindergarten?

3. Discuss Ms. Johnson's interaction with Julie's parent and the early notification that their daughter was struggling academically in school.

4. What factors do you believe should be included in decisions about promotion or retention?

RESOURCES

Denton, D. R. (2001). *Finding alternatives to failure: Can states end social promotion and reduce retention rates?* Atlanta, GA: Southern Regional Education Board.

Roderick, M. (1995). Grade retention and school dropout: Policy debate and research questions. *Phi Delta Kappa Research Bulletin, 15,* 1–6.

Shepard, L. A., & Smith M. L. (1989). *Flunking grades: Research and policies on retention.* New York: Falmer Press.

U.S. Department of Education. (1999). *Taking responsibility for ending social promotion: A guide for educators and state and local leaders.* Washington, DC: Author.

CHAPTER 4

SAFETY AND
PROSOCIAL BEHAVIORS

All children come to schools with different experiences with their families and communities. As educators, this contextual information about students provides meaningful information about the elements of the children's environments that may impede or promote their success in school. Even very young children have experiences in their families and neighborhoods that many adults have not had. Yet a child who has been physically abused or neglected, has been sexually assaulted, has been exposed to drugs, or has witnessed traumatic events brings other concerns to the learning situation. Many theories on the psychological development of individuals have focused on the physiological, safety, and security needs of children that must be met before children may realize their academic needs. Different children come to school with different experiences, so a "one size fits all" approach to working with a group of students is not a realistic goal. Each child needs individual attention and nurturance to be able to reach his or her potential. In this chapter, a series of cases is presented that focus on some very typical and some atypical experiences concerning safety and prosocial behavior in the classroom that teachers have had with students.

In the first case, "Teasing the Traumatized Child," Jill Barber and Mary W. Armsworth reflect on their experiences helping a third-grade boy who from a very young age experienced abuse and neglect from the members of his family. The authors carefully present how the young child's constant level of hyperarousal impacts all of his actions in his third-grade classroom. The authors conclude with helpful insights for the teacher on how to interpret the behavior of and support the needs of children who are victims of abuse and neglect.

In a second case on abuse and neglect, David K. Grant asks us to consider the long-term consequences of early exposure to drugs and alcohol. The child in this case, in a retrospective view of his early experiences, causes the reader to think about the systems of support that are necessary for children to be happy, healthy, and successful in school. In "The Inconvenient Child" we are moved to think about the experiences that young Sean has and how those experiences impact his performance in the classroom.

Just as children are victims of physical abuse, unfortunately children are also victims of sexual abuse or exposure to inappropriate material of a sexual nature that is not intended for young children. In "Anna's Undergarments," Victoria Person reflects on her experiences with a young child in a second-grade classroom. Over the course of a year, Person details her interactions with Anna and her interpretations of Anna's behavior. She presents her interactions with Anna's parents and the school counselor. Despite Person's ability to focus on and perceive Anna in a very positive light, the reader is asked to consider what else might be happening to Anna.

Although children can be victims of abuse, abuse is often defined quite narrowly. Children who are exposed to drugs and alcohol are also victims of neglect who need support in their schools. Two school psychologists and a fifth-grade teacher, Vicki Bunke and Tara Terry-Childers and teacher Aaron Childers, present a case of two students who are both using banned substances. In "You Can't Judge a Book by Its Cover: Mr. Smith Confronts Drug Use among His Students" the classroom teacher's reaction and the reaction of one of his mentors causes the reader to consider the typical images we have about children who use drugs and alcohol. In a twist, however, another student's drug use that goes unnoticed in the same classroom challenges us to reconsider our assumptions.

Most teachers have concerns about the emotional and behavioral needs of students. In one case, a teacher confront a situation in which a child presents a physical and immediate danger to the rest of the children in the class. Jennifer Hargrove writes about her experiences with safety in the classroom in "I'm Not Going To...." The case describes the behavior of a young second-grade child and challenges the reader to think carefully about the security needs of the child who is engaging in dangerous behavior as well as the needs of other children in the class. The case highlights the need for systemic support for the child in the school and home.

The need for belonging and affirmation from peers is presented in the next case by Carson McCutcheon. McCutcheon, a first-year teacher, presents her experience in dealing with graffiti inappropriate for school. In "To Tell the Truth" the reader is asked to critique the teacher's handling of the situation including her first-year teacher status and the ownership for behavior that she placed on her students.

The final two cases of the chapter deal with traumatic events that children experience. The experiences highlighted in these two cases impact the children in the cases for the rest of their lives. In "Moving On As Best We Can" Jeannelle Carlisle present her son's experience of having an elicit substance added to his drink at lunch without his knowledge. The resulting injury to her son, in light of her family's attention to a member of the family who was ill, coupled with the school's response causes the reader to think about the systemic influences on a family in crisis. The last case in this chapter presents a situation where students in a second-grade class lose one of their classmates to a fatal car accident. Written by Sylvia Hutchinson and Michelle Graham, "Sudden Tragedy" presents a teacher wrestling with her own feelings of loss as well as her role in that loss.

CASES

CASE 4.1

TEASING THE TRAUMATIZED CHILD

Jill Barber
Mary W. Armsworth

Each day, millions of children in the United States face abuse. The most recent data on child abuse indicate that more than 800,000 new cases of abuse were substantiated in 1999, adding to the millions of children already recorded in the nation's tracking system (National Child Abuse and Neglect Reporting System, 1999). Regardless of the living arrangements made for children who are abused— whether they remain in their homes, are placed in foster care, or are placed with their relatives—the majority will continue to attend school and be a part of your classroom. Although psychological trauma resulting from abuse affects the whole child, the observer often sees only changed behavior that may be confusing or complex to understand (Armsworth & Holaday, 1993; Pynoos, Steinberg, & Goenjian, 1996). Understanding the impact of this trauma provides the teacher with an additional "set of lenses" to view and to make sense of the effect that abuse has on learning and classroom behavior.

A child who lives in an abusive home exists in a constant state of chaos, fear, and often terror that destroys his or her sense of a "safe place." This existence results in feelings of helplessness, vulnerability, and loss of control. A child abused by one or both parents, suffers from the loss of nurturing and protective individuals who for other children provide comfort and care. The difficulties a child in this type of environment faces in moving through normal developmental processes while simultaneously living immersed in fear, with little or no support, are enor-

Contextual information about students shared among teachers provides meaningful insight about the elements of the children's environments that may impede their success in school.

mous. Recent research by Perry (1997) on children exposed to constant abuse has yielded information that adds to our understanding of such children. Perry has documented changes in the central nervous system that are continuously active when a child is responding to constant threat. This state results in the child being hypersensitive to external stimuli (e.g., noise, movement, voice tone, and cues that are similar to earlier trauma) and being hypervigilant (having a heightened awareness of possible threat or attack). Pynoos and colleagues (1996) emphasize the importance of understanding any cues that are traumatic reminders of any aspect of the previous abuse. When activated, the child behaves as if the trauma is reoccurring in the moment. The more threatened we are, the more regressed our thinking and behavior become. The child's ability to concentrate, to process information, and to learn is affected. According to Perry (1995), "the key to understanding traumatized children is to remember that they will, at baseline, be in a state of low-level fear—responding by using either a hyperarousal or dissociated adaptation" (p. 4). Consider this information as you read the following case about Thomas.

Thomas Burch was a nine-year-old third grader in an elementary school in rural Texas when we met. I was a traveling school psychologist assigned to several elementary schools in a large county. Thomas was in a special education class and had been identified as having both learning and emotional difficulties. Thomas's teacher, Mrs. Moore, reported that he had little tolerance and was easily frustrated, got into frequent fights, seemed not to pay attention, did not complete tasks without many requests, and had academic abilities that seemed to "come and go." Mrs. Moore told me that at times he could read well, but at other times he needed to sound words out and was not able to remember what he had read. Mrs. Moore was both frustrated and puzzled. Thomas was in her classroom, a self-contained special education class, for five of the six periods of the day.

Thomas lived with his biological mother some of the time, but at other times, because of her substance abuse and other stressors, Thomas and his siblings lived with their maternal grandmother. Thomas had a history of being both physically and sexually abused by his biological father who lived in the same community and who had not been prosecuted for the abuse. At times, Thomas seemed to idealize his father. His father owned a local business and had a nice car. At other times, he became enraged and denied that his last name was Burch. According to reports from the local Child Protective Services, Thomas had been sexually abused starting about age four and had been physically abused for most of his life. He was removed from the custody of his mother at one point because she refused to deny his biological father access to Thomas and his siblings. Thomas and his siblings refused to testify in court against their father and so, according to the Child Protective Services worker, nothing could be done to prosecute Thomas's father for the abuse. Thomas continued to have some contact with his father in supervised settings. He also continued to alternate between being angry and being fearful in interpersonal interactions at school. He also struggled with academic tasks.

One challenge Mrs. Moore faced typifies the way children who are abused often handle conflict and may be useful to consider. One morning, Thomas came to school late and seemed to be distracted. His teacher welcomed him, got him settled into his desk, and started on the morning reading task. Thomas seemed to welcome the routine of his classroom. He worked well for about thirty minutes until Jose walked by his desk, knocked his pencil to the floor, and bumped his arm. At this point, Thomas became explosive. He jumped from his desk, shouted at Jose, shoved, and hit him. Mrs. Moore quickly intervened and separated the boys. Her assistant, Mrs. Rodricus, took Jose to a time-out spot in the classroom and Mrs. Moore took Thomas outside the classroom to calm down. Thomas seemed inconsolable. He was crying and was unresponsive to Mrs. Moore's questions. He walked away from her and then began running to an outside door. Mrs. Moore followed him and, after catching up with him, put her arm around him. He slowed down but still was not talking. She walked around the playground beside him until he calmed down. Although Thomas could not tell Mrs. Moore what had upset him, he was able to return to the classroom, physically. After being invited, he chose to sit at a table near the teacher's desk. He was unable to return to his class work. Thomas daydreamed and drew until it was lunchtime.

TEACHING NOTE

Thomas Burch's history documents a life of abuse, pain, and fear resulting in a child who has attempted to survive physically and emotionally under conditions that produce confusion and anxiety. Both parents engage in behavior that is harmful to Thomas and to them. Thomas's situation leaves him trapped in the wake of his parents' refusal to accept responsibility for their behavior, or to allow their child to receive help from Child Protective Services. The absence of a protective person who can be counted on leaves this young boy in a helpless, vulnerable situation over which he has no control.

The trauma Thomas has experienced for at least six years as a result of physical abuse, sexual abuse, abandonment, and neglect has come at critical stages of his development. Thomas's surroundings provided few, if any, basic needs. The six basic needs for (1) security or safety, (2) control and effectiveness, (3) positive identity and self-esteem, (4) positive connection and trust in others, (5) autonomy and self-trust, and (6) comprehension of reality (Pearlman & Staub, 1999) have been ignored by the significant adults in his life.

As with many children who are abused and neglected, when the family institution fails the child, outside resources, such as school, peers, church, and other relationships, become the means of filling these basic needs. The time spent in a classroom is often the safest situation children who are abused experience on a regular basis. School provides opportunities for the child to experience predictability and structure; to observe interactions between adults and children that are healthier than those modeled at home; to view another reality besides destructiveness and irresponsibility; and to experience relationships that may provide trust, positive connections, and positive esteem.

Trauma resulting from abuse, neglect, and loss has the potential to alter the physiological, emotional, cognitive, social, physical, and spiritual functioning of children (Armsworth & Holaday, 1993). An adage often quoted by individuals who work with children who are abused is "When abuse begins, childhood ends." The normal progression of development is derailed, and sometimes permanently changed. Because Thomas's abuse is long-standing and his home situation is unstable, he has had to adapt to pervasive fear and learn to cope with the resulting anxiety. Thomas displays behaviors that indicate he is attempting to cope with strong feelings of fear and anger but with limited coping mechanisms and skills. As Perry's (1995) theory indicates, Thomas is always in a low-level state of fear, and his behavior alternates between periods of hyperarousal and dissociated adaptation. This parallels the "fight or flight" human response to fear. The behavioral patterns appear to be responses to what is occurring around Thomas at the moment, or as a result of retraumatization by his father, or the reactivation of memories or feelings related to the abuse.

Thomas's academic abilities that "come and go," his inability to remember what he has read, and his lack of attention are the types of behavior exhibited when a person makes use of dissociative adaptation, a means to "flee" at least internally from a fearful situation. Dissociation is a mechanism that allows the child to get distance from feelings, thoughts, and sensations that are too overwhelming or that feel uncontrollable (Barber, 1997). Dissociation is a normal behavior that we all have experienced. The mild range includes behaviors such as daydreaming, highway hypnosis, and total absorption in a good book or film. At the more severe range are behaviors such as "spacing out," feeling remote from the environment, drastic changes in behavior, unexplained outbursts, and disorientation (James, 1989). Barber (1997) found that individuals who experienced trauma at during early and middle childhood were more dissociative than those who experienced similar events during adolescence. Additionally, those who experienced multiple types of trauma, including sexual abuse, incest, physical abuse, and the loss of a parent were more dissociative than those who experienced a single type of trauma. Increased dissociation can be understood as protective for children who are overwhelmed with experiences that are painful and outside their control. Although the behavior helps the child keep away from uncomfortable feelings and thoughts, defensive dissociation interferes with the ability to focus, retain information, complete tasks, hear instructions, and develop a consistent pattern for learning.

The incident related to Thomas's being bumped by Jose and Thomas's explosive response illustrates behavior resulting from hyperarousal. The low-level fear that is always present in Thomas, coupled with hypervigilance that keeps him on guard for attack, sets the stage for uncontrolled behavior, or the "fight" component in the human response to threat. The traumatic reminder that activated Thomas's explosive attack on Jose was likely the bump on the arm, a cue for reminders of bodily attack from parental abuse. Thomas lacks the ability to regulate his emotions in a healthy manner, a situation that has developed because of a lack of positive modeling from his parents, and he reverts to regressed thinking and behavior, as noted by Perry (1995). Some children internalize the overwhelming feelings and "implode"; others externalize the feelings and "explode." Thomas could not tell the teacher what had upset him possibly because the cues signaling possible threat or attack often operate outside the child's conscious awareness.

The implications from the case are clear for the classroom teacher. In order to help children like Thomas, teachers should provide consistent and predictable environments, discuss expectations for behavior, help children identify triggers that result in negative thoughts and feelings, help children focus on their own strengths and resources, provide a source of nurturance and comfort for children, and allow children to make choices to foster a sense of control. The issues surrounding abuse and neglect are complicated. Yet the teacher is one source of support and guidance for children.

QUESTIONS FOR REFLECTION AND DISCUSSION

1. How could a classroom teacher help Thomas focus so that he could learn at his maximum potential?

2. What techniques would be helpful to calm Thomas when he becomes upset?

3. How could Thomas be involved in understanding what helps him learn and perform best in school and in creating those conditions for himself?

REFERENCES

Armsworth, M. W., & Holaday, M. (1993). The effects of psychological trauma on children and adolescents. *Journal of Counseling and Development, 72*(1), 49–56.
Barber, J. S. (1997). *A log linear analysis of variables which explain dissociation in women with histories of incest.* Unpublished doctoral dissertation, University of Houston.
James, B. (1989). *Treating traumatized children: New insights and creative interventions.* New York: Lexington Books.
National Child Abuse and Neglect Reporting Systems (NCANDS). (1999). Online. www.acf. dhhs.gov/programs/cb/publications/cm99/high.htm/htm
Pearlman, L. A., & Staub, E. (1999). Understanding basic human needs. Online manuscript. www-unix.oit.umass.edu/%7egubin/rawanda/lec1.htm
Perry, B. D. (1995). *Principles of working with traumatized children: Special considerations for parents, caretakers, and teachers.* Unpublished manuscript, CIVITAS Child Trauma Programs, Baylor College of Medicine, Houston, TX.
Perry, B. D. (1997). Incubated in terror: Neurodevelopmental factors in the "Cycle of Violence." In J. Osofsky (Ed.), *Children in a violent society* (pp. 124–149). New York: Guilford Press.
Pynoos, R. S., Steinberg, A. M., & Goenjian, A. (1996). Traumatic stress in childhood and adolescence: Recent developments and current controversies. In B. van der Kolk, A. C. McFarlane, & L. Weisaeth (Eds.), *Traumatic stress: The effects of overwhelming experience on mind, body, and society* (pp. 331–358). New York: Guilford Press.

RESOURCES

Holmes, M. M., Mudlaff, S. J., & Pillo, C. (2000). *A terrible thing happened: A story for children who have witnessed violence or trauma.* Washington, DC: Magination.
James, B. (1989). *Treating traumatized children: New insights and creative interventions.* New York: Lexington Books.
Johnson, K. (1998). *Trauma in the lives of children: Crisis and stress management techniques for teachers, counselors, and student service professionals.* Almeda, CA: Hunter House.

CASE 4.2

THE INCONVENIENT CHILD
David K. Grant

Sean, a child who is impulsive, disruptive, and troubled, is being examined for special education placement after his first year of kindergarten. His family has a multigenerational record of abuse and neglect. He cannot fit in the mainstream classroom. Where can he be served? How can he be served? By the time he reached his teen years, he was an inmate at a youth detention center. This case examines Sean's psychological profile, educational experience, and home life and poses questions to the reader regarding best practices and possibilities.

Does nothing work? Is the life path of a child certain and immutable, decreed by the fates? For Sean's kindergarten teacher nothing worked. She tried everything: rewarding him, paddling him, counseling him one on one. When she ran out of ideas, she sent him to the principal's office. Then came the drugs that would become the center of his educational plan for the rest of his life (Ritalin, Dexedrine, Mellaril, Tofranil, to name a few). For ten years after kindergarten nothing had worked. Now he is in a youth detention center, heavily medicated, obese, moving from class to class slowly, and staring blankly into space. Occasionally, he lights up, grunts, squeaks, and engages in repetitive activities that keep him seated and relatively quiet. He prefers to use a calculator and tally up answers to math questions in long continuous columns on his paper. On a computer he will do the same word and letter matching games. He creates no disturbances. He is a model prisoner.

Before his incarceration and in order to prepare Sean for first grade, a special education planning meeting was held in August following Sean's year in kindergarten. In the minutes of his first individualized education plan (IEP), Sean's behavior was described. The team consisted of his mother, his kindergarten teacher, the principal, the school psychological coordinator, and his psychological services socials worker.

Sean was in a regular kindergarten classroom. There were many difficulties. According to the teacher, "He could not sit still and he wouldn't stay on task for more than a few seconds." She added, "He stole things for no reason. He chewed on his fingernails and would remove his shoes and socks and chew on his toenails while the other kids would laugh. He didn't care." She continued to describe how she couldn't get him to follow the class rules.

He appeared disinterested in forming relationships with other students and, when they laughed and ridiculed him for his actions, he showed no reaction or emotion. He was oblivious to the other students and was not interested in playing with them. After moving about from activity to activity, he would find a quiet place to be by himself. Sometimes in his quiet times, he would place himself near his teacher.

The psychologist's report described Sean's anxiety. He had recorded that Sean had a record of being cruel to animals. He threw kittens into a pool, drowning them. He put another kitten's head into a cup of coffee. He stepped on a small dog because he wanted "to hear the sound it made." His testing brought greater questions about the gap between his ability and his performance. The psychologist predicted that he would score much higher than he actually scored.

His mother believed Sean had not been learning much in school. He knew how to write his name as well as his alphabet and could count but had lost ground in his first year of formal education. Sean's home life, however, was much more problematic than his time in school. During his kindergarten year, there were two different men living in the home. He has siblings fathered by two other men as well. He had not seen his own father since he was six months old.

Her own father had sexually abused his mother when she was young. Since Sean was born, there have been five different men in his mother's life. The children services agency had been called several times. The first visit occurred when Sean was two years old. All of the adults who spent time in Sean's home had a history of heavy drug abuse. His mother had a history of drug abuse and addiction from early childhood. Although his mother denied using drugs when she was pregnant, she had been severely depressed and lost a lot of weight during the pregnancy; however, Sean weighed nearly eight pounds at birth. Drugs, alcohol, and sexual abuse were a family tradition. Sean was the latest heir of this legacy.

Home life for Sean and his mother was chaotic. The men came and went; her jobs waitressing were subject to time changes and often resulted in leaving Sean with these different men. When she was gone, the lover would drink, smoke tobacco and marijuana, watch TV, and abuse Sean. Long before the social workers contacted the family when Sean was two, he had been given drugs and alcohol to quiet him down, to "see what he would do." Typically, he would be given street drugs mixed with his food as an "experiment" or placed in a bag as an infant and marijuana smoke would be blown into it, "to mellow him out." He provided great amusement for these adults in the home. His mother, who desperately wanted and needed relationships, refrained from intervening for fear that the men would leave.

His mother moved many times, both before and after his birth. She abandoned her children and first husband after he had physically abused her. She has no contacts with her other children. Sean and his mother have moved at least three times since he was born. Some of these moves may have been a result of violent outbreaks between the lovers and her, causing difficulties in the neighborhood. Police intervention and the suspicion of drug abuse made the family's presence unwelcome. Sean had also become involved at an early age in taking things from the yards of neighbors. His thievery and his mother's involvements made them unwelcomed.

Both Sean and his mother participated in some counseling but never stayed more than a few sessions. The medications prescribed for Sean were not given regularly, and there was suspicion on the part of social workers that others were using the medications in the home for their narcotic effect. The mother participated in Alcoholics Anonymous for a few visits but couldn't keep it up. She attended some revivalist religious activities where cures were promised and frenzied displays of babbling, shaking, and fainting occurred as the musicians and speakers worked the audience into a lather. Sean's mother felt equally hung over and depressed after these episodes. The emotional high and level of caring attention offered never lasted long enough to meet her needs or expectations. She moved both Sean and herself like nomads between various cures—approved medication, self-medication, formal counseling, religious events, and continual attempts to find a stable home life and a family that modeled itself on the promise of the middle class. She never stayed with any one program or person long. Instead, she found the same family she grew up with and was training Sean to follow in her footsteps, no matter how she tried to stop that from happening.

There was little structure in the home to bolster what was being developed at school. There was little or no literature. Mom had some fashion magazines and the men had some light pornography. The TV and top-forty radio were the main sources of media. The violent drug-amplified arguments and fights that occurred in the home were the models Sean used to construct his responses to others. School and home were two different, conflicting cultures. Sean was the center of attention when he was awake at home because he was either being abused, chastised, or used as a source of entertainment. It was a feral upbringing in a suburban setting. He learned to take care of himself first because no one else in his life could be trusted. The line between need and want blurred. For Sean, what is perceived as needed must be taken now, without delay, because the opportunity may never come again. This is what he brought with him to the schoolroom.

QUESTIONS FOR REFLECTION AND DISCUSSION

1. Can the traditional classroom meet the needs of Sean?

2. What environmental design adjustments in the classroom may make a difference?

3. Children who are treated with behavioral drugs often must depend on them for the rest of their lives; at what point do drug regimens become abusive? Are they for the child or for the teacher's benefit?

RESOURCES

Foucault, M. (1977). *Discipline and punish, The birth of the prison.* New York: Vintage Press, Random House.
Freire, P. (1970). *Pedagogy of the oppressed.* New York: Continuum Press.

WORLD WIDE WEB RESOURCES

Office of Juvenile Justice and Delinquency Prevention (http://ojjdp.ncjrs.org)
United Nation's Office of the High Commission for Human Rights—Guidelines for the Prevention of Juvenile Delinquency (www.unhchr.ch/html/menu3/b/h_comp47.htm)

CASE 4.3

ANNA'S UNDERGARMENTS
Victoria Person

Anna is a second grader who exhibits very interesting and mature behavior regarding sexual material and knowledge. Anna's teacher recalls the year-long pro-

cess of addressing Anna's concern in a public school. The case highlights the struggles of a teacher with the suspected sexual abuse of a young child.

The first day of school eight-year-old Anna entered my second-grade classroom proudly wearing a new, though a bit too tight, skirt and blouse. The first morning melted into afternoon and recess time finally arrived. As the class lined up to go outside, Anna asked if she could change her shoes so as not to get her new ones scuffed. I was glad she changed into her play shoes as I watched her actively jump and run from the gym equipment and chase her classmates. Suddenly, Anna slipped and fell. Her new skirt flew over her head revealing a ruby red thong panty. This would be the first of many exotic undergarments Anna would wear to school that year.

I watched Anna mature the year before as I looked down the first-grade hall. Her name was a familiar word in the hallway every time her teacher lined up the class. Anna was often not following directions and refusing to cooperate. She was physically a very heavy girl with a pleasantly pretty face. As bright as she was stubborn, Anna's math and reading levels were average. It wasn't Anna's style to talk back; she simply, quietly did not do what she was asked. Her reputation was willful, but pliable when spoken to sternly. She generally self-corrected in time. Her teacher didn't recall Anna wearing any provocative undergarments in the first grade. Anna's teacher called on the Student Support Team (a precursor to special education referral) to help her with Anna's behavior. It was recommended that she be tested for a behavior-related problem in the second grade. Despite the image of Anna provided her, I generally found her to be one of my most interesting students. She was challenging, yet somehow she and I were able to work well together.

By October of second grade, Anna was wearing a piece of her mother's revealing clothing at least twice a week. When I contacted her mother concerning the undergarments, she would assure me she would correct Anna. Yet, Anna continued to wear the undergarments to school. Like Anna, her mother was a large woman well into plus sizes. The undergarments Anna wore were very large on her. Her mother came to school several times to collect the inappropriate clothing, but Anna would come back to school the next day wearing something else revealing. When I asked Anna why she wore the undergarments to school, she told me she thought the panties and teddies were pretty. After her mother would leave for work, Anna would go into her mother's dresser drawer and find something that she thought was pretty and wear it to school.

By January, Anna's mother's boyfriend has been released from jail and all Anna's mother's attentions were diverted from Anna and her little sister to the boyfriend. Anna's behavior problems escalated and the undergarment situation skyrocketed. I was unable to contact Anna's mother. By this time, most of Anna's drawings included a man with a penis showing. She was scratching and writing the word "ass" on desks, walls, and especially the bathroom walls. She stopped wearing thong panties, but started wearing her mother's bras that were very large on her. At recess she would run behind the slides and ask the boys if they wanted to see her privates. Recess was chaotic. Things were escalating sexually with Anna. The counselor was talking with Anna several days a week concerning language and sexual behavior. All the while, Anna lovingly came to the classroom every morning and hugged me. She never talked back to me; she simply quietly refused to do what I asked.

Because Anna's mother wanted privacy with her boyfriend (the boyfriend was the father of Anna's younger sister), Anna was sent to live with her grandmother. Anna was very hurt and jealous that the younger sister lived with her mother and that Anna was moved. Anna's grandmother also had an older granddaughter living with her. The eighteen-year-old cousin had a whole drawer full of exotic underwear that she invited Anna to wear. New underwear, her mother moving her out, and her ever developing behavioral issues sent Anna into a new personality I wasn't expecting. Anna was tested for emotional and behavioral problems in late February as I awaited the results of testing for resource placement.

Anna began talking back to her teachers in early April. She started hitting other children on the playground, her written obscenities grew from "ass" to "fuck," "shit," "I want to have sex with you," and others. Her mother was of no assistance. The counselor and I decided it would be best to call social services and ask them to make a home visit to find out what was going on in Anna's home life. Because of the large caseload in the social welfare system, it took six weeks for social services to contact Anna's mother and grandmother. Anna's mother became worried that social services would take her children, so she brought Anna back into her home. Anna was much happier with her mother.

When Anna moved back into her mother's house, she calmed down a great deal. She was no longer feeling abandoned and threatened by her baby sister. She stopped talking back and became the silently stubborn Anna I had always treasured. Her sexual behavior calmed down. She still loved to wear the bras and teddies that were way too big for her, but at least wearing the thong underwear had stopped. I learned to ignore her "selections" as long as the undergarments didn't interfere with her classmates or her learning.

Anna's testing came back in early June; her tests showed a great deal of depression and anxiety. Her IQ was normal. No medication was recommended. She was slated for three one-hour resource segments to address her behavioral issues. Anna is one of those children a teacher never forgets.

QUESTIONS FOR REFLECTION AND DISCUSSION

1. What communication could the first-grade teacher have had with Anna's new second-grade teacher?

2. What are some strategies that Anna's teacher could have used to allow her to collect information about Anna's change in behavior?

3. What discussion or conversation could Anna's teacher have with other students in the second-grade class about Anna's choice of clothing?

4. Although the counselor was intervening with Anna, are there signs in this case of sexual abuse?

5. What other strategies could the teacher have employed besides calling Anna's mother to alleviate the problem of wearing inappropriate clothing at school?

RESOURCES

Kleven, S. (1998). *The right touch: A read-aloud story to help prevent child sexual abuse.* Bellevue, WA: Illumination Arts.
Prendergast, W. E. (1996). *Sexual abuse of children and adolescents: A preventive guide for parents, teachers, and counselors.* New York: Continuum.

WORLD WIDE WEB RESOURCES

Klaas Foundation for Chlidren (www.klaaskids.org)
The National Council on Sexual Addiction and Compulsivity (www.ncsac.org)

CASE 4.4

YOU CAN'T JUDGE A BOOK BY ITS COVER
Mr. Smith Confronts Drug Use among His Students

Aaron Childers
Vicki Bunke
Tara Terry-Childers

This case describes a teacher who discovers the use of marijuana by a fifth-grade student and must decide how he should handle the situation. The teacher realizes that there are several dilemmas he must resolve when determining his best course of action. Discussion questions are designed to help the reader analyze this teacher's reactions and responses, and predict their own behavior given similar circumstances. The case is followed by resource reading suggestions relevant to drug and alcohol use among youth.

Children in the United States are confronted with stressful situations at an early age. Unfortunately, some children turn to drugs or alcohol for relief from the stresses that they encounter. Drug and alcohol abuse continues to be a salient issue among school-age children. Statistics indicate that illicit drug use in the year 2000 remained stable for the fourth year in a row (Greenberg, 2000). Synthetic drugs, such as Ecstasy, have gained in popularity during this same time, although there have been decreases in the use of inhalants and hallucinogens. The perceived risk of smoking cigarettes and using smokeless tobacco increased,

Alternative school settings, such as this intergenerational program where preschool children participate with seniors, are often a good fit for students with unique social backgrounds.

whereas perceived risk of taking crack and powder cocaine and using alcohol have decreased (Johnston, 1991).

We would like to think that all children who use and abuse drugs and alcohol come from abusive homes, have parents with drug addictions, and live in bad neighborhoods. What else would cause these children to act in such self-destructive ways? The truth is that although some children who use drugs do experience these problems, many do not. Some children exhibit typical signs of substance abuse such as attraction to deviant peer groups, failing grades, rejection of family and nonusing peers, and changes in behavior and dress. Others do not neatly fit into our predetermined categories of children who use drugs or alcohol. All children are placed at risk for substance abuse, and early identification of these students may be our first line of defense. Children spend much of their waking hours at school. Therefore, educators need to be aware of these risks and the warning signs of substance abuse. They also need to be mindful that the causes of substance abuse are complex and, for this reason, one cannot always judge a book by its cover. With this background, we introduce Jarrod and Megan. Both Jarrod and Megan are eleven years old. They are students in Mr.

Smith's fifth-grade class in a suburban public school. Jarrod was identified as emotionally/behavior disturbed in the second grade but has since been mainstreamed for the majority of his classes. He has had a history of attention problems and as a first-grade student his diagnosis was attention deficit hyperactivity disorder, combined type. Further, his behavior patterns were described as oppositional and impulsive. He was placed on stimulant medication at the age of nine years. Testing records indicated an average IQ with potential for academic success; however, he was failing all of his academic subjects. Although Jarrod has a history of difficulties, he has recently changed his appearance and attire. Specifically, he has begun to dress in black, pierced his ears, and dyed his hair blue.

Jarrod comes from a single-parent family. His mother works long hours, although she is at home at night. Jarrod, however, make a practice of always arriving home before his mother. Jarrod's parents were never married. His father left when he was born and has never had contact with Jarrod. Jarrod's seventeen-year-old brother dropped out of high school in the eleventh grade and lives in the home when he is out of work and in need of a place to live.

Megan, however, is a straight A student. She has been on the honor roll since the first grade and never gives her teachers a difficult time. She comes from a two-parent, upper-middle-class family. Although both her mother and father work, they are heavily involved in Megan's academic activities and volunteer for after-school functions. Megan has been tested for the gifted program but did not qualify. She serves on the safety patrol and is president of the student council.

"Another day, another forty-seven cents," said Mr. Smith as he sat down to enjoy his thirty-minute lunch. "What are you having today, Ms. Jones?"

"Just the usual Lean Cuisine instant meal," the older woman answered.

Mr. Smith and Ms. Jones are both teachers at Parkview Elementary School. Ms. Jones teaches fourth grade, and Mr. Smith is a fifth-grade teacher in his second year. Their lunch times overlap and Ms. Jones, a twenty-one year veteran, has taken Mr. Smith under her wing. He goes to her whenever he has a question about something.

"Anything new today?" asked Ms. Jones.

"Not really. Well, kind of. Do you know Jarrod?"

"Yeah, I had him last year. He's a pain in the butt. If I remember correctly, he doesn't do his work and likes to argue back whenever you ask him to do anything."

"That's him. Normally, I can put up with his behavior, but this week he's been even more difficult than usual. He did really poorly on the most recent test and I know that he understood the material. Yesterday, we got into an argument because he wanted to draw circles on his math sheet instead of answering the problems. I had to sit him in the hall until he could calm down. After that, he and Megan Riley got into an argument."

"Megan is such a sweetie. Good student. Straight As for me last year. Her mother is the PTA vice president, you know."

"I did know that. But Jarrod seems to be really on edge. I was thinking about calling his mom."

"Well, good luck on getting any help from that home. His mother works all the time and she'll never come up here for anything. That child needs to be at the alternative school."

"He's not that bad. He just needs some help. He is an angry little kid and he doesn't have any idea how to deal with those feelings."

"What he needs is some discipline. That mother needs to get him under control. And he should be in a self-contained class."

Mr. Smith thought about this while finishing his lunch. Was Ms. Jones right? Should Jarrod be sent somewhere else? Ms. Jones seemed to know what she was talking about; she certainly had the experience, but he didn't always agree with her views on certain students. So what if Jarrod dressed a little bit off, had colored hair, and was a tad argumentative? Does that make him a bad kid? Mr. Smith looked up and realized that it was time to get his students and head back to class.

Mr. Smith stood in front of his class. "OK, does everyone understand the centers and what they're supposed to do?"

Most of the class nodded.

"All right then. Let's get started. You have ten minutes for your first center." For a few seconds, the class was in chaos with twenty-three fifth graders all moving around in different directions, trying to be the first one at the centers. Then, a relative calm settled in and the students began working. At one of the centers, Jarrod arrived last and stood at the edge of the group.

"Oh *great!* We got stuck with Jarrod. That means one less person to help us with the work," moaned another student.

"Shut up!" snapped Jarrod and he grabbed the center directions and tore them in half.

"Mr. Smith! Jarrod ripped the directions!" Megan yelled.

Mr. Smith came over, "What's going on here?"

"We were trying to work and Jarrod ripped up the directions," Megan informed.

"Is this true, Jarrod?" Mr. Smith asked.

"This activity is stupid. It's all stupid," Jarrod mumbled.

"That's it. Jarrod, go to the principal's office."

"But…"

"Now! I'm not dealing with you right now. Go!"

"They started…"

"OUT!" Mr. Smith yelled, pointing toward the door. Jarrod stormed out and slammed the door. *I have got to do something,* Mr. Smith thought to himself. He walked over to the coatrack to try and find Jarrod's backpack and, hopefully, his assignment sheet. *Maybe his mom will see this note and get back to…* that thought immediately left his head when he looked inside the pocket of Jarrod's backpack. *Oh no. What do I do now?* Mr. Smith was not certain, but he was pretty sure the dried green stuff in the plastic baggy was not oregano.

Mr. Smith went next door and asked Ms. Roberts to watch his class. He took the backpack and knocked on Ms. Jones' door. "I have a situation," he told her when she opened the door.

"What's up? You looked very worried."

"I found this." He opened up the backpack and motioned for Ms. Jones to look in. She too recognized the drugs. "What do I do?"

"You've got to take this to the principal immediately."

"What if it's not his? Shouldn't I talk to him first? Give him a chance to explain?"

"Who? Whose backpack is this?"

"Jarrod's."

"That figures. No, you can't. This has to go straight to the principal."

"I…I guess you're right, but I…he…"

"This is Jarrod we're talking about. This is just the kind of thing we need to get out of here. You have got to go to the principal." Ms. Jones turned and went back into her class.

"At the very least, it's an automatic ten-day suspension." Mr. Smith, unsure of himself, headed toward the office.

Mr. Smith got back to his class. "I have some bad news, class. Jarrod will not be coming back for a few days. He…ah…has some family stuff to deal with at home. So anyway, we still have a lot of work to do here, so let's get busy."

He watched the students continue with their work. His mind was racing with thoughts of what he could have done to prevent this, how could he have known, and what signs might have given him some clues.

In the corner, a group of students was working and talking quietly to each other.

"What do you think happened with Jarrod?" one student asked.

"I don't know and I don't care," said Megan. *The only thing I was worried about was when Mr. Smith was over at the coatrack earlier,* Megan thought to herself. *I just knew he was going to find those pills I have hidden in my backpack."*

QUESTIONS FOR REFLECTION AND DISCUSSION

1. How well did Mr. Smith handle his dilemma? Did he make mistakes? Use good judgment?

2. How would you have reacted in this situation? What would you have done the same? Differently?

3. Are there signs that signal drug or alcohol use by students? Are they always evident?

4. How do the policies of your school or school district impact your decisions regarding substance abuse and the children in your class?

5. How do you handle a situation in which the local school policy conflicts with your personal philosophy about handling drugs and alcohol use?

6. How do you approach a student that you suspect is using or abusing drugs or alcohol? Their families?

7. To what extent do you consult with other teachers about your students?

8. Are there professionals in the school system that could offer support?

REFERENCES

Greenberg, R. (2000). Substance abuse in families: Educational issues. *Childhood Education, 76,* 66–69.

Johnston, J. (1991). *It's killing our kids: The growing epidemic of teenage alcohol abuse and addiction.* Waco, TX: Word.

RESOURCES

Arterburn, D. (1989). *Drug-proofing your kids.* Pomona, CA: Focus on the Family Publishing.

Beman, D. S. (1995). Risk factors leading to adolescent substance abuse. *Adolescence, 30,* 201–208.

Chen, L., Anthony, J. C., & Crum, R. M. (1999). Perceived cognitive competence, depressive symptoms, and the incidence of alcohol-related problems in urban school children. *Journal of Child and Adolescent Substance Abuse, 8*(4), 37–53.

Covington, H. (1999). Community involvement: Substance abuse prevention for teens. *Nursing and Health Care Perspectives, 20,* 82–87.

Dishion, T. J., Capaldi, D. M., & Yoerger, K. (1999). Middle childhood antecedents to progressions in male adolescent substance use: An ecological analysis of risk and protection. *Journal of Adolescent Research, 14,* 175–205.

Fowler, R. E., & Tisdale, P. C. (1992). Special education students as a high-risk group for substance abuse: Teachers' Perceptions. *School Counselor, 40,* 103–108.

Margolis, R. D. (1996). Reeling in the years. *Insight, 17.*

McGee, R. S., Springle, P., & Joiner, S. (1991). *Overcoming chemical dependence.* Waco, TX: Word.

McLaughlin, T. F., & Vacha, E. F. (1993). Substance abuse prevention in the schools: Roles for the school counselor. *Elementary School Guidance and Counseling, 28,* 124–132.

Polson, B., & Miller, N. (1983). *Not my kid: A parent's guide to kids and drugs.* New York: Avon.

Strack, J. (1985). *Drugs and drinking: What every teenager and parent should know.* Nashville, TN: Nelson.

Thomas, C. S., & Schandler, S. L. (1996). Risk factors in adolescent substance abuse treatment and management implications. *Journal of Child and Adolescent Substance Abuse, 5*(2), 1–16.

WORLD WIDE WEB RESOURCES

Addictions and More (www.addictions.net)
Free Vibe (www.freevibe.com)
Gotta Quit (www.gottaquit.com)
National Institute on Drug Abuse (www.drugabuse.gov)

CASE 4.5

"I AM NOT GOING TO…"

Jennifer Hargrove

This case presents a child who has behavioral and emotional outbursts in her classroom. Although Janice is intelligent and appears to be "fine," she brings a lot of safety issues and concerns with her to the classroom. Her behaviors may cause a teacher to rethink a whole plan daily and create alternate activities should an issue arise. The classroom teacher may even have to adjust the system for readily having daily supplies available for the children to use when they need them. There is the issue of who will take care of the "other" children while a teacher frantically deals with "the one." Who watches the children of the teachers who have to come to the rescue of another teacher in a time of crisis? This presents another safety issue as well. All of these things should be considered heavily in a plan to help children with social and emotional needs.

Janice is an eight-year-old second grader. She appears to be quite delightful, intelligent, happy, well adjusted, and worldly. She comes from a middle-class military family and lives on the military base with her mother, stepfather, and middle school–aged brother. Her mother is Caucasian and her stepfather is African American. Her biological father is Caucasian and lives in Florida. He is not involved with Janice's daily life; however, she talks highly of her father and goes to see him at Christmas and during summer vacations. Despite the fact that she now lives with parents of different races, backgrounds, and cultures, it does not seem to have presented any unique situations for her. Janice's stepfather is very involved in her life at home and at school. She appears to love him and respect him greatly. He has been a part of her life since she was only one year old.

Janice is a very creative child and she enjoys drawing and making things. She likes to bring little gadgets to school that she plays with when I am not looking. She is obsessed with combing her hair and does not like to be asked to put her brush away. Janice came to Brookwood Elementary School this year from another school in the same county. She made friends easily. Although it seems as though one particular African American girl is her "best" friend, she plays with a variety of children in our class and other classes. Janice has good leadership qualities and often organizes games and activities on the playground and during breaks in class. She is an excellent reader and a great math student. Things tend to come naturally to her academically; she easily grasps new concepts.

As a teacher, I was delighted to welcome a new student with a folder that looked as good as Janice's. I thought immediately that she would be delightful to have in class, a positive influence on other children. As time went on, I found out that my well-adjusted, delightful, intelligent child was not going to be as easy to work with as I had first thought. Janice had other issues. She brought things to my attention that I never thought I would have to deal with as a second-grade teacher. The most serious rethinking I had to do concerned safety, not merely the physical safety of the student but also the physical safety of the other students and myself. I also had to rethink the arrangement of supplies, furniture, and other children in the classroom. To document Janice's behavior, I began to keep a journal record of her activities, my intervention, and Janice's responses.

Monday. Janice comes into the classroom and appears to be happy and carefree. She walks in and puts away her book bag and coat and tells me she is leaving to go to breakfast. When I explain to her she cannot go eat breakfast because she has arrived at school after the tardy bell and no more breakfasts can be served, Janice loudly responds that she hated what her mom fixed her for breakfast and "therefore must eat or she will starve to death." I explained that we have to follow the school rules, but that I had some crackers in my desk and would be glad to give her some. The response was a head down on the desk and a loud "That is not good enough!" So, I simply put the crackers down on her desk and let her know that she could still have them until it was time to start language arts instruction when our morning work time was over.

The day progresses and we approach language arts around 9:00. Janice has done nothing up until this point but keep her head down and swing and stomp her feet. When I called her group to the floor for guided reading, she decided she would then eat the crackers and skip reading group.

I said, "Janice, snack time is now over and you must come to the reading group with your materials and wait until break time." Janice gave no response and kept opening the crackers.

I started my reading group and gave her time to readjust but she didn't so I reminded her of my request again. Janice replied, "I will not come to group. I am hungry and I am going to eat."

When I approached Janice to help her get her materials, she threw a pencil across the room. Then as I got her materials together, she clenched the desk and would not let go.

Despite my request to join the group again, Janice simply gripped the desk harder and pressed her lips together. I rang to the office to get the behavior specialist teacher to help with Janice while I returned to reading with the other children. Janice had to be physically removed from the room, kicking over chairs as she desperately tried to grab hold of anything in order to stay in the room. The specialist had to put Janice in a bear hug to be brought to the floor. Two additional adults and the behavioral specialist finally removed the eight-year-old child from the classroom.

As this scene has happened many times before, the other children were accustomed to it and were almost able to ignore it and continue with their work. Despite the children's efforts, the episode was still quite distracting. Janice did not return for the rest of the day and was suspended the next day. Her mother did not return with her to school on Wednesday. Janice, her mother, and stepfather came in on Thursday morning for a meeting to discuss how to help Janice. These behavioral outbursts had been occurring from the second week of school. It is now the fourth month of school and things are getting progressively worse. Janice does not appear to be happy to be back at school. She apologizes to me and says she will follow school rules and do as she should for the rest of the school year. She hugs me and I let her know that she is still welcome in our class. I reinforce the notion that she is a smart girl and that she should set a good example with good compliant behavior.

Thursday Afternoon.   It is time for math and Janice wants to sharpen the new pencil she has just been given by a friend. Our class rule is that we sharpen pencils in the morning unless they are broken. I decline her request to go to the pencil sharpener. She had already interrupted my math lesson when she blurted out that she wanted to sharpen the pencil. This denial made her angry. She put her fingers in her ears and refused to cooperate and do the activity. My thought was to let her suffer the natural consequence of her refusal by letting her figure out the math on her own when she "got around to working on it." This she did not like. Janice demanded that I help her with her math when we were moving on to social studies. I explained to her that I couldn't at the moment and that she would have to wait until the end of the day. When I told her to get out her social studies book, she started stabbing herself with her pencil in the arm. I asked her not to do that because it was dangerous to her body. She continued. As I approached her, she tried to stab me with the pencil. I was able to successfully get the pencil from her grip using techniques I was taught in a behavior management class. Taking away the pencil only made her more angry.

Janice then began name calling, cursing, and threatening to kill me if I didn't give her her pencil back. I called for help from the front office. She told me she was going to tell her mom that I was stealing her things and lying about her all the time. When help arrived, I lined up the rest of my class by the second door in the room that led to the garden. This I did in response to the fact that Janice had moved to the classroom door as she tried to run away. As the other two teachers arrived to once again restrain her, they decided to deal with her in the classroom rather than taking the chaos into the busy hallway. Her audience had been removed when I sent the other children into the garden with my paraprofessional. The episode lasted about an hour before they could get things under control with Janice. I did not see Janice the rest of the day. She was allowed to return to school the next day because her parents decided that she only acted up because she wanted to be home or go to work with one of her parents rather than going to school.

Friday.   Janice came in looking rather tired and upset. Her mom came in with her and made her apologize to me. She made me some really cute pictures that said "I love you" and "I am sorry." As her mom prepared to leave, Janice began trying to go home with her mom because she didn't have to work that day. Janice's mom told her that she had to stay at school. As the school day began, Janice immediately started agitating other children. She would walk by other children's desks and say mean things or knock things off their desks. She threw books across the room and refused to sit and do any of her class work. I tried talking, offering rewards, and threatened punishment. She did not respond to any of it.

I once again had to call for help. When the behavioral specialist teacher arrived to help me, the new plan was to immediately remove Janice from the situation into a time-out opportunity to think things through and calm down. Although she had agreed to the plan that we came up with as a team (the principal, her parents, Janice, and me), she did not conform. Ugly words started flying out of her mouth at us, racial slurs were being spoken, and curse words were coming rapidly. She had to be removed immediately. This time I had to help.

We had secured both arms, but in the process Janice had managed to kick me extremely hard in the shin. She was out of control; she knocked the behavioral specialist off balance and the teacher fell hard down on her knee. We finally had to restrain her on the floor in the hall. It took both of us to hold her. All this time my other children were alone in the room. After this episode, Janice spent quite some time at home.

This is just an example of one week of Janice's behavior at school. She has since been referred to receive the special services and attention she deserves through special education. However, it took an entire year to get these services for her. In the meantime, many other issues were created in and around her in the classroom and everywhere Janice went in the school. Safety became a great concern for everyone involved with Janice, around Janice, and even for Janice herself. Safety is a huge concern for teachers and the school systems. Children need to be safe before they can learn.

Schools are packed with many supplies and tools that may be used as weapons and could potentially be dangerous. When Janice decided to throw a fit, whatever she had in her hands could be dangerous to her and all of those around her. How do you keep these things from becoming potentially dangerous when she and other students need them for their work at school? As time passed, I was able to recognize when something was beginning to set her off and tried my best to remove anything that may cause harm or danger to Janice, myself, or other students.

The times that Janice would become physically out of control with her body were another whole issue. She would expend so much energy on these fits that she would physically collapse when she finally gave up the fight. These episodes could last for minutes or hours. Sometimes it would take more than one or two adults to help her. This put other people in danger as well. Children in a fit of rage can be so strong that it may take several people to contain that anger. While containing that anger, you have to make sure not to hurt yourself or the child involved. Teachers can take classes on how to safely restrain a child so the child, the adult, and the other children do not get hurt in the process; however, how can you ensure that this will work every time and keep everyone safe in the process? We try our best and think before we act, keeping the child's safety first in our minds.

Another issue teachers should consider is that of a student physically inflicting harm on him- or herself. When children do this, they are screaming for attention and help. Still, safety has to come first when approaching a delicate situation such as this. You want to make the child safe, away from whatever is causing the pain. Teachers also have to consider personal safety in making sure the "weapon" is not turned on them while trying to help. At any moment children out of control may also turn on other children.

In addition, the physical setup of the room must be considered. Supplies have to be available to all students, but they can be potentially dangerous in the wrong hands. Children have to sit in desks and furniture has to be in the room, but this equipment may also be potentially dangerous and cause serious safety concerns. Most importantly, we have to worry about the safety of the other children. As Janice started lashing out at teachers in a physical way, she could also have turned her focus to other children. Taking the other children out of the room and allowing the specialists to help Janice in the classroom reduces the risk to Janice, those dealing with her, and the other children around.

Although Janice presented a number of concerns to me as a teacher, she still deserved the right to an education. Each day, Janice and I started a new slate. I quickly realized that the basics of teaching also include the participation of many other professionals. Janice probably would be considered a challenge to any teacher. It is important for teachers to access the resources available to them to enable each child to benefit from their schooling experience.

QUESTIONS FOR REFLECTION AND DISCUSSION

1. What apprehensions do you have about a child in your classroom with emotional and behavioral problems?

2. What are the implications for the teacher and other children in the class when Janice was having an outburst?

3. What observational data the teacher has collected document the antecedents of Janice's behavioral outbursts?

4. How could Janice's family have been involved more?

5. What are your thoughts on the amount of time that it took for Janice to be evaluated for emotional and behavioral difficulties?

6. What limitations with regard to classroom activities might be suitable given that Janice was a student in the classroom?

WORLD WIDE WEB RESOURCES

Council for Exceptional Children (www.cec.sped.org)
National Information Center for Children and Youth with Disabilities (www.nichcy.org)

CASE 4.6

TO TELL THE TRUTH

Carson McCutcheon

Carson McCutcheon, a first-year teacher, demonstrates her responses to a "word" left written under one of the tables in her classroom. She allows the students to provide her with a solution to her dilemma.

I am a first-year teacher in a school in the Southeast. My school's student population includes enough children who live in poverty that 93 percent qualify for free and reduced lunch. In a school that is populated primarily by African American and Hispanic children, I teach half-day remedial language arts to nine third graders and language arts to nine fourth graders that are on grade level. These classes are part of a pullout program that meets in a trailer in the back of the school.

One Thursday afternoon as the students were packing up their belongings to return to their homeroom classes, I noticed one of my third-grade girls, Isha, cleaning up the underside of one of our tables. I asked her what she was doing and she informed me that she was wiping off a "dirty" word. I told her that I would deal with it later and that the students needed to go back to their home-rooms because we were late. I had a billion things on my mind at that moment, so it was not unlikely that I would forget to check out "the word."

The following day, the same attention was given to the table when it was time to transfer classes. Isha was again cleaning the underside of the table. Given all the attention paid to the table and the fact that all the children were now reading the "bad word," I decided to check it out. I looked under the table and there was the word *fuck* written in chalk along side two pictures of hands with the middle finger raised. As the children and I walked back to their homerooms, I asked if anyone had any information concerning the "bad" word. The children denied seeing anyone write it, and, to be honest, I believed them. The students are very quick to tell on each other and, because no one was willing to tell me anything, I thought that they really did not know who did it.

In the ten minutes between my language arts classes I went to speak to the counselor, partly because I was so upset about the incident, and partly because, as a first-year teacher, I honestly did not know what to do. I told the counselor that I assumed it was a fourth grader because no one in the third-grade group would tell on each other. I also knew that the fourth-grade teachers were having trouble with some of the students writing the same word and the same pictures on notes that had been confiscated. She and I discussed some strategies on how to encourage students to share information about the word and drawing. Then I went to pick up my fourth graders to return to our classroom.

As class began that Friday, I explained to both my third and fourth graders what I had seen and how distressed I was about the word and the drawings and that no one was willing to confess. Looking around the room as I spoke, I began to feel foolish because I realized that these children had neither the motive nor the opportunity to do this in our room. My fourth graders didn't have any free time while in the room, and they would think it was rude to do such a thing to me. My third graders wouldn't have realized that it was an insult to me although my fourth graders would have. Looking back, I remembered that my third grad-ers took a standardized test in the room the week before and had some free time once the test was over. I knew immediately that it had to be a student in the third-grade group and I began to develop a mental list of possible suspects.

On Monday, I began the class by discussing how vandalism made me feel. I didn't yell or accuse them but I let them know how truly upset I was. I told them that it hurt me that someone would write something so profane and also that no one would tell me the truth. Some variations of what had happened began to surface. I drew a graph on the board showing how little I cared about vandalism and how much I cared about the students making up stories (not telling the truth). I left them with these thoughts and told them that if anyone had any information to let me know. They whispered for a few minutes about what I had said and soon a child yelled out that a student named Jesus had done it. I was pretty sure that Jesus wouldn't have done it so I asked a few follow-up questions and it soon became clear to all the students that it wasn't him. I left it alone for the day. They asked on the way back to their homerooms if I knew who the culprit was. I told them that I might have an idea but I wanted to let the person confess.

The following day Maria was absent. Eduardo told me that she was absent because she was the one who did it and she didn't want to come to school to face me. I asked Eduardo for some additional information. He told me that he and Maria were best friends and she told him the day before. Several other children chimed in, saying they thought it was Maria. I told them that it wasn't fair to accuse her because she wasn't there to defend herself and they had no proof.

Before they came to my class on Wednesday, I compared Maria's handwriting with the word under the table. I really couldn't tell if it was her writing or not so I decided to try something new. I wrote several sentences on the board, each beginning with a letter from "the word," and also including another letter somewhere in the sentence. For example, I wrote, "Frogs hop into cold ponds." "Umbrellas open in the freezing rain." I did this because I couldn't tell if the letters under the table were upper or lower case. I had the students copy the sentences and circle the nouns. They assumed it was simply a regular language arts lesson. They finished and we moved on to the day's lesson. As we lined up to leave, I told the students that I had them do the noun exercise so I could compare handwriting. I was going to compare the handwriting after I dropped them off, so if anyone had anything to tell me, this would be the time. I reminded them that they would be in less trouble if they confessed. I could see Eduardo and others whispering to Maria encouraging her to confess. She finally did. She said, "Ms. McCutcheon, I have something to tell you. I did it and I am very sorry." I told her, "I am so glad you told me. I have to report this to the principal, but I will be sure to tell her that you told the truth."

The principal never had time to speak to her about this problem, so the next day I had her clean the bottom of the table. I told her how proud I was that she had told the truth. I spoke to her homeroom teacher when I dropped the children off that day. I explained to her what had happened and that Maria had confessed. Maria's mom was coming the following day for a conference, so she said she'd talk to her about it. After the conference, her teacher said she and her mother agreed that this was a problem but they were both proud of Maria for telling the truth. I don't know if Maria was in any trouble at home, but her teacher and I thought the incident had been handled properly and we decided not to punish her any further.

QUESTIONS FOR REFLECTION AND DISCUSSION

1. Would you have chosen the same strategies as the teacher?

2. What kind of knowledge do third and fourth graders have about such words? Do you think they understand their meaning?

3. Did the teacher focus on the character issue or the vandalism?

RESOURCES

Berenstain, S., & Berenstain, J. (2000). *The Berenstain Bears and the big blooper.* New York: Random House.

Wood, A., & Wood, D. (1988). *Elbert's bad word.* New York: Harcourt.

CASE 4.7

MOVING ON AS BEST WE CAN

Jeannelle Carlisle

In this case, a fifth-grade child is the victim of a malicious act by another group of fourth-grade boys. The reader is asked to respond to questions of zero drug tolerance and classroom accommodations.

We live in a small town in the desert Southwest, a place where everyone knows everyone else's business. I work as a teacher and my son attends the fifth grade in the same system. Our lives were in turmoil because my husband was losing his battle with cancer.

My son, after eating his lunch in the school cafeteria, got up to put away his tray, leaving his drink on the table. While he was gone, two fourth-grade boys slipped some pills into the soda can. He returned and picked up the drink chugging most of it down. While he was drinking, another boy told him to stop because some pills had been put in the soda. It was too late. Most of the drink was gone. It was no big deal. Peer pressure is a powerful force. Nobody told an adult.

At the end of the school day, my son came into my classroom as he usually does. He looked pale. He told me he wasn't feeling well, had a bad headache, and was dizzy. I asked him how the day had gone and that's when he told me what the boys had done. It was 3:02. It had been three hours since lunch. I immediately took him to see the principal where he reported the incident.

I called a neighbor to stay with my husband, and took my son to the emergency room. By now his speech was slurring, his color pale, and his eyes had a dazed far away look to them. The nurses took his vital signs and blood samples then asked if he had hit his head. The doctor examined him then called me outside. He asked me what had happened. I told him everything my son had told me. He had a physical two weeks earlier to qualify for sports, received a clean bill of health, and was given consent to play ball. The emergency room doctor told me that now my son was very ill and was slipping into a coma. Did I know what the pills were? No, but I knew where the boys were. They were at the ball field where everyone else was on a Friday night. He advised me to call the sheriff's department and have the boys picked up and questioned. He wanted to take more blood samples to see if it could be determined exactly what the pills were, but there was not much time. He would have to start flushing out my son's system with intravenous fluids or my son would become comatose. It was 6:30 P.M.

I called and reported everything to the sheriff's department. They had not heard anything about it from the school but agreed to send a deputy to look for the boys. The deputy picked up one of the boys and his mother from the ball field. The other boy could not be located. In the meantime the hospital performed drug tests on my son's blood. It was negative for acetaminophen (Tylenol), aspirin, and any derivatives. It was negative for street drugs. The doctor then contacted a toxicologist. It was reported that there were several kinds of heart medications, antidepressants, and antipsychotic medications that could cause these same symptoms if taken in overdose. My son was becoming unresponsive so the decision was made to start intravenous fluids immediately.

I tried to contact my husband and the school's principal. My neighbor brought my husband to the hospital. I could not get in touch with the principal, so I called the assistant principal and left a message. When she called back, I told her the situation. I gave her the names of everyone who had been sitting at the table and told her that my son said that some of the boys had also taken these pills. She responded that it was late at night and that she didn't want to unnecessarily upset anyone so she wasn't going to call anyone that night. It was 10:00 P.M.

The doctor came back into the room and remembered treating my husband only two nights earlier. He had recognized me, but he didn't realize who I was until then. He said that during all this testing a blood sugar analysis had been done on my son's blood. A normal blood sugar is 100. The normal range is 80 to 150. My son's was 985. He needed to be admitted and have fluids continued until it was back in the normal range. It was 10:30 P.M.

The sheriff's department called and reported that the boy said the pills were Tylenol. The doctor spoke with the deputy and told him Tylenol was not what was in my son's blood. The boy was lying. My husband and I were standing right there at the counter. We heard the doctor say this. When he hung up the phone, I asked him if my son could die. He looked right at me and then at my husband. He said yes. I started to cry.

As they were wheeling my son into his intensive care room, a nurse from the emergency room entered. She said that they had located the other boy. He was in the emergency room having his stomach pumped. He had taken some of the pills that night. I called the school's assistant principal and told her this, but she still did not want to contact any of the other parents. I told her that I would want to know, that it was her responsibility. She said it was a judgment call and that it had been made, by her. My sister came to the hospital to take my husband home. I stayed with my son.

Early the next morning, another doctor came to see my son. My son was groggy and looked worn out, but his blood sugars were back in the normal range. I was relieved and thought the crisis was over. Then the doctor asked to see me outside. He said that my son needed to stay in the hospital at least for the day. If his blood sugars remained normal, he would release him but we would need to be prepared. We would have to monitor his blood sugars for the next three days. If they remained normal, good. If not, it was very serious, and we would need to get him to the hospital right away. He said that it was very possible that my son's pancreas had been damaged and that my son was no longer producing insulin. He could be diabetic. If this was the case, then the same symptoms would occur. The doctor also told me that the deputy brought some pills to the hospital. The hospital pharmacist could not immediately identify the pills and asked to send them off to a toxicology lab. The deputy said he needed them for evidence and could not leave them; he took the pills with him. This sounded to me like the sheriff's department was conducting an investigation and that people would be held accountable for what had happened.

My son was released late that afternoon. When we got home, my husband told me not to answer the phone. Everyone was calling and asking a lot of questions. From what he could tell, the boys at the cafeteria table had gotten together at the ball game and again that morning at another event. The story was that they had told my son the pills were in the drink before he drank it. They had put the pills in to watch them fizz, and the pills were Tylenol. They were saying that my son said that he didn't care and drank the soda anyway, knowing the pills were in the can.

I called the sheriff's department to find out what they were doing on my son's behalf. I was told that the boy had confessed around 10:00 P.M. that he and another boy had traded the pills for candy. The boy then took the deputy to the school playground where he had ditched the pills. They found two of the pills, which the deputy took to the hospital to be identified. They couldn't immediately identify what the pills were so the deputy left them to be sent to a toxicology lab. I reported to the sheriff what the doctor told me the night before. The pills had been taken back by the deputy to keep as evidence. I asked if that was protocol. I was told if there were two pills, one would be kept in the evidence locker and one would be given to the hospital. I asked him to check the locker. He did and told me that there were no pills there.

The phone rang all day. Not one call was from the two boys or their parents. I was to attend a conference in a nearby city on Monday and Tuesday of the next week. I called the hospital and asked it there was a problem with my taking my husband and son with me. I was told I could because there were several hospitals nearby, including a well-known children's hospital.

That night I was contacted by the state Bureau of Investigation. The school had never reported any of this to the sheriff's department. I told the investigator everything. I told him specifically the results of the tests on my son's blood and advised him that he could verify this with the hospital. I told him about my conversation with the school's assistant principal, and about my conversation with the sheriff's department. I knew that the deputy was friends with the parents of the boy who had been picked up.

I packed all of us up and left on Sunday. Monday I attended the conference. We stayed in the same hotel the conference was held in so I was able to check on my family all throughout the day. My husband was coughing a lot and having some pain. He thought it was the strain of all that had happened and only wanted to rest. My son's blood sugars were in the normal range. Later that evening we decided to go out to eat. While at dinner, I thought that my son didn't seem quite right. We had checked his blood sugars just before leaving for dinner and they were in the normal range. We decided to get back to the hotel and check his blood sugars again just to be sure. They were at 400. I rushed my son to the children's hospital about five minutes away. I told them all that had happened and gave them permission to contact the first doctor, which they did. They admitted my son and started the intravenous fluids.

My husband called. He was now throwing up blood. I called my brother-in-law who lived in the same town. He took my husband to another hospital, where he was admitted. I stayed with my son.

The doctor came into the room and called me outside. He said that he thought he should give my son insulin. If the problem was diabetes, the insulin would bring down the blood sugars. If it wasn't diabetes, then he was in the hospital where they could deal with the effects of the insulin. I gave permission. The insulin worked. My son was hospitalized for a week. So was my husband. I went back and forth between them.

On Tuesday I called the school to find out what action was being taken against the boys. I spoke with the principal. He said that all of the boys had told the same story. The two boys would be suspended for ten days, but he would allow them to make up all of their work. He told me that my son could be expelled for taking the drugs. I reminded him that all of these boys had been together at the ball field and could have made this story up. They were lying about the pills being Tylenol and the proof was in the blood tests taken at the hospital. I also reminded him that our school had a zero tolerance drug policy. My son should not be punished for someone else violating that policy and the two boys should be expelled. He told me that he had decided to do me a favor and let my son off because he had already faced a consequence. The two boys would face suspension. He stated that I needed my job because I needed the medical insurance. He told me that he had spoken with the state Bureau of Investigation and explained that the incident wasn't reported because it was Friday afternoon and the students wouldn't be back until Monday. This was a school problem, and he would handle it within the school. He was sure that I would be satisfied with that. He said that I had enough to deal with and that I should concentrate on my family. He had already started the process for me to take emergency family medical leave for the remainder of the school year. I had enough leave time that this wouldn't affect my paycheck or my insurance. He said that my job would be waiting for me in the fall. I said that I wanted to think about it. I then called the sheriff's department. The sheriff told me there was no evidence and that it was my son's word against all of these boys. He told me to do what the principal suggested and not make a fuss. Nothing good would come out of it. I should take care of my family and return to my job in the fall. By then everything would be back to normal. My insides crumbled.

My husband died at home in my arms five months later. My son is a brittle diabetic. His blood sugars rise and fall hundreds of points in a very short period of time. He has been admitted to the hospital with life-threatening diabetic ketoacidosis six times. I can't tell you our names or where we live because I am afraid. I know that the school system would go to any length to discredit me and my son in order to protect themselves.

I thought about moving. My family is here. My husband, my son's father, is buried here. Our friends and our church are here. My son does not want to leave the only school he has ever attended, the only home he has ever known. Within five months, I lost my husband and my son was poisoned, changing our lives forever. Did I now want to put us through a long battle in court? Could we withstand any more of the incredible stress under which we had been? It would divide the community. Some people would support us, some would support the other boys. How would this affect us at school and at home? Would the price we would pay be worth it?

I decided to let my son stay until he graduates from high school. It's been two years since this happened. We were in counseling for more than a year. He now has an insulin pump that helps regulate his blood sugars. The boy who was responsible for bringing the pills to school has been in a lot of trouble and he has now left the school system. My son has never taken matters into his own hands, but the other boy is afraid. He has been shunned by most of the other boys at that dreadful table. My son is highly respected, makes good grades, stays out of trouble, and is active in the school band, where he is the section leader by talent and by peer recommendation. We have tried to move on as best we can. It is very hard.

QUESTIONS FOR REFLECTION AND DISCUSSION

1. Describe your reaction to this case.

2. What steps could have been in place for monitoring the lunchroom to prevent this episode?

3. How do you feel about the school's reaction, despite the existing zero tolerance policy?

4. How might your classroom need to be modified to accommodate a student with diabetes?

WORLD WIDE WEB RESOURCES

American Diabetes Association (www.diabetes.org)
Juvenile Diabetes Research Foundation International (www.jdrf.org)

CASE 4.8

SUDDEN TRAGEDY

Sylvia Hutchinson
Michelle Graham

Billy and Kevin are very excited about the class skating party and the idea that Billy won't have his little sister tagging along. Unfortunate tragedy strikes on the way home from the skating rink and their teacher Ms. Campbell is left in shock.

On a cloudy October Wednesday, Mary Jenkins and her daughter, Sus (short for Susanna), complete their weekly grocery shopping and head for the checkout counter. Almost everyone in town tries to do their "big" grocery shopping on Wednesday. Wednesday is double coupon day. Lots of people observe this "tradition," consequently, they bump into friends in every aisle of the store. Everybody stops to talk and joke. They look at one another's babies, and complain about their relatives, or the weather, or work. Grocery shopping may take most of the afternoon and often looks like a town meeting. Mary always takes a few minutes to visit with her good friend, Betty Cramer, a cashier at the Piggly Wiggly. The line is never too long for Mary and Betty to exchange just a bit of news, the kind of conversation known so well to really good friends. This Wednesday, however, it is not simply chatting. Betty and Mary have to make plans for their children's school party. They agreed last week to drive the boys over to the skating rink for the big event. As Mary rolls her cart to the counter, she is aware of the line of customers behind her. She and Betty are accustomed to exchanging personal information in this public arena. They have a kind of code built between good friends over years. They are both talking at the same time, while Betty's "rapid fire" fingers race over the cash register keys. Within a few minutes, they decide that one car will be fine. They can all go in Betty and Joe's car. After all, a minivan has plenty of room for the whole crowd and the children love to play in the back. Mary and Bill drove last time, so Betty says "it's only fair that we drive this time." Sus waves goodbye to Betty. Mary and Sus load the groceries into the car and drive home to start dinner.

Betty and Joe have only one son, Kevin, who is a good student and a "better-than-average" athlete. Bill coaches Kevin in Little League and talks frequently about how he and Kevin's dad, Joe, will one day go to a big league ball park to see their boys play. Mary and Bill have two children. "Little Billy" has just turned seven years old, is in the second grade, and looks so much like his dad that it is always a topic of conversation with family and friends. Billy plays second base and is a strong batter. Although Susanna is a four-year-old, her mother describes her as a terminal "terrible two." Susanna always tries to follow her brother Billy. Sus frequently embarrasses him with her boisterous attempts to do everything he does. Mary was already worried about taking her along on Thursday evening for the skating party. She knows that Sus will try to get out on the ice with Billy. Billy is very patient and really quite loving to Sus, but there is a limit, even to Billy's patience.

So many times Mary has heard Billy's pleas, "But Mom, nobody else has to have his little sister with him all the time. Why does she always have to go with me? It is soooo embarrassing! Nobody else has a little brother tagging along all the time, much less a little sister. Can't you do something to keep her here…at least once in a while, please?" Mary heard all this and more as she was putting the finishing touches on supper.

After supper, the table was cleared and Mary and Bill talked as they did the dishes. They really did understand and sympathize with Billy's feelings. So they hatched a plan. They told Sus that they had a great surprise for her. Mary in her most excited voice said, "We'll go by Video Mart after dinner tomorrow night and rent your favorite video and then we'll watch it together. We'll have popcorn and your favorite chocolate drink. It will be a real party for just the three of us." Sus was impressed and agreed that it sounded like a party to her. She was so excited at the idea of a party that she didn't seem to notice the phrase "…the three of us."

After Sus was in bed, Billy hugged his mom and dad over and over. "Thanks, thanks so much. I hope I can do something special for you sometime. Oh boy! This is going to be great. Just Kevin and me on the rink…. We'll show the guys some great tricks tomorrow night. Boy this is going to be a great party." Billy was so excited he had a tough time getting to sleep that Wednesday evening.

Mary called Betty and told her the revised plan. Betty was disappointed. After all she and Mary didn't have that much time to just sit and visit. She had looked forward to sitting in the stands and talking to her old friend. However, she knew that Billy and Kevin would enjoy a "night to themselves." Much as everyone loved Sus, she admitted that Sus was demanding.

Thursday was a very long day in the classroom. Although Ms. Campbell had taught long enough to know that the day of a field trip, let alone a party, was not a day to ask intensive concentration of the pupils,…there were some things that needed to be done on this Thursday. Kevin and Billy were swapping notes and whispered messages all day. They were excited about the party. Both were ready to show off their skating skills for the rest of the class. They had even perfected a trick or two. They liked being partners on the baseball field and the skating rink. Finally, the bell rang and they reviewed the plans for meeting and how much fun it would be to have the entire back of the minivan to themselves. Almost as exciting as the party was the awareness that there would be "No Sus" tonight. Billy met his Mom at the cafeteria to head home. Kevin took the bus.

Dinner consisted of a quick sandwich because they were leaving early. At 6:00, Kevin and his parents arrived. Billy grabbed a sweater and his mother added a warm coat. Even though it was only October, it was an unexpectedly rainy and quite chilly. Sus was surprisingly calm and focused on the family video party to come. Mary and Bill walked Billy out to the car. Joe rolled his eyes as the boys clamored to the very back of the station wagon and remarked to Bill that it may be a "long night." Bill offered to trade places and let Joe stay home to watch the video with Sus. Joe immediately replied, "I don't think so." They laugh easily, knowing that Sus can sometimes be both a delight and a dilemma.

Kevin and Billy are calm and seem eager to please their parents and get the trip underway. They do not want any delays. Joe pulls out of the driveway amid waves and shouts of "Be careful," "Remember your manners," and "Be sure to thank Ms. Campbell for arranging this party."

The trip to the skating rink seems long to Billy and Kevin, but the arrival is sweet. Some of their friends are already at the rink and yelling as Billy and Kevin "hit the door." Betty and Joe retrieve the dropped coats and sweaters as Billy and Kevin yank on their skates. They make their grand entrance to the floor and immediately begin to demonstrate their "dynamic duo" spin. They spend every possible minute on the rink and only pause briefly to eat a few snacks. The evening for the boys seems all too short. It is time to leave long before they are ready. Even the parents seem to have enjoyed the evening more than they might have expected. Betty and Joe visited with Ms. Campbell and their other friends but now are yawning as they think of the long workday on Friday. Everyone begins to move toward the parking lot. They wave goodbye to Ms. Campbell and Betty says to Joe, "It's always a treat to talk with Ms. Campbell. She's almost like family, isn't she?" Joe nodded and Betty snuggled a little closer as they walked to the car.

Ms. Campbell watches the cars drive away toward Markward. She is a veteran second-grade teacher nearing retirement age, although no one in the community considers retirement an option for her. She has taught most of the parents of the children in her class this year. The community is small and relatively stable. Many of the teachers went to school in the same building in which they now teach. Few of the teachers have taught longer than Ms. Campbell and no teacher is more respected. She is the one who mentors new teachers. Unspoken exchanges in faculty meetings clearly point to the collegial expectation that Ms. Campbell is the one who should end prolonged discussions by casting the deciding vote. She is what is sometimes called an "informal change agent." Although the principal is well liked, Ms. Campbell is often the one to whom other teachers look for direction. Although she doesn't actively invite this mantle, everyone knows it belongs to her. Even the principal looks to her for advice and is aware that he needs her loyalty and approval to successfully get many ideas implemented. Although Ms. Campbell is a bit flattered by the confidence that her colleagues give her, she admits it can be burdensome at times.

She moves to her car while wrapping her coat round her shoulders and shifting the heavy tote bag. She is relaxed at the thought that she only has a few blocks to drive. Her sister lives nearby and she is staying with her tonight. She will have to rise a little earlier in the morning to make the drive to school, but she is quite content with that prospect. The rain probably will have ended and she can collect her thoughts on the early morning drive

Ms. Campbell had a lovely visit with her sister and arrives early for school. She is excited about some activities she has planned. She used the skating party last night to design some spelling and writing small-group work and is quite pleased with her creativity. She is thinking that the pupils will enjoy the activities based on last night's party. She's smiling to herself as she rounds the corner and turns into the school office. When she sees the light in the office she feels reassured at the predictability of her workplace.

No matter how early she arrives, Thelma Dietz, the school secretary, is already in the office with her work spread about busily humming to herself. However, this morning, Thelma is not humming. Ms. Campbell is startled because it looks as if Thelma is crying. "What on earth is wrong?" Thelma is obviously upset and struggling with a "right way" to tell Ms. Campbell what has happened. She begins but chokes on some of the words. Ms. Campbell hears recognizable names (Kevin, Billy, the Cramers) but cannot get a clear sense of events. She thinks Thelma said there had been an accident. Then words begin to tumble out…automobile wreck, critical condition, ambulance…My God…Did Thelma just say that the Cramers are dead? That Billy Jenkins is dead? That Kevin is in critical condition? In shock, Ms. Campbell tries to understand. She finds herself asking question after question, not allowing any time for answers. "What happened? When did this happen? How could this be? I just talked with Betty and Joe last night…and the boys were there skating…spinning in a circle with some trick…. This can't be true." Thelma responded, "I thought you had heard…I know Mr. Burchett, the principal, tried to call you…. He called as many people as he could. Oh, no, we forgot that you stayed in Markward last night…. This is so horrible. I didn't want to be the one to have to tell you." Ms. Campbell responding from her state of shock, mumbled the question no one could answer, "How could this have happened?" Thelma, in a shaky voice, tried to use the most ordinary logic, "you know October…a little rain mixes with that top layer of oil and the roads are unpredictably slick." But in the next breath she admitted in a series of sentence fragments that it was all quite unbelievable, "I still can't believe it…such a nice young family…it's so wrong…so unfair."

Ms. Campbell weaves down the empty hall toward her classroom. She is grateful for the wall but not sure it will be there as she reaches out to steady herself. She eventually reaches her room, which should provide familiar solace, but instead the room is flooded with disturbing memories and images. She immediately sees Billy's desk and then Kevin's. All the desks are empty, but these two peculiarly so. Without warning, she can see Bill, Joe, Betty, Mary…not as mature parents but as second graders in her class so many years ago. And all at once she wonders what she could possibly say to Mary and Bill, to Sus…to the grandparents. "Oh dear God, what will I say to the children when they arrive this morning?" Ms. Campbell has to leave the room to get a much needed cup of coffee and to try to draw answers from the silence of the hall. A young teacher catches Ms. Campbell walking toward her classroom. "Ms. Campbell—please may I talk with you?" Ms. Campbell turns to see the woman crying and before she can say anything, the young woman says, "My own parents died when I was Sus's age. I wish I could talk with her but I wouldn't know what to say. I can't imagine what I will say to my own class. What if I start to cry? I keep thinking of Sus, Billy, and Kevin, the Cramers, and my own parents. If I do start to cry will I be able to teach? What can I do? What do I tell my class of first graders? Should I say anything or should I just "leave it" for their parents? Many of my students know Kevin, Billy, and Sus.... What if they ask what happened? What do I say? How should I approach the topic so they will understand and not be afraid?"

Ms. Campbell's class day begins and the children are in the room. She has been told that the district school psychologist, social worker, and counselor have been notified of the tragedy and will arrive later this afternoon, but, in the meantime she worried how she would address the topic. The day began with Jodi meeting Ms. Campbell in the hall with a note. Her parents want Ms. Campbell to deliver a note to Billy's parents. She put the note in her pocket with some resignation. When she looked around the room she saw an uncharacteristically quiet class, none of the usual movement and chatter. Simon, the class "cutup," simply sat in his desk. Jacob usually occupied every spare moment with taunting or bullying some smaller or less confident child, but this morning he sat eerily still with his desk turned away from the rest of the class.

All of a sudden Simon burst forth with a flood of questions, "What happened to Kevin and Billy? Where are they? Are they hurt? Mama wouldn't tell me anything." Steven added that "his family drove past the wreck on the way home from the skating party. I was half asleep and at first, I heard Mom and Dad ask whose car it was and then they got real quiet and Mom started to cry. That woke me up...but good. I could tell someone was hurt real bad, but they wouldn't talk to me." Maggie added, "I saw the car. I thought maybe it was Kevin's mom's car but I wasn't sure. Everyone got real quiet when I asked and that made me scared." Fran added "OK, what happened? Billy and Kevin are...my friends." Josh said, "I heard Billy and Kevin were wrestling in the back seat of the car...that is why it crashed...is that true?"

The confusion and emotional demands extended beyond the school day and into the evening with phone calls from parents and friends. A parent called to talk with Ms. Campbell, asking what to "say" when she saw Billy's parents around town.

QUESTIONS FOR REFLECTION AND DISCUSSION

1. What could Ms. Campbell say to the second graders? How could she answer their questions about the event, their fears, and what she knew to be the death of one friend, the critical injury of another, and the death of his parents?

2. How does she help the students recognize, understand, and deal with their reactions to this tragic loss? What "signs" of grieving should she watch for with the students? How does she answer the spoken questions and the unspoken fears?

3. Should the children's parents be informed of this tragedy? Why or why not? By whom? If so, how?

4. What resources plans, policies, and/or professional personnel, such as a school psychologist, nurse, social worker, or others can be provided by the school? If these are not available, how should the school compensate?

CHILDREN'S STORIES

Buchanan-Smith, D. (1973). *A taste of blackberries.* New York: Crowell.

Henkes, K. (1998). *Sun and spoon.* New York: Penguin Putnam Books for Young Readers.

Kransky, L., & Brown, M. (1996). *When dinosaurs die: A guide to understanding death.* Boston: Little, Brown and Company.

Little, J. (1984). *Mama's going to buy you a mockingbird.* New York: Viking Kestrel.

Park, B. (1996). *Mick Harte was here.* New York: Random House.

Paterson, K. (1977). *A bridge to Terabeithia.* New York: Crowell.

Rylant, C. (1992). *Missing May.* New York: Orchard Books.

Rylant, C. (1997). *Cat heaven.* New York: Scholastic.

RESOURCES

Corr, C. (2000). Using books to help children and adolescents cope with death: Guidelines and bibliography. In C. Grollman, S. Bertman, & K. Dokas (Eds.), *Living with grief: Children, adolescents, and loss* (pp. 295–314). Alexandria, VA: Hospice Foundation.

Grollman, C., Bertman, S., & Doka, K. (Eds.). (2000). *Living with grief: Children, adolescents, and loss.* Alexandria, VA: Hospice Foundation.

Hogan, N., & Graham, M. (2002). Helping children cope with grief. *Focus on Prek & K, 15*(1), 1–8.

Maierman, N. (1997). Reaching out to grieving students. *Educational Leadership, 55*(2), 62–65.

McGlauflin, H. (1998). Helping children grieve at school. *Professional School Counseling, 1*(5), 46–49.

Miller, K. (1996). *The crisis manual for early childhood teachers: How to handle the really difficult problems.* Beltsville, MD: Gryphon House.

Westmoreland, P. (1996). Coping with death: Helping students grieve. *Childhood Education, 72*(3), 157–160.

Winter, E. (2000). School bereavement. *Educational Leadership, 57*(6), 80–85.

CHAPTER 5

SOCIAL ISSUES

In today's schools what we find more and more is that teachers are regarded only as information dispensers. The teacher–student relationship is being dehumanized. Effective teachers must be more than purveyors of information, they must be people who help children learn the skills of self-control and motivation; develop a sense of genuine caring for themselves and others; learn alternatives to cheating, lying, violence, and human exploitation; and develop tolerance, acceptance, and a valuing of the unique worth of every person. These are core values on which our sense of community rests. These are also teachable and learnable skills. Our goals as teachers should be to help children become good people and function effectively in this world.

Kevin Ryan and Karen Bohlin (1999) describe seven competencies teachers need to develop to become character educators: (1) Teachers must be able to model good character and character building themselves; (2) teachers must make the development of their students' moral lives and characters a professional responsibility and a priority; (3) teachers must be able to engage students in moral discourse about the "oughtness" of life—they must be able to talk to students about what is right and wrong in life; (4) teachers must be able to articulate clearly their own positions on a range of ethical issues while not unnecessarily burdening students with their views and opinions; (5) teachers must be able to help children empathize with the experience of others—in effect, help them to get outside of themselves and into the world of others; (6) teachers must be able to establish in their classrooms a positive moral ethos, an environment characterized by high ethical standards and respect for all; and (7) teachers must be able to provide activities, in school and in the community, that will give students experience and practice in behaving ethically and altruistically (pp. 153–154).

The first three cases in this chapter highlight a variety of social issues encountered in early childhood classrooms that involve values, morals, ethics, and virtue. In the first case, "A Trip to Reality: An 'Everyone' Story," Rebecca Mann wrestles with an incident of anti-Semiticism that she experienced as a fifth grader. In the second case, "Dealing with Dishonesty," Pat Nickell discusses the dilemmas that emerge for two elementary teachers when they are confronted with a fifth-grade student who exhibits a consistent tendency to be dishonest. The third case, by R. C. Carter, is entitled "Ostracizing Rich." In this case Scott is student teaching in a fifth-grade classroom when rumors of possible violence by a student spread throughout the school. Unexpected outcomes lead Scott to question how the administration and other teachers ultimately responded to this situation.

As teachers we must be constantly challenged to find meaningful ways to raise student aspiration, to heal human hurt, and to help in the task of optimizing every child's potential. Education is a vital component to that end. Research indicates that education is the best antidote for intolerance (Avery, 1992). Because schools bring together children of different ethnicities, cultures, genders, religions, and socioeconomic strata, teachers have the opportunity to incorporate into their lessons an emphasis on acceptance of difference, toleration of and respect for the beliefs of others, and the skills of reasoned dialogue.

Another component in the task of optimizing each child's potential is the child's parent(s) or caregiver(s). By forming effective partnerships with parents, teachers can get a boost in helping students to succeed. Research shows that effective communication between parents and teachers is vital to student achievement and a successful school experience. Parents' involvement in their children's educations is positively associated with academic performance, higher attendance rates, lower suspension rates, greater teacher satisfaction, improved parental understanding and parent–child communication, greater empowerment for parents, and improved school climate (Henderson & Berla, 1994; Winters, 1993). With the changing nature of today's families, and as classrooms become more and more diverse and challenging, communication and collaboration between teachers and parents has become more difficult than ever. But it is important to note that research has found that it is teachers' attitudes and practices, not the marital status, educational level, or work status of the parent, that determine whether families become productively involved in their children's schooling (Epstein, 1996). The next two cases involve communication issues between teachers and parents. Dee Russell and Paige E. Campbell, in "Go on into the Hall—You're Excused from the Celebration: Religious Observance in a Public School Classroom," describe parents who are Jehovah's Witnesses and are concerned about how their first grader, Sarah, feels after she has been excused from the classroom for a birthday celebration. The classroom teacher questions how she should respond to the parents' request that she talk to the other children in the class about why Sarah goes away when there are birthday parties. Stacy Schwartz, in "The Difficult Parent," describes how Laquisha Davis begins prekindergarten as a bright, energetic, and eager four-year-old but by the second grade is exhibiting behavior problems and is recommended by the classroom teacher for testing and referral to the behavior disorders classroom. Laquisha's mother is confused, saddened, and discouraged by the kindergarten, first-, and second-grade teachers' lack of communication and collaboration with her.

The chapter concludes with a case by P. Elizabeth Pate entitled "Student Stress: It's 10:00 P.M. Do You Know Where Your Kids Are?" in which two teachers share their frustration and dismay at the physical and emotional behaviors exhibited by stress as a result of stress.

REFERENCES

Avery, P. (1992). Exploring political tolerance with adolescents. *Theory and Research in Social Education, 20,* 386–420.

Epstein, J. L. (1996). Advances in family, community, and school partnerships. *New Schools, New Communities, 12*(3), 5–13.

Henderson, A. T., & Berla, N. (1994). *A new generation of evidence: The family is critical to student achievement.* Washington, D.C.: National Committee for Citizens in Education.

Ryan, K., & Bohlin, K. E. (1999). *Building character in schools.* San Francisco: Jossey-Bass.

Winters, W. G. (1993). *African American mothers and urban schools: The power of participation.* New York: Lexington Books.

CASES

CASE 5.1

A TRIP TO REALITY
An "Everyone" Story

Rebecca Mann

In this case, Rebecca Mann reflects on an elementary school experience in which she was teased for being Jewish. As you read the case, critique the reasons Mann may have been frustrated and the responses of her teacher and parents. Brainstorm a list of strategies that you could use to foster acceptance for all religions in your classroom.

I always knew that I was different from other people. I was shorter, my hair was curlier, and I was Jewish. Each individual trait was rather insignificant, but, combined, I felt overwhelmed. As I grew and learned, I began to realize that my differences made me special. It was my unique combination of characteristics that made me who I was and I became proud. Of all my individual traits, being Jewish was always important to me. I had been raised in a traditional household where God was kind, good things happened to good people, and being Jewish was a

Schools bring together students of different ethnicities, cultures, genders, religions, and socioeconomic strata.

wonderful thing. It was, however, not something you advertised. My parents had grown up in a time when anti-Semitism was acceptable. They both have shared many stories with me about their experiences with prejudice. My dad was denied job promotions. My mom had to listen to hateful words. That was not the kind of life they wanted for their little girl. Even today, I have kept my faith private except around people whom I trust. The only reason I share my story now with you is so you might have an understanding of people of the Jewish faith and the sometimes reluctance with which they identify themselves as being Jewish.

Perhaps you have experienced such an incident, perhaps you have a friend or loved one who has been hurt by another's words. No matter what the case, I hope you conclude this reading with a greater understanding of the pain that ignorance may cause. I was raised in a household that not only had strong religious convictions but also had high moral expectations. As a young girl, I was not allowed to play with toy guns or even to make pretend guns out of my thumb and forefinger. I was not allowed to watch excessively violent television shows. If I raised my hand to hit a fellow family member, I was sent to my room until I calmed down. By the time I was in the fifth grade, I knew that violence was not the way to solve problems. I was capable of using my words to tell someone how I felt instead of hitting or kicking them.

I have always loved learning. Getting up for school was always difficult for me, but once I was in the building, I was ready. I always did my homework. I responded to my teachers, but my biggest academic problem was my mouth. Every report card I have received made some reference to the need to control my talking. I loved to socialize because I felt that talking and listening was one of the best ways to learn. School has always come pretty easily to me; I have had to work but not very hard.

I was in the fifth grade. I had just moved to Atlanta, Georgia, from Toronto, Ontario. I was adjusting to the new surroundings, but the transition was difficult. Atlanta was like a different world to me. People talked slower and with a strong accent. Also, there were more people who believed that my religious convictions were their business. The majority of my closest friends knew that I was Jewish and what being Jewish meant to me. But I did not think it was necessary for the whole school to know what I believed. One afternoon, I was sitting in my science class in the second seat back right in the middle of the room. The teacher had finished her lesson and we were to be working independently on a worksheet. I was minding my own business when the boy in front of me turned around to face me. I chose to ignore him. He was not my friend or even a person with whom I spoke, he was simply a boy sitting in front of me. He proceeded to drop a penny on the floor. I continued to ignore him. Then he looked straight at me. I raised my eyes already aggravated at his drawing me off task.

"Aren't you gonna pick it up, Jew?" As soon as the words registered, I reacted. Without thought, I drew my hand back and as he turned around to face the front of the classroom, I let my hand loose. As my hand smacked him straight in the back of the head, I heard my name being yelled.

"Rebecca Mann, go straight to the office." I did not even argue. I knew that my response had not been acceptable and that I had I reacted on impulse but I was not ashamed of what I had done.

As I sat waiting in the office, I became a little nervous at the thought of the different punishments I might receive. This was my first time and only time waiting to enter the principal's office because I was in trouble. The more I sat, the more angry I became. Should I have simply sat there and taken the harassment? What would have happened if I said something to the teacher? Had my small and truly harmless act of violence made an indelible mark on this other's child's life? Would he think before he said that sort of thing again? I did not know. The visit with the principal is somewhat foggy. I do remember my parents being called. Because I was a first-time offender, I was let off with a warning. "Rebecca, you are too bright a student to use violence to solve your problems." I was pleased that I had not been unreasonably punished, but what about the boy? Nothing happened to him. There was no retribution for his anti-Semitic remark. How was that fair?

QUESTIONS FOR REFLECTION AND DISCUSSION

1. Did the teacher react appropriately?

2. Was it right for the teacher to send Rebecca straight to the office? Why? Why not?

3. What punishment should Rebecca have received, if any? Should the boy have been punished?

4. How can we better prepare teachers to work with this type of situation in the classroom?

5. Have you ever had a similar experience? Would and could you share that with your classmates now?

6. How should a child's faith, with regard to promoting children's understanding, be presented in an elementary school classroom?

7. What sorts of experiences might the boy have had or what might have influenced him to make such a remark?

8. Script a dialogue that the teacher might have with the class regarding this incident.

RESOURCE

Isaacs, R. H., & Olitzky, K. (1994). *Sacred celebrations: A Jewish holiday handbook.* Hoboken, NJ: KTAV Publishing House.

WORLD WIDE WEB RESOURCES

The Jewish Network (www.shamash.org)
Judaism 101 (www.jewfaq.org)

CASE 5.2

DEALING WITH DISHONESTY

Pat Nickell

One of the most challenging tasks that teachers face is supporting children in the development of character, values, morality, and ethics. As they grow, most children come in regular contact with admonitions of what is good and bad in terms of their behavior. When a new class arrives in August, teachers quickly note that some of their children have a more integrated sense of right and wrong, good and evil than others. The following case study is based on events that actually took place in the mid-1970s; the author was one of the teachers. In it, a fifth grader exhibits a consistent tendency to be dishonest. This tendency appears to be so ingrained in Paul that he is unable to quell it, even when it threatens to cost him something very important. Perhaps the teachers should have sought professional help for Paul. Perhaps the teachers should have developed a different kind of behavior management system or set up special rules for Paul. Perhaps this "special trip" was more than fifth graders can handle. What do you think?

Cornish Elementary School was a four-year-old school on the south side of a medium-sized midwestern city. The school served its surrounding suburban neighborhoods, most of which were middle class and predominantly white. The school also served residents of three mobile home parks and a rural farming area that extended to the southern border of the county. Cornish housed about 900 students in kindergarten through fifth grade and was considered to be one of the more progressive schools in the district, known and respected for its award-winning principal and staff who were highly committed to continuous improvement in student performance. Jerry Bosch, the principal, took great pride in "his" school, "his" teachers, and "his" children, and made school–community collaboration "his" hallmark.

Amy Rankin and Barb Keller, two of Cornish's most innovative teachers and strongest child advocates, had only six years experience between them in the classroom. Nonetheless, their growing success with parents and children gave them confidence and their team-teacher relationship served as a catalyst for trying new ideas. This time, it was to be an extended environmental education field trip. By the beginning of February, Amy and Barb had spent weeks making plans, creating forms and letters, and gathering district approvals. It was time to announce the trip to the children and parents. At first, their two classes of fifth graders thought their two well-loved teachers were teasing them, but soon reality began to sink in and student excitement began to exceed Barb and Amy's. Barb had attended a workshop the previous summer sponsored by the science education department at the local university during which presenters had described a plan for multiday field trips that allowed for in-depth student research and other exciting innovations in outdoor education. The two teachers attended follow-up training together and soon were hooked on the idea of involving their students in such an experience. They would take their students to a state park that offered many opportunities for environmental studies, provided a well-respected naturalist and guide for support both in planning and implementation phases, and provided an affordable lodge that could house the teachers and children on the park property.

Taking 56 fifth graders on a three-day two-night field trip into the "wilderness" seemed like educational hari-kari to most of their colleagues. However, Barb and Amy enjoyed challenges and were reciprocally motivated by one another's commitment to progressive teaching ideas. They soon found themselves deeply engrossed in in-class and out-of-class preparations, not the least of which was preparing the students for the kinds of behaviors they would need to exhibit at all times in this free and open environment. The two teachers could not afford an accident on this trip; they were setting a precedent for their rather conservative school district and needed to "prove" to all concerned that this trip was not only worthwhile educationally for this age group, but also posed no threat to the students' physical or emotional well-being.

Thus, a major part of pretrip classroom preparations had to do with implementing an elaborate system for enabling the children to "earn" their passage. The teachers decided to take a positivist approach and let the students know that as of two months prior to the trip, all students had the teachers' permission to attend as long as their parents agreed. But in order to continue as a participant, the students would be required to maintain 180 of the 200 points that they were each given at the beginning of the two-month preparation time. Points could be lost in a number of ways, but Barb and Amy made every attempt to make sure point losses were clearly related to behaviors that might actually threaten the success of the trip. "Success of the trip" was described up front for students, parents, and administration in terms of objectives such as "building a stronger class community," "showing respect for our natural world," "learning new things through independent as well as collective effort," and "taking responsibility for one's words and actions." Thus, points were taken away for such actions as hurting a classmate's person or feelings; being disrespectful of other people's property; littering; not taking responsibility for class assignments; and saying and doing things that negatively impacted the group, its members, or its academic progress. The teachers believed that the trip should be an opportunity to develop more than simply knowledge about the environment they would be exploring. It should also serve as an opportunity to develop social and civic responsibility before the students moved on to middle school.

> Challenge: Create a list of objectives for a three-day outdoor education field trip for fifth graders. What expectations would you create for pretrip classroom behavior that would help prepare students to succeed on the trip objectives? Is honesty an important behavior for this field trip setting as it has been described, or is it simply something we want children to be, but that has little to do with safety, learning, and other, more important criteria?

Paul Hamilton was in Amy's class. Like most of the others, he was eleven years old, but he was less mature socially and emotionally. He was the younger of two sons in a two-parent middle-class family. His father taught in the pharmacy department at the university and his mother was a practicing pharmacist. Dr. Hamilton had been a guest speaker for the two classes earlier in the year and had enthralled the children with his stories of living for two years in India as a member of the Peace Corps.

Paul was short for his age and slightly stocky, but he had beautiful skin and a cherublike face. He was both extremely active and highly intelligent, excelling in most sports and games as well as winning spelling and geography bees, essay contests, and other academic competitions. Nonetheless, he was a difficult child to like because often he purposefully did things to irritate or hurt others, particularly when no one was looking. He seemed to take great pleasure in trying to outwit classmates and teachers by creating a problem and then projecting absolute innocence. His immature and childlike appearance seemed to make his deviousness all the more repugnant. At his best, he was quite deft at hiding his actions. At his worst, he would be caught in the act but refuse any responsibility. It was this latter behavior that was the most offensive to both Amy and Barb because it seemed to them that not only must he realize that he was the obvious miscreant but also that he was caught in a lie. No amount of public scolding or private counseling seemed to help. He unequivocally denied responsibility for any misdeed and he capped that by denying denial. The students looked to Amy to "take care of" Paul when he hurt or angered them, yet over and over again, she found herself grasping for some retribution that would satisfy the students and her while causing the desired responses to emerge from Paul—admission of guilt and remorse. Over and over Amy failed.

> Challenge: Would Paul, or children like him, be a problem for you? Why is this behavior difficult for teachers to handle? What is wrong with this behavior? Think of some strategies that you would use with such children to help them realize that deceit is socially unacceptable and to help them learn better ways of relating to classmates and teachers.

Paul's father took a more active role than his mother in Paul's schooling, appearing for conferences and returning phone calls made by teachers. Amy had met with Paul's father on three occasions between September and December regarding Paul's hurtful actions and accompanying deceitfulness, but Dr. Hamilton insisted that this was not a pattern for Paul at home and refused to accept that it was a pattern at school. When Amy related specifics, Dr. Hamilton disdainfully relegated them to "typical behavior of kids." ("Don't all kids try to avoid trouble when they can?!")

> Challenge: Do you believe that all kids "try to avoid trouble when they can" by lying? If so, how will you handle this? If not, how would you respond to Dr. Hamilton? Plan a parent conference with Dr. Hamilton. What would be your goals? How would you begin? How would you handle his refusal to accept your concerns as worthy of any action on his part?

Paul was given the same 200 points as the rest of the class and was told, along with the others, that he would need to maintain 180 of them in order to participate in the field trip. Within two weeks, Paul had already lost nine points because of clear infractions of the standards set by Amy and Barb. Each time, Amy spent time trying to get Paul to admit that he had misbehaved and to recognize that if he continued to lose points his participation in the field trip was in jeopardy.

On the Monday after Paul lost the ninth point, Dr. Hamilton appeared at Amy's door after school, Paul in tow.

"Mrs. Rankin, I understand that you have told Paul that you don't want him to go on the field trip to Brighton Park," he stated without emotion.

"Dr. Hamilton, come in and have a seat.... Is that what Paul told you?" Amy asked. Without waiting for a response, she began, "Dr. Hamilton, what I have told all of my students is that they have 200 points…"

"I know all of that, Mrs. Rankin. I read your letter about your point system and Paul has explained it as well. My question is, why did you tell Paul that in the end you will make sure that he won't be allowed to go when, if I understand correctly, he still has enough points to participate."

Amy considered the importance of her response.

> Challenge: Paul, once again, has lied. He has told his father that Mrs. Rankin is going to "make sure" he doesn't get to go on the trip. Why do you suppose he did that? Might he think that he probably isn't going to be able to keep enough points, so he wants to set the situation up so that his father begins to question Mrs. Rankin's motives early in preparation for when he loses his twentieth point? What should Amy say? Script the rest of this parent conference to achieve the best outcome you believe can come of it.

After the conference, Amy went home completely exhausted. She and her husband discussed her situation and possible outcomes.

Amy decided to tell Barb about the conference and let it go at that for the time being. Paul lost three more points during the following week, one of which was taken away by the physical education teacher in whose class Paul forced a ball away from a classmate in order to start a new game. He then said the child offered him the ball. Other children witnessed the incident and agreed that Paul was not being truthful. Two other points were taken away because Paul failed to complete two separate assignments, one of which caused his science team to get behind in their work. His teammates were furious.

When Paul had lost seventeen points, his father appeared in Mrs. Rankin's room after school again, stating that Mrs. Rankin had continued to take Paul's points away not because it was deserved but because she did not "want" Paul to go on the field trip—she "had it in for Paul." Amy asked Barb to step in for this conference and the two of them tried to assure Dr. Hamilton that each point Paul had lost was because of rule infractions, primarily a failure to "take responsibility for one's word and actions"—and that both teachers had made multiple vain attempts to convince Paul to cease breaking rules. But more importantly they wanted Paul to be honest so that he would stop losing points. Dr. Hamilton would not be convinced. It was clear that he believed his son.

A cafeteria worker reported to Mrs. Rankin that Paul took the salad dressing dispenser to his table when he forgot to put dressing on his salad at the salad bar. This was not only an infraction of cafeteria rules but Paul also denied taking the dispenser, saying that a classmate had done it and he only used it once it was there. All the other children at the table agreed that Paul had been the one to bring the dispenser to the table. Mrs. Rankin removed Paul's eighteenth point and tried one last time to talk with him. After more than twenty minutes, he tearfully acknowledged that he knew he was close to losing his right to go on the trip but that he wanted very much to go. He stated that he was willing to turn over a new leaf and show everyone he deserved to go with the class. Mrs. Rankin silently held her breath.

> Challenge: Based on what you have read, what would you do at this point? Would you do anything to help Paul mend his ways?

On a Friday morning during reading class, ten days before the trip was to begin, Paul asked Mrs. Keller if he could be excused to use the restroom. Robert, another student in Barb's class, had left a few moments before. Barb Keller warned Paul to go ahead but hurry back.

In a few moments, Robert came running into Mrs. Keller's room and from the tone of his voice, Amy knew that something was wrong. She rushed next door to find Robert white-faced in fear. Breathless, he stumbled for words but managed to communicate that Paul was "in trouble" in the bathroom—something about the light switch. At that moment, a child appeared in the doorway whom neither of the teachers recognized. As the child spoke, they became aware that it was Paul, minus his eyelashes, eyebrows, and bangs. According to Paul, he had gone into the bathroom where a student from another fifth-grade class was "messing with" the light switch (a somewhat antiquated switch that requires a special tool to turn it off or on) with a paper clip. He had stood watching the student until suddenly "there was a blast and the lights went out." The blast had obviously hit Paul in the face, singing off all his facial hair and some of his skin. He was frightened and beginning to feel the pain. After rushing Paul to the office for medical attention and reporting the incident to the principal, Barb returned to her classroom. Amy had the two groups together and was attempting to restore a semblance of peace by reading the next chapter in *Bridge to Terabithia*.

Barb interrupted. "Robert, the principal wants to see the boy who was playing with the light switch, but Paul is in severe pain and he isn't able to remember exactly what happened or who the other boy was. Can you come with me to the office and tell him what you saw?"

Robert became visibly frightened. "Mrs. Keller, there wasn't anyone else in there. It was just me and Paul. Paul was the one who stuck the paperclip in the light switch; I swear!"

> Challenge: What will happen? What do you think Paul will do? Should you take him on the overnight field trip? What will you say

to his father? How should teachers deal with children who use dishonesty to resolve their problems? Is Paul's problem "too big" and in need of professional counseling? How would you find out if this is the case?

WORLD WIDE WEB RESOURCES

Moral Values and Spirituality in Children's and Young Adult Literature (http://falcom.jmu.edu/~ramseyil/moral.htm)
Teaching Virtues: Building Character across the Curriculum (www.teachingvirtues.net)
The Character Education Partnership (www.character.org)

CASE 5.3

OSTRACIZING RICH

R. C. Carter

Scott was entering teaching as a second career, a profession he rediscovered after being asked by some children to teach Sunday school. Usually, he was the oldest student in his college classes with the least amount of educational experience. Age, however, had provided a counterbalance to his lack of teaching experience. Age had afforded him a greater amount and variety of opportunities, which helped shape his vision of the teacher's role. He regarded students as equals in the learning process. He and they differed only in that age had permitted him more opportunities for growth and experience, assets he hoped would help him connect with the students' worlds.

Time and work experience also advanced his social status. Thirty years ago he was easily identified as a person who came from the wrong side of town—a "kid" from the projects, a young man whose constant skirmishes with trouble would not have been tolerated if he hadn't been blessed with athletic ability. College had been much more than a textbook education. He learned outside as well as inside the classroom.

In a few minutes Scott would begin today's fifth-grade social studies lesson. He had reached the point in his student teaching that he was taking over portions of the class. He listened to his cooperating teacher, admiring the natural ease the man took in presenting the material and running the class. Scott took a deep breath to calm his butterflies. His gaze shifted from the classroom, over several empty desks, beyond the tops of the teachers' parked cars to focus on the dogwoods in bloom. It was a scene considerably more tranquil than a few days earlier.

Off to the left, near the flagpole the morning prayer group was disassembling. This group, comprised mainly of concerned parents, prayed for the safety of students inside the building. The daily vigil grew out of a meeting with the school superintendent. Held in the school parking lot, the gathering included several influential community members and school supporters. Their concern was students', or more specifically their children's, safety. For two days there had been a steady stream of vehicles picking up students. There was concern by the second afternoon that the school might close from low attendance.

Rumors raced throughout the community that a student had made threats thought to jeopardize other students. The threats had not been directed toward any specific person. Rather, the threats were a general response to taunting questions made by other students. On the third day the superintendent met with parents who were demanding some sort of action. A month ago, such rumors could have easily been dismissed. However, Columbine was fresh in the public's mind. A similar incident in metropolitan Atlanta the previous week further heightened public concern. These events had peaked public awareness to the extent that the smallest rumor that something may have been said was treated as a fact in reality. It was repeated over and over, becoming scarier with each retelling.

Scott knew many of the students' parents. They were neighbors, previous co-workers, and fellow church members. Their reactions to the rumors surprised and startled him. Yesterday morning after hall duty he ran into a friend of several years. They had helped each other with moving and home improvement projects. The man was picking up his three children. They discussed the necessity of his doing so. His friend asked what Scott would do in this situation. Scott responded that he would keep his son in school. His friend's reply was to the contrary, "I think you're wrong. There's no way you can protect all the kids at this school." The children were taken home.

Walking toward Scott's classroom the other students walked past an administrative office where Rich was sitting passively; Rich was the focal point of the current uproar. He was in the office as a form of protective custody. A student with a quiet personality, he didn't outwardly appear to be troubled by all that was going on around him. An investigation had determined the alleged threats were actually statements of self-defense in response to leading and self-serving questions. His answers then were taken out of context, used as instruments of ostracism and further ridicule by his tormentors. They also provided the basis for the current turmoil.

Standing at his door monitoring the hallway traffic, Scott could hear students talking about Rich. "He wears the same shirt and pants everyday." "I bet he doesn't even change his underclothes." "I hear his Mom is a witch." "So is his grandmother." "He never eats lunch." " I bet he can't afford it." And on it went. What Rich heard was probably worse. These were comments students made regardless of who was listening. It was doubtful that the comments made personally to Rich, without an adult present, were less hurtful.

Scott had become aware of the importance of, and the need to ameliorate, the effects of negative peer pressure. He had learned students who lack independent judgment can feel as if they have to wear the right clothing, use the "in" slang for expression, and create school work that doesn't stand out from their peers. To these students being different was a social disaster. Their self-esteem was attached to the opinions of others. In this instance, inclusion in the peer group and the commensurate building of self-esteem created a weeklong disruption of education and further ostracized an innocent person. Students were conforming by passing on opinion and speculation as if it were fact. When this phenomenon was combined with parental awareness of recent safety problems in other schools, it exacerbated community fear.

Scott remembered an administrator's description of Rich as a very polite young man. He did dress differently. Rich wore clothes and fashion items that made statements or were presumed to make statements. It appeared this young man was chosen because he was different. Scott recalled his own days of bell-bottom pants, banana collar shirts, and eight-inch-wide polka dot ties. He hadn't worn signs or symbols, but he grew long hair, a handlebar moustache, and a beard. He had kept the beard since 1974. It had caused him some problems and closed more than one employment door over the years. Conversely, he had jobs where he was the first employee to have facial hair. He had refused to shave out of the conviction that the worth of an individual was more than skin deep.

The present atmosphere at school stirred a mixture of emotions and memories. It wasn't the first time Scott had experienced situations in which the differences between people and ideas became problematic. He remembered a walk down Main Street at 2:00 in the morning. Thousands of college students were reveling amongst the broken pieces of plate glass that had been parts of restaurants and storefronts. He watched a student body vice president jubilantly waving a bottle of wine and shouting hoarsely, "We shut it down!" Scott thought to himself that this group failed to realize they had not only closed the university but also they had shut down the forum for their ideas and hopes. The reaction to destructive civil disobedience would become a tool against their causes. Tears welled inside him. The emotional muddle he felt then might reemerge during this current controversy. People were being caught up in something without fully understanding the consequences of their actions.

However, this was different. This strife fed on fear rather than a coopted cause. There is a saying that if three people agree with the same rumor it's a fact. If people hear the same thing often enough, it'll become the truth. The scenario had life in the instance. Scott had to view this current circumstance from a new perspective. He was no longer a spectator but a shareholder in the responsibility for establishing the parameters in which learning from this setting could take place. What was the best way to turn misguided energies into a learning model? Perhaps he could develop links to the students through his personal experiences, thereby explaining parallels to the past few days.

Scott was active in campus and community affairs in college. When asked to play Santa Claus at a party for underprivileged children, he gladly agreed. He was a volunteer in a free school program for community and migrant worker children to provide early education. Monies from student activity fees and community donations funded the program. The donations included a marginal dwelling (refurbished with eclectic student leftovers) in which volunteers conducted after-school and weekend classes.

As Scott, replete with pillowed girth and green bags bulging with toys and candy, was about to enter the house, a social alarm rippled through the hosts. A member of the ladies' clubs giving the Christmas party noted that almost all the children were African American. A short frantic discussion concluded it would be worth Santa arriving a little late to have him look more appropriate. The children could be kept busy playing games. A phone call yielded prop makeup from the theater department. Satisfied they had avoided a potential faux pas the hosts dashed inside to announce Santa's arrival.

Santa stepped into the room with a hearty, "Ho, Ho, Ho!" Children began running toward him eagerly wanting to know what was in the bags. Everyone that is except for a little boy who stood to the side crying. As the hosts helped the children return to their seats so Santa could get to his chair, Scott approached the crying boy. "Ho, Ho, Ho. You shouldn't be crying with Santa here." With an anguished expression and the bitterness of disappointment the little boy said, "You're not Santa, Santa's White." It was a long walk to Santa's chair.

Later that same academic year Scott was co-coordinator of Choice '68. Sponsored by *Time* magazine, it was a nationwide program to poll college sentiment on the upcoming presidential election. *Time* arranged the speakers' itineraries in preparation for mock elections on the selected campuses. Scott sat on the speaker's platform next to Paul Butel, the Socialist Workers' Party candidate for vice president, whom he had just introduced. Mr. Butel stood and solemnly asked the audience to bow their heads in remembrance of Dr. King who had been slain days earlier. Suddenly, a fire and brimstone shout shattered the silence and beseeched, "Brothers and sisters get your guns." Mr. Butel went on to decry the White man's pollution of the Black man, of their heritage, their culture, and their very being. To illustrate the White man's contamination of the Black race, he instructed the audience to look around the room, at "all the different shades of us." The crowd erupted with roars of power shouts. A sea of clenched fists waved over their heads. In response, campus security closed and locked the ballroom exit doors from the outside. Scott was one of only four or five pollutants in the room. It was a long speech.

Scott decided the best approach to address the current issues would be to cast himself with the students in the role of investigator, problem solver, and communicator. He would incorporate the experiences of Santa Claus and Dr. King's persona with the contradictions of the Progressive Era to connect the students with the issues of diversity—learning about others and social status. A lack of exposure to such issues may lead to the unconscious assimilation of norms prior to the development of critical thinking. For example, when he was a kid a commonly used phrase was, "The only good Indian is a dead Indian." Some of his first plastic toys were soldiers of blue and Indians of red, green, and yellow. He built forts from Lincoln Logs and made mounds of dirt with cherry bombs and firecrackers underneath them. When the Indians attacked, he'd blow up the hills, just like John Wayne at Fort Apache.

For Scott the best approach to overcoming inappropriate socialization had been to take personal strides to identify and to investigate social inconsistencies. Experiential strides he could share with his students today while making a link to the current school happenings. The connection might even yield a teachable moment on the responsibility of maintaining your own identity as a contributing member of society. He believed this was the bottom-line obligation for social studies teachers. Especially if they were going to help students become members of society who would be critical thinkers and reflective, competent citizens. Through his experiences he would encourage the application and expansion of student knowledge and involvement in the recent events. By connecting with their actions and interests he hoped to help them develop a sense of the responsibility for the power they will have over their lives.

By modeling and encouraging students to look at issues from as many ways as possible he could help increase the potential for this understanding. He wanted them to perceive themselves as having intelligence and being capable of personal growth. He hoped they would discover the ability to identify issues, to investigate their social worlds, to exercise their rights, and to carry out their responsibilities with other members of society regardless of another's social status. Perhaps, they could avoid some of human nature's tendency to distinguish and to sort human being into one group or another. Maybe then it would be possible as Bing Crosby and Paul Whiteman sang in the 1920s, that "The Blue Birds and the Blackbirds Got Together."

At least that was the plan last night. The contradiction of Jim Crowe Laws in the Progressive Era, his personal experiences with Santa, toy soldiers, and a political candidate had been the ingredients for today's lesson. It's amazing the number of thoughts the mind can process in a few short minutes. During hall duty this morning he was informed that teachers were not to avoid the current school circumstance, but they should not bring it up. Whenever students mentioned it, the teacher was to dispose of it as quickly as possible. His cooperating teacher also believed that when a teacher revealed any personal indecision or past mistakes, she or he lost credibility in the eyes of the students. He felt Scott's personal experiences would be inappropriate. Therefore, Scott's plans to incorporate them into the lesson would have to be dropped as well.

The disappointment intensified as he passed one of the empty student desks. It belonged to a student he knew very well. She was an honor roll student and one of the children who had asked him to be her Sunday school teacher. A child who became so caught up in the rumors and hysteria that she unwittingly became a major contributor to the misrepresentation of Rich. She was serving an out-of-school suspension because of her actions. With a sigh he mentally ran over the revised lesson for the day. The lesson would be students getting the mail for their parents as a result of Thomas Watson's Rural Free Delivery Act. How innuendo, rumor, and saying stuff just to be part of the crowd can ostracize a person or a whole group of people just because they look different or don't dress the same was shelved.

QUESTIONS FOR REFLECTION AND DISCUSSION

1. Did the downplaying of the school situation ignore a teachable moment?

2. If, as commonly held, teaching is a social act, how do we connect socially with our students?

3. Is it really the students' world we attempt to connect with or our conceptions of how we think they view the world?

4. How does our socialization and perceived social status of others influence classroom decision making?

5. By sharing their failures and mistakes do teachers model risk taking and express openness to experience and a tolerance for ambiguity? Or, do we reveal a weakness for students to exploit and render our efforts something less and perhaps efforts that may be ignored?

6. How do we help students understand norms that were socialized before they could critically think?

7. How is the "appropriateness" of a norm determined?

8. How are our actions toward and involving others premised on how we view them and the status we accrue to them?

RESOURCES

Glasser, W. (1992). *The quality school: Managing students without concern.* New York: Harper Perennial.
Manzo, A. V. (1998). *Teaching for creative outcomes, why we don't, how we can.* Retrieved July 13, 1999, from http://europa.galileo.gsu.edu:40000/…New Article+html/Article.html
Schmuck, P. A., & Schmuck, R. A. (1997). *Group processes in the classroom.* New York: McGraw-Hill.
Starko, A. J. (1995). *Creativity in the classroom: Schools of curious delight.* White Plains, NY: Longman.

WORLD WIDE WEB RESOURCES

Diversity Works (www.cultural-concepts.com)
Native Child, Inc. (www.nativechild.com)

CASE 5.4

GO ON INTO THE HALL—YOU'RE EXCUSED FROM THE CELEBRATION
Religious Observance in a Public School Classroom

Dee Russell
Paige E. Campbell

Many teachers say they wish parents were more involved in their classrooms. Here is a letter from a father, concerned about his daughter, who offers some suggestions

Parents and teachers, working together, can nourish understanding about religious differences between children.

about what might happen in the classroom. John Miller, a Jehovah's Witness, is concerned about how his first grader, Sarah, feels after she has been excused from a classroom birthday celebration.

Ms. Hopgood has taught first grade in this same school for five years. In previous years, she has had children who were Jehovah's Witnesses in her classroom and is sure that she has shown her respect by letting them stand silently when the class recites the Pledge of Allegiance and by letting them leave the room when treats are brought to school. This is what the Millers asked her to do when they came to open house—and she is doing it!

This is the first time she has ever received a letter like the one sent from John Miller. She really wonders what this father expects her to do—how can she do more than she already is? Surely, talking about Sarah's religion would be against the law—wouldn't it? What would other parents say when they heard that she had let Sarah or her parents talk about what being a Jehovah's Witness means? She is a little fearful about having a meeting with the Millers because they may demand she do things that are against her conscience—after all, she does not share their beliefs. Following is the letter from John Miller.

November 23, 2002

Dear Ms. Hopgood,

I want to begin by assuring you that I am very pleased with the growth that I have seen this school year in my daughter. I believe that your first grade is just what Sarah has needed. The way that you encourage children to read has been so good for Sarah. She comes home every day with something to tell us about a new story that she learned.

But (and I am sure you could guess that there would be a "but" somewhere in here) I am concerned about another part of the class—a part of which you may not be aware. You already know from our first visit at open house that we are Jehovah's Witnesses—and I know that you have tried to honor our beliefs. You have excused Sarah from having to say the Pledge of Allegiance to the flag each morning. You also excuse her from the classroom each time a child brings a treat to celebrate a birthday. Sarah goes into the hall and waits until all the special treats are gone.

I am not sure that you fully understand why we have asked you to excuse Sarah, how we want to make sure that God alone is honored, that no thing and no person will be honored before God. We know that you have followed through on our request.

Apparently, Sarah was excused from class again yesterday. We didn't know that at first, but we did notice that Sarah was quieter than usual when she got home. When we asked her what she had done at school, she suddenly burst into tears. "I had to go stand in the hall again," she said. "The other kids had special cupcakes for Emily's birthday and I couldn't have any. It's not fair that I can't eat any." Emily is Sarah's best friend. I think that made the whole situation more difficult. She felt as if she had been excluded from a celebration that was important to her friend.

We asked her whether she knew why she could not eat the special treat. And she told us that it was because God would be mad at her, if she did. I think this is the way that she could put it into words for herself. We have talked about this before and we told her again that God wanted us all to worship only Him. Celebrating birthdays was honoring a human as being more important than God.

She nodded her head and said she knew that. But still it wasn't fair that she had to stand in the hall. None of the other kids ever had to. And no one in the class knows why *she* has to. Sarah said, "They think I go out there because I have been bad—so bad I never deserve to eat a special treat!"

My wife and I talked more about this after Sarah was in bed. We were both raised as Jehovah's Witnesses and we remember doing the same thing that Sarah has been asked to do. Our teachers sent us to the hall, too, when there were birthday parties. We would see a mother come in with a tray covered in aluminum foil and our teachers would look at us and tell us to go into the hall. Just the same way they told bad kids to go into the hall. There was never a reason, just that matter-of-fact command: "Go on out into the hall."

We both remember how lonely it was there in the hall and how embarrassed we were—we were sure that other teachers walking by would think we were bad kids because we were standing out there in the hall.

I know it must be hard to have so many children in one room and that you cannot think about all of them all the time. But we would like to talk to you about this situation. Is there somewhere else that Sarah could go when there are parties? Is there something she could do that would not seem so much like a punishment?

Would you be willing to talk to the other children about the reasons that Sarah goes away when there are birthday parties? Couldn't that help other children understand more about Sarah? We do not want her to be ashamed of our religion. Perhaps if it could be talked about a little bit, more people would understand a little better.

My wife and I would like to come some afternoon to talk to you about this. I would be willing to take some time off work, if you would let us know what day is best for you. This is important to us and we do not want to let more of the year go by with Sarah feeling the way she does.

Sincerely,
John Miller

QUESTIONS FOR REFLECTION AND DISCUSSION

1. If you were in Ms. Hopgood's place, how would you respond to this letter? How would you prepare for your conference with the parents?

2. To what degree is Mr. Miller expecting too much of a teacher and a classroom? Is it appropriate to talk about a student's religion in the classroom? In what ways can a teacher help support a discussion of religious beliefs without overstepping boundaries? Should all celebrations be prohibited in the classroom?

3. Teachers often claim to be interested in developing self-esteem, but for many people, religious belief is an important part of who they are. To what degree should teachers address religious issues, especially as they relate to a student's sense of self?

RESOURCES

Ward, H. H. (1988). *My friends' beliefs: A young reader's guide to world religions.* New York: Walker and Company.
Jehovah's Witnesses prepare a pamphlet especially for teachers that explains important beliefs that may affect children in public schools. The pamphlet is available at any Kingdom Hall.

WORLD WIDE WEB RESOURCE

Teaching Tolerance (www.splcenter.org/teachingtolerance/tt-index.htm)

CASE 5.5

THE DIFFICULT PARENT

Stacy Schwartz

This case examines the complex relationships between teachers and parents. Often-times we think of parents as supportive of the school, but there are other factors that need to be considered. Schools need to consider what roles they have generally offered parents and how they might broaden their definition of parental involvement. In addition schools need to consider the ways that they might support families of their students. Teachers, students, and their families could benefit from more equitable relationships between home and school.

Laquisha Davis was the glimmer of any teacher's eye. A bright, energetic, and eager four-year-old, she was willing to attempt anything in prekindergarten. The girl with her hair in braids accessorized with bright red bows thrived with all that was going on in her busy classroom. She especially enjoyed being able to write (draw) her stories and have an adult add the dictation—to put her exciting words on paper! When she was not writing or drawing stories, she was in the book center mimicking her teacher, Ms. Ann, reading to the class. She would line up the dolls (or even her friends) to hear the story of the day—and boy, could she tell a story!

Not only did Ms. Ann enjoy watching Laquisha learn in the classroom, but so did Laquisha's mother. Ms. Ann's prekindergarten class had an invited time for parents to come to school every other week and Mrs. Davis was always there. She was nervous about sending Laquisha off to the big school, but Ms. Ann's welcoming presence helped calm her fears. Ms. Ann, the prekindergarten teacher, had made it clear to all the parents that they were always welcome in her classroom. Ms. Ann knew that many of the parents had to work just to make ends meet, so she was flexible with the parents' schedules. She also made home visits to learn more about the families and to show that she believed the parent–teacher partnership was two way. Ms. Ann was creative in her work with families and found a way to make the parents feel special about their roles in their child's education. Over the year, Mrs. Davis continued to support and be supported by Ms. Ann. The relationship they had built was valuable to each of them as well as to Laquisha.

The following year Laquisha moved to a school closer to home. The kindergarten teacher was kind and caring but did not share the same enthusiasm for Laquisha's spirit that Ms. Ann did. Laquisha's high energy and strong will resulted in a lot of time in "time-out." The same pattern continued in first grade, and there were even fewer times for her teacher and Mrs. Davis to interact. This lack of interaction resulted in less opportunity for Mrs. Davis to be welcomed into the classroom and less time for her to converse with the teacher about Laquisha. Mrs. Davis was confused and saddened by this. Just two years earlier she had played such a vital role in her child's education, and now she felt that there was little room for her.

Troubles in school continued for Laquisha in second grade. Mrs. Thomas, the second-grade teacher, had little tolerance for parents and families in her classroom. After all, she was hired to teach the children. *Working with* families to her meant having *families work for her.* Checking homework, chaperoning field trips, and donating to the class parties were the best activities for families.

Laquisha's mother had to increase her hours at work to pay for rising rent and other bills. Their financial responsibilities left little time to be donated to the school at the end of the month. Her mother continued to check Laquisha's homework every night and read through her Friday folder every week. Mrs. Davis began to notice that Laquisha was getting time-out more often and missing recess almost daily. She only wanted the best for her child. When she tried talking with the teacher about Laquisha's achievement in school the teacher's only response was, "Laquisha just needs to try harder." Mrs. Davis was discouraged with no specific feedback from the teacher and how her child could be successful in this second-grade classroom. When Laquisha returned to school after the winter recess break, Mrs. Thomas sent an envelope home in her Friday folder. After an increasingly frustrating year with Laquisha's behavior and low grades, Mrs. Thomas had referred Laquisha for testing and referral to the behavioral disorders classroom. When Mrs. Davis received the letter her heart sank. She felt that she had stayed in close contact with Laquisha's teacher and checked her daughter's homework carefully. She knew her daughter was not a meek and mild little girl. She understood that Laquisha had a lot of energy, but Mrs. Davis had watched other children be labeled by the school. She had seen the special education classrooms and noticed they were often populated by children from minority families. She knew that the situation was more complex than labeling her daughter and placing her outside of the regular education classroom. Needless to say, Mrs. Davis fought and resisted the attempt to place her child. She had wanted her child to have the same access as the other children. Mrs. Davis refused to sign the papers.

This decision came with a price for Mrs. Davis. Mrs. Davis came to be viewed as "one of those" difficult parents. Although Laquisha's mother thought her decision was a good one in the long run because Laquisha would not be labeled, Mrs. Davis was now the one with the label. Although she continued to be involved in Laquisha's schooling in as many ways as she could, such as making class games and other projects that the teacher requested, she longed for that connection she had with her daughter's first teacher. She only wished her child's teacher could understand what she was asking her to do. More importantly, she wished the teacher could understand her decision, her daughter, and her family.

QUESTIONS FOR REFLECTION AND DISCUSSION

1. What kinds of things can we do, as teachers, to support families and children?

2. What are some ways that teachers can learn from parents about how to meet children's needs?

3. How might teachers' definitions of "normal" and "good" affect the way they interact with children and families?

4. How could Laquisha's next teacher rebuild relationships between Laquisha's home and school experiences?

RESOURCES

Arnold, M. S. (1995). Exploding the myths: African American families at promise. In ⌐. ⌐.
Swadener & S. Lubek (Eds.), *Children and families "at promise": Deconstructing the discourse of risk* (pp. 143–162). Albany: State University of New York Press.

Cook, D. A., & Fine, M. (1995). "Motherwit": Childrearing lessons from African American mothers of low income. In B. B. Swadener & S. Lubek (Eds.), *Children and families "at promise": Deconstructing the discourse of risk* (pp. 118–142). Albany: State University of New York Press.

Quint, S. (1994). *Schooling homeless children.* New York: Teachers College Press.

Shockley, B., Michalove, B., & Allen, J. (1995). *Engaging families: Connecting home and school literacy communities.* Portsmouth, NH: Heinemann.

Valdes, G. (1996). *Con Respecto: Bridging the distances between culturally diverse families and schools.* New York: Teachers College Press.

CASE 5.6

STUDENT STRESS
It's 10:00 P.M. Do You Know Where Your Kids Are?

P. Elizabeth Pate

In this case, two first-year, fourth-grade teachers share their frustration and dismay at the physical and emotional behaviors exhibited by their students as a result of stress. Mrs. Mayse and Miss Trotter describe what most teachers experience in their day-to-day teaching: students reacting both physically and emotionally to stress. Follow along as these two novice teachers learn about sources of student stress and ways to alleviate stress.

Scene 1. Wednesday afternoon, teachers lounge, Sixth Street Elementary School. Mrs. Mayse is sitting at an old cafeteria table with papers spread around her. Miss Trotter enters the lounge and immediately sinks into the worn sofa. Miss Trotter starts the conversation.

"Wow, what a day! I'm pooped. I do not even know what is wrong with my students. Yummmmm…who brought the brownies today?"

"I think Kate did. She's the one around here who likes to cook." Mrs. Mayse asks, "What's going on with your students?"

"Well, to begin with, Shana and Michael didn't do their homework last night, again. Then, when I asked Chris if he brought back the note I asked his mother to sign, he just stood there with tears streaming down his face. No sooner had I calmed him down, than Jackie and Wayne started a shoving and yelling match over who could put away the map supplies! Honestly, I don't know what's set them off. Is it already a full moon again?"

"No, we just had a full moon," laughs Mrs. Mayse as she continues to sort papers. "Sounds like the kids and you had a rough day. My students were exceptionally quiet today. It's as if they were lethargic or overtired, or something. It was like pulling teeth to have them share anything in class."

"I'm tired of these behaviors. I think we need to find out what's going on that's making them so stressed," responds Miss Trotter as she reaches for another brownie.

Scene 2.   Two days later Mrs. Mayse and Miss Trotter are at computers in the media center searching for web sites on student stress.

"This is a good one," shares Miss Trotter. "It has basic information about stress." Mrs. Mayse leans over and together they read.

> Stress occurs when tension or pressure is placed upon someone. Stress involves both physical and emotional reactions and can be positive or negative. Often, adults remark that "they tend to work better under stress," such as when they are up against a deadline. This "works better under stress" type of reaction is positive. However, for elementary school-age children, stress oftentimes manifests itself in negative ways. Some physical and emotional behaviors in classrooms may be negative reactions to stress. Sources of stress, or stressors, in children's lives could include the family (e.g., divorce, poverty and homelessness, fast-paced family life), child abuse and neglect, health concerns, death (e.g., understanding of, bereavement), and substantiated or unsubstantiated fears.
>
> Additional sources of stress may be related to schooling itself. Lack of resources, homework support, and anxiety over testing may cause students to act out or become withdrawn in class. Some students have parents who work at night or have no access to educational resources, and for them homework often goes uncompleted. A student's after-school schedule and home environment can play a large role in whether homework gets done. Uncompleted homework leads to poor grades, low self-esteem, hopelessness, and high stress levels. Educators must make sound decisions on homework based on student, family, and community needs. To alleviate stress, do make attempts to:
>
> - Create tools to help identify potential stressors. Have student draw concept maps depicting life around their home and neighborhood. Utilize interest and concern inventories to find out about student fears and needs. Have students keep a weeklong hour-by-hour journal to get a sense of how and where time is spent both in school and out of school.
> - Identify associated stressor behaviors. Look for patterns of behavior. If a student seems more lethargic on Mondays than other days of the week, it may be that the child is getting home from perhaps going between parents on weekends.
> - Cut back on homework or eliminate it altogether. This might help those students that don't have support at home to keep from giving up. Some teachers utilize homework activities that families may work on together.
> - Teach coping strategies to students. Humor, problem solving, discussion, drawing, and physical activity often helps to ease stress-related tension.

- Communicate with the child and parents or caregivers. Without prying, find out what is happening in each child's life that may uncover sources of stress. And correspondingly, talk with parents and caregivers about concerns you have regarding physical and emotional behaviors of students.

Remember, don't:

- Attribute all behaviors to stress. Don't always assume that everything a child experiences is stressful.
- Make generalizations. Don't erroneously assume that students from intact, financially secure families have stress-free lives or that students from poor families live in continual stress.

"I think this is great information. Let's have our students make concept maps. I also like the idea of having them complete interest and concern inventories. I think I have one my professor at the university gave me we can use. Let's also have them keep a weekly log," remarked Mrs. Mayse.

Miss Trotter responded, "Great, let's get started. If nothing else, it will help us learn more about our students."

Scene 3. The following Friday the two teachers are in Mrs. Mayse's classroom. They are sharing their students concept maps, interest and concern inventories, and weekly logs of activities.

Mrs. Mayse asks as she looks at a concept map, "Look at this one. Who is this student? This can't be right."

"That's Shana's. She lives in one of the apartment complexes on the east side of town. Look at how she depicts her neighborhood," responds Miss Trotter. Shana's concept map shows her apartment building crudely drawn in the middle of the page. Lines radiate out from the apartment. At the end of one line is a drawing of a police officer. Another line indicates a robbery. A third line depicts a shooting. Other lines show families, stray animals, a swing, and a school bus.

"Look at Michael's. He lives in one of the historic neighborhoods. His father is a professor at the university. His mother works as a consultant for the hospital," says Mrs. Mayse. Michael's concept map centers around a large two-story house. He has lines drawn toward a soccer field, drum lessons, a baseball field, tennis courts, a playscape, the university, three dogs and a hamster, and families.

The two teachers picked up the completed interest and concern inventories and began scanning through them. Miss Trotter says, "Question 18, 'What concerns you most about home?' is such a simple question. But, just look at what the students are saying. Chris says that he's concerned that his mom will have to get a third job. Michael's concerned about not making good grades. Jackie's concerned about his parents divorcing and wondering with whom he will live."

Mrs. Mayse says, "I was surprised to see that a lot of my students, in response to the question, 'What concerns you most about school?' said they were afraid they would fail the standardized tests and be retained in the fourth grade."

The camaraderie between the two teachers quickly changed from one of casualness to concern. "You know, these help explain some of the behaviors we have been seeing. If I were in the fourth grade and I had to worry about being home alone, being too involved in extracurricular activities, having responsibility for my siblings, and wondering what was going on outside my apartment, I would probably be stressed and act out or not care about school. These kids are dealing with a lot at home, not to mention all the stuff that goes on at school," said Mrs. Mayse.

The two teachers continued to sort through answers. Miss Trotter found out that Shana receives little or no support in completing her homework. Michael, however, is so involved with extracurricular activities that there is little time left for his homework. Chris's mother continuously has to work extra shifts at the bakery to make ends meet and was not around to sign that note for which Miss Trotter was asking. Jackie was acting out as a way to release frustration caused by verbal abuse at home. Wayne was simply reacting to Jackie's outburst. Mrs. Mayse found out that her students claimed to be "practically brain dead" because they were stressed about the weekly tests she had them take in preparation for standardized examinations.

"I think we are making progress toward understanding the lives of our students and identifying stressors that may explain some of their behaviors," said Miss Trotter.

Mrs. Mayse replied, "I agree. I had no idea. This is another piece of the puzzle for me. I focus so much on getting everything covered and getting them ready for the tests that I lose perspective."

"It's a problem alright. Now what?" answered Miss Trotter.

QUESTIONS FOR REFLECTION AND DISCUSSION

1. This case ends with the question, "Now what?" The reality is that these two teachers have only limited control over some of the factors that lead to student stress. So what do teachers do to address or alleviate student stress?

2. Economic and technological divides in our society today exacerbate student stress. What does this statement mean? Is it accurate or misleading? Why?

3. The web site on student stress mentioned several do's and don'ts. Conduct an Internet search for more do's and don'ts to add to the list. Which do you think you would use in your classroom and why?

4. In what ways can Mrs. Mayse and Miss Trotter use the information gathered from the concept maps, interest and concern inventories, and weekly logs of activities?

WORLD WIDE WEB RESOURCES

The American Institute of Stress (www.stress.org)
Promoting Stress Management: The Role of Comprehensive School Health Programs (www.ed.gov/databases/ERIC_Digests/ed421480.htm)
Raising Children to Resist Violence: What You Can Do (www.apa.org/pubinfo/apa-aap.html)

CHAPTER 6

SPECIAL NEEDS

Under our federal legislation, all children are entitled to access to a free and appropriate education in our nation's public elementary schools. All teachers face the challenge of meeting the unique needs of children with special needs in their classrooms. The different types of disabilities and chronic medical conditions are often categorically presented to teachers in their preservice preparation programs, but the strategies that teachers would use to assist children are often not. Parents, resource providers such as occupational and speech therapists, teachers, and counselors all play different but important roles in accommodating a child with a special need in a classroom. The following four cases highlight some of the experiences of teachers and parents in their work with children with special needs.

In "Fighting for Robert," Barbara Bradley summarizes her experiences with a preschool child, Robert, and the unique needs that he brought to the classroom. She describes her emotional interactions with Robert and advocacy for his learning and development in the classroom. Linda Lord and Patricia M. Hentenaar describe how typically developing children assist and view children with special needs. In "Dr. Kent! Justin Is Being Mean…," the authors help children process through a difficult situation.

These two cases focus on the education of two specific children with special cognitive, social, and emotional needs. In "A Year Full of Challenges: Teaching a Student Who Is Deaf in a Regular Classroom," Susan B. Cardin explores how her whole class is impacted by having a child who is deaf enrolled in her class. Cardin describes her growth and development as a teacher and the modifications that she made to her classroom. She describes how she relied on the deaf educators to assist her in interpreting not what children know but what they mean.

In the final case, "Chronic Illness and the Art of Juggling Medications, Instructional Activities, and Transportation," Yvette Q. Getch presents a mother and her son as the mother advocates for her child's needs in an elementary school. The case highlights the contextual changes that should be made for a child with chronic and multiple medical conditions. The case urges readers to consider how many individuals in the school must work in concert to provide the least restrictive environment for the child.

CASE 6.1

FIGHTING FOR ROBERT

Barbara Bradley

This case documents the advocacy efforts of one preschool teacher on behalf of a student with special needs. The case presents the needs and rights of the student along with the dilemmas the teacher faces. What are some of the emotional boundaries that teachers must negotiate?

For most of the fourteen years I worked with preschool children who had special needs, the final day of the school year was the same. As the last school bus departs on the final day of school, I find myself grinning as the past nine months become a nostalgic blur and my thoughts turn to lazy summer days, except for one year. That year I cried. My co-workers and I engaged in some good-natured teasing, but they understood my sadness and they had tears too. That was the year the school boundaries changed and I hugged Robert good-bye knowing he would not be in my class for another year of preschool. My story is about Robert.

When I first met Robert, he was three-and-one-half years old, lying in a corner of our classroom banging one foot against the wall and tapping his head with one hand. We quickly learned that Robert was doing what he always did, avoiding social interactions and engaging in self-stimulating behaviors. Thus, my first objective, with the help of my educational assistant, was to encourage Robert to explore toys and play in closer proximity to his peers. I knew this might be a challenging objective, but I had no idea what was to come. Robert, with his significant cognitive and motor delays and a profound hearing loss, launched into an uncontrollable trauma when I moved him from the safety of his corner. I was horrified along with the other staff members who came to my class to find out what was happening. Robert had pulled off and pulled apart his hearing aides, scattering the pieces across the room. As the hearing aides squealed electronically in the background, Robert kicked his legs and flayed his arm, tears and mucous rolling down his face. Finally his crying stopped and he simply lay on the floor in an exhausted heap. As my panic subsided, I realized I needed to

Teachers work together with parents, counselors, and other resource providers to make classrooms inclusive for children with special needs.

make a decision: either allow Robert to remain in the safety of his corner until he was ready to participate or expect him to be an active member of our class. Based on the prognosis of his syndrome, Charge Association, I knew waiting was not an option. Robert was a member of our class and I expected him to participate in activities. Although I questioned my decision several times during Robert's first few tantrums, the alternative was not acceptable and soon we noticed that his tantrums were less severe and less frequent. By the end of the first year, Robert would still get angry but he rarely had a tantrum and, more importantly, he was participating in a variety of class activities.

We began the following school year in prekindergarten by encouraging Robert to explore a variety of sensory materials. He was extremely tactile defensive. For example, Robert would play at the rice table but he would only pick up objects with his fingertips and would avoid touching the rice. With guidance and support from our speech therapist and with occupational therapy, we also developed an oral–motor sensory stimulation program. Although Robert had been tube fed his entire life, we wondered if he could learn to drink from a straw or cup and eat soft foods, not as his primary means of nourishment but in the hope that one day Robert could go to a restaurant and enjoy a soda with his family and friends. We did not know, however, if Robert was physically capable of eating or drinking. I discussed this issue with Robert's mother, Ms. Martinez. She was excited by our ideas and my offer to contact Robert's physician and clarify our staff's concerns. Robert's physician was agreeable to meeting and suggested I confer with several members of Robert's medical team. The team reviewed Robert's medical records and our proposal. They concluded that medically there was no reason for us not to attempt to introduce liquids or soft foods. They did want their psychologist, however, to review Robert's case and to give him additional assessments. In the meantime we began implementing the next phase of our program.

We placed eating utensils in front of Robert that, at first, ended up quickly on the floor. Eventually, Robert explored the utensils, so we began to pour little puddles of liquid and place soft foods on his plate. That too ended up on the floor but soon Robert was tapping his spoon in the liquid and food. We were pleased with Robert's progress so we were shocked and upset when we received the report from Robert's psychologist stating that Robert was not emotionally ready to attempt liquids or soft foods. As we read the report it was obvious what happened; Robert had had one of his infamous temper tantrums during the evaluation. I contacted Robert's mother to discuss the report and our belief that Robert was not suffering emotionally from our program. Ms. Martinez supported our attempts and was eager for Robert to learn how to eat and to drink. Consequently, I contacted Robert's physician, but, understandably, he supported the recommendation of his team member. Again, I contacted Ms. Martinez and we decided to continue with our program. By the end of the year, Robert would tolerate oral stimulation with a Nuk brush and he would tap a Nuk brush dripped in juice against his face and lips and occasionally would place the brush in his mouth.

After two years in our program, Robert, five-and-a-half, was now leaving us but we were pleased by the progress he had made. With minimal physical support, Robert would stand at an easel and paint, although there are still stains on the rug from his initial introduction to painting. Robert would also crawl onto an adult's lap for comfort and he would occasionally communicate by taking an adult's hand and moving it toward a toy he could not reach or could not make work. Of course, I remembered the tantrums and cleaning up the many messes he created. But as the bus pulled away, I also remembered wiping away his tears and much of the hard-won progress that we had made on his behalf. There had been much progress, but so much more could have been accomplished. I knew Robert would be taking his first steps and I would not be there to see him. But I also knew that this sadness is often the lot of teachers who work with children with special needs.

The following school year I would occasionally hear about Robert's progress; he was walking short distances independently and he continued to participate in certain play activities. However, the news I received early in winter was disturbing. Robert's educational team did not believe it was appropriate to introduce liquids or soft foods to him and they did not think he should eat with the other children in his class. Although I did not agree with their choice to discontinue the program we began, I could empathize with the educational team's decision. There is often not clear agreement among well-meaning professionals about the most appropriate instructional goals and strategies for children, especially children with such severe and difficult-to-solve problems. However, I admitted to myself that I was angry about their decision to exclude him during mealtimes. Robert's current educational team believed that Robert's classmates would be upset by the tube feeding and, consequently, they fed Robert in a small room adjacent to the class. While his classmates ate lunch, Robert was allowed to play.

In the two years that Robert was in my class, his peers, the volunteers, parents, and visitors who came to our class never appeared upset by how Robert received his nourishment; curious yes, but not offended or disgusted. I debated what to do and regrettably never contacted Robert's teacher. I decided she was now responsible for Robert's education and was doing what she thought was best for Robert and her other students. I have always been torn by my decision not to contact Robert's teacher or Ms. Martinez while at the same time questioning some of my own beliefs. My objective for Robert was for him to be more like other children, but he *was* different. Robert had significant developmental delays and significant medical problems.

Was I creating false hope for Ms. Martinez and myself? Parents of children with special needs have hopes and dreams for their children as do all parents. Although I believe, as a teacher, I need to support parents' hopes, I also believe I need to help parents come to terms with their children's limitations. By focusing on feeding issues, was I suggesting to Ms. Martinez that one day Robert would not need to be fed through a tube and would be able to go out with friends to a fast-food restaurant? Did my hopes and dreams for Robert exceed his developmental abilities? Was I setting Ms. Martinez and Robert up for failure? Or, by choosing not to contact Robert's new teacher, did I fail Robert and his mother by not continuing to advocate for his needs? I am not sure what would have happened if I had intervened. My answer would have only been possible if I had tried.

QUESTIONS FOR REFLECTION AND DISCUSSION

1. What concerns might you have with a child such as Robert being placed in your class?

2. What education or training might have to take place with the other students in the class?

3. Describe the value of this teacher's intense efforts with Robert.

4. Discuss how multiple professionals were necessarily involved in Robert's care.

WORLD WIDE WEB RESOURCES

Charge Syndrome Foundation (www.chargesyndrome.org)
Council for Exceptional Children (www.cec.sped.org)
ERIC Clearinghouse on Disabilities and Gifted Education (www.ericec.org)

CASE 6.2

"DR. KENT! JUSTIN IS BEING MEAN..."
Linda Lord
Patricia M. Hentenaar

This case presents a look at an activity in a classroom in which children with disabilities are misunderstood. The teacher's response to a situation in the classroom creates confusion for another child.

Craig had been out for several days and had missed the children's activity of making "Christmas coupon books" for their parents. "Craig hasn't made a coupon book yet, Dr. Kent," a student informed me. Craig noticed the white pieces of paper that had been placed on his desk on the day of this activity. I ignored the student's comments, hoping that we could simply avoid having Craig think up ways that he could physically "help" his parents. Craig is a child with cerebral palsy. He has physical limitations and requires assistance from a paraprofessional during the school day. He wouldn't be able to vacuum, sweep, or do so many of the physical things that the other children had offered on their coupons. The whole idea of the activity was to allow the children a chance to offer help for their parents in a way that would really help them. I had stated emphatically that students were not to offer "help" that would require their parents' assistance. Of course, there were probably ways that Craig could help his parents but not in the way the other children had conceptualized the assignment. I didn't want Craig to feel uncomfortable about the assignment by highlighting what Craig could not physically do.

Later on that day, I told the children that it was too cold to go outside and we would have to stay in for recess. "Anyone who has been absent and needs to make up work should take care of this during recess. Those who have unfinished art projects need to finish them and those who have finished everything may choose a learning center in the closet." Craig, whose desk I was standing next to, then said, "I haven't done one of those books." I saw he was looking at the blank white coupon pages that had been piled with all of his make-up work. Before I could reply, Aishia spoke up, "I will help Craig."

Now this was an interesting situation. Aishia had been experiencing difficulty lately getting along with others. She was picking on other children and making hurtful statements to her classmates. Her behavioral problems compounded with her learning disability in reading made her a challenging student to have in the classroom. I knew that Craig, a strong reader, really should make one of these booklets and Aishia, needing more practice in reading and writing, really needed the experience of helping someone. I figured they could help each other.

I pulled Aishia aside and carefully said to her, "Now, Aishia, you must help Craig think of things he can do. This is slightly different than the way you made your coupon book. You know that Craig has difficulty walking and getting around. Could you help him think of other tasks he could help his parents with?" I paused for a moment, looking at her to see if she understood what I was implying. I then repeated, "Aishia, you know Craig can't do some of the things we listed on the board when we did this activity in class." Aishia looked at me intently and said, "OK, I know what you mean."

Aishia pulled a chair next to Craig's desk and began working with him. As I watched them, I noticed that Craig became very involved in the task and I hoped that he could think of things that he could really do for his parents. I noticed that Aishia worked diligently with Craig to brainstorm different tasks he could do. To see Aishia involved in this way with another child was very satisfying. I was glad to see that she had understood my message of how to handle this situation in a considerate and sensitive way. Craig was not only learning to offer help to others but Aishia was also learning to refine her social skills in working cooperatively with others. In a self-contained class for children with special needs, and varying special needs at that, this was sometimes a difficult task.

They worked together for about ten minutes as I continued to direct others in making up their work. Aishia suddenly called to me in an alarmed fashion, "Dr. Kent! Justin is being mean. He is saying mean things about Craig." I looked up and saw Justin, who sat directly next to Craig, looking partly bewildered and partly alarmed at me. Ever since the rush of the holidays began, Justin had been rather disorganized and sometimes unpredictable. "What could he have said?" I thought to myself. I knew that Justin would never consciously hurt anyone, but sometimes he could be unintentionally inconsiderate. "Justin said that Craig can't do things," Aishia told me in a disgusted tone. "Oh, brother," I thought. "After all the work I have done in getting the point across to Aishia and now Justin has to confuse the situation." Aishia was understandably upset by Justin's comment. After all, Mrs. Hinton, her other special education teacher, and I were constantly trying to instill in her a sense of consideration for others. She was only reporting to me something that I had made very clear to her was wrong and inconsiderate. "Justin," I said very firmly, "Why did you say that?" Immediately, I noticed that Justin's eyes began to convey the kind of panic that people have when they know that they have unintentionally done something wrong or unacceptable but don't know what that something is. Justin could tell that I was frustrated. "But I was just stating a fact," he said quickly. Suddenly the information that I had been reading about Asperger's syndrome flashed into my mind. Mrs. Hinton and I had discussed how people who have this syndrome often state exactly what they see. They have a difficult time viewing the world from another person's perspective. I recalled how she and I had seen Justin play this out in our classes. As tears began to well in Justin's eyes, I knew that once again, he was feeling misunderstood and very alone because behavior interpreted by others in a way never intended by him. I quickly said, "Justin, I understand. That is fine, Justin. You didn't mean it in an ugly way. I understand." As Justin's coloring came back, Aishia looked at me bewildered and confused. I went to her and said, "Aishia, I appreciate you sticking up for Craig that way. We have to be careful of what we say to others. Justin did not know that this was something that might be rude to say. He did not mean to hurt anyone." She looked at me, still confused. Craig watched this whole exchange without saying anything. He continued to work with Aishia and finished his project.

QUESTIONS FOR REFLECTION AND DISCUSSION

1. How could the teacher help with Aishia's confusion?

2. What support strategies could the teacher have provided for Justin?

3. How might the teacher have arranged this activity differently?

WORLD WIDE WEB RESOURCES

Asperger Syndrome Coalition of the U.S. (www.asperger.org)
Council for Exceptional Children (www.cec.sped.org)
United Cerebral Palsy Organization (www.ucpa.org)
West Ed Center for Prevention and Early Intervention (www.wested.org)

CASE 6.3

A YEAR FULL OF CHALLENGES
Teaching a Student Who Is Deaf in a Regular Classroom
Susan B. Cardin

At the beginning of the year, teachers face many challenges. One teacher found herself looking anxiously toward a year of new experiences and expectations after finding out she would be teaching a student who was deaf. After a period of apprehension, she approached the situation with an open learning attitude and found this to be one of the best years of her second-grade teaching career.

There are desks to arrange, labels to make, letters to write, supplies to organize, bulletin boards to put up, lessons to modify, texts to read, and the list is not exhausted. Everything has to be done in only a few days, and then there are the many meetings. I had already learned that our school would have a class for students who are deaf and hard-of-hearing, but I knew that this class wouldn't really affect me. After all, I was new to this school. I was also desperately trying to finish graduate school at night. No, the class for deaf and hard-of-hearing students would be interesting to have in our school, but it wouldn't really affect me this year. Maybe I would learn a little sign language if I had time.

With my class list in hand, I rapidly began preparing the room. On one of my many passes through the office, I was informed that I had a student added to

Teaching a student who is deaf in a regular classroom can be both a challenge and a very rewarding experience.

my roster. My list had grown to twenty-one students, predominantly African American and female. My class also included several students who spoke English only at school and Spanish outside of school. I wondered about the new student. Already this year had included many new experiences—trying to learn a new school and attempting to communicate with Spanish-speaking parents when I speak only English. I added the name and kept on moving. Not until later in the day did I find out that my new student, Kristin, was deaf. How was this going to work?

Armed with a handful of questions, I approached Ms. Winn, the teacher of the class for the deaf. She seemed nice and pretty helpful. That was when I found out just what I was about to become involved in this year. Little did I know how it would change my approach to teaching!

What I found out was overwhelming. As a teacher of a student who was deaf (Kristin is almost totally deaf), I would be expected to turn in lesson plans along with accompanying materials at the beginning of each week, if not sooner, to the special needs teacher and to the interpreter. I would be teaching Kristin math, social studies, and science every day. I would need to try to adjust my lessons so that there was limited reading and writing involved in any activities. Many students who are deaf are not able to read and write at grade level in elementary school. I needed to coordinate my teaching with Ms. Winn each week in order for her to preteach any difficult skills or vocabulary. The interpreter, Nancy, needed the materials to verify any vocabulary or signs needed to properly interpret for me. This was only the beginning of the many things I would learn.

In the classroom, Kristin had to sit in the front and there also needed to be room for the interpreter to sit or stand near me when I taught. I needed to speak a little more slowly (I do typically speak fast), and I needed to pause occasionally for the interpreter to keep up with what I was saying. Also, many students who are deaf, particularly those who have been deaf their entire lives and who use almost exclusively American Sign Language, learn conceptually. Therefore, I tried to adjust my teaching methods accordingly. This was a challenge at times. Manipulatives were extremely important, especially for math.

This was a lot for me to remember. When making my lesson plans, I had to be careful to think about the activities I had planned. Many traditional worksheets were not conducive to Kristin's learning style. Most of the textbooks in my classroom were too hard for her to read independently. How was I to overcome these challenges?

After much contemplation, I made a few realizations. These are things that are true for teaching those students who are deaf, hard-of-hearing, or have any other special needs. First, I decided I wouldn't be intimidated. I had faced many challenges in my time as a teacher, and this certainly couldn't be the most demanding. If I started out small, then eventually I would climb the mountain of responsibilities before me. For the first month, every day after school, I checked in with Ms. Winn to see if she had any feedback or ideas. She was a wealth of knowledge and compassion. I took this teaching challenge one day at a time until my confidence grew.

This led me to my second realization. I had to believe in myself and in those around me. Whether I was a first-year teacher or an accomplished veteran facing a new student, I knew more than that which I was giving myself credit. I drew on my knowledge of teaching four-, five-, and six-year-old children to gain insight and ideas into ways to teach new concepts. I pulled out old supplies and found new ways to use them. I consulted the different parts of my textbooks for ideas. It was amazing what materials I had that could be modified.

When working with students with special needs, I always found others who were willing to help me. Ms. Winn was an invaluable resource. She had an idea or suggestion for every situation that I encountered. Many days she simply let me sit and look around her room while we shared humorous or, at times, frustrating stories. Even late in the year, I turned to Ms. Winn to guide me when I was stuck. Other classroom teachers offered new approaches or materials to use when teaching a skill. One teacher reminded me of a wonderful set of fraction pizza and pie manipulatives in the media center. Ms. Winn shared a fabulous idea for solving word problems. I copied posters she had created for identifying commonly used terms from word problems. This helped not only Kristin but also other readers who were struggling when facing these difficult problems.

I discovered that I was not expected to completely change my classroom, my teaching style, or my life in order to accommodate Kristin. She, like many other students with special needs, was very capable and did not need to be babied. Kristin's lack of ability to hear did not mean she couldn't learn or needed to be treated differently from other students. On the contrary, she was often dependent on others to help her and needed to learn independence whenever possible. Kristin was only one member of my classroom community. That community did not revolve around her unless I let it happen. Yes, I did teach a student who is deaf. But I also taught students who had learning disabilities, chronic medical conditions, and other special needs. I treated Kristin as I would any of these students, with respect, and with the expectation that she could and would learn while in my class.

How was my classroom this year? I believe I have learned more from Kristin than she has learned from me. I have learned a great deal of sign language. Kristin is just as eager for me to sign as I am to learn. We spend time while waiting in line learning signs for things nearby. Kristin delights in my efforts and I can often sign without an interpreter. In fact, sometimes Kristin forgets that I can't sign like she can. We often laugh when she has to repeat the same sentence two or three times so that I can understand. She corrects my signs and Nancy, Kristin's interpreter, and I laugh later when I realize what I may have accidentally signed in my efforts to try too hard.

Nancy loves to teach the students in my class so that they can sign. It is amazing how fast they learn! I have Nancy teach words related to our unit in social studies before the unit gets underway. That way the students can listen to me instead of staring at Nancy as she interprets.

By my respecting Kristin for the person she is, she respects me as a teacher. Kristin has learned much this year beyond academics. She has learned how to be an integral part of our classroom community. We still have our occasional discipline challenges as with any other student. Though it would be tempting to "give her a break" because she is deaf, that would be unfair to Kristin (though if asked she wouldn't agree). Kristin has many friends and her absence is noticed when she is sick.

This year, I have grown as a teacher. I have learned that resources are available when you look for them. I have been reminded that not every child has the same needs. Kristin's needs are similar to the needs of many of my other students. When I have been frustrated with the thought of trying to teach students with so many different learning styles, I have discovered that it is possible to adapt activities so that many different learning styles are incorporated without a great deal of extra work, only a little creativity.

Had Kristin not been in my class this year, I would have had an entirely different class and experience. My class is much more accepting of students who may be different. They sign remarkably well and have a different attitude about those who face physical challenges. It is my belief that my students have received a more developmentally appropriate education. I have not fallen back on easier teaching methods, such as worksheet after worksheet. Instead, I have looked for better ways to teach new concepts in a more meaningful manner. With only a little effort, I have become a better teacher.

I have also become a better person this year. I have learned that my need for simplicity is not always the best plan. Learning sign language has helped me to appreciate what it is like to live in a world where only a few others speak your language. At times I feel like my toddler son who is just learning to speak and making so many mistakes. I have become much more aware of how I communicate with people and what my nonverbal communication says. Best of all, I have renewed my love for teaching in a diverse classroom. How boring it would be to surround myself with only those who are like me!

Yes, I am expected to go beyond the traditional responsibilities of most teachers. Preparing materials a week ahead of time is difficult. Sometimes I fall behind and other times I can be far ahead. I have to find video materials that are closed-captioned. Is it a hassle some days? Yes! But as Ms. Winn has reminded me, "It's not the biggest hassle in my day." I reserve that honor for all the mounds of paperwork I deal with daily! And as I teach my students, that which is hard makes us better and stronger.

QUESTIONS FOR REFLECTION AND DISCUSSION

1. How might you react to a child who is deaf or a child with special needs being added to your class unexpectedly? Should teachers be expected to regularly perform additional duties such as those required is this case without compensation?

2. How might this classroom be different with two or three students who are deaf, rather than only one? Would these changes be positive or negative?

3. What resources or experiences do you have on which you might fall back to help in a situation such as this? Where might you go and who might you ask for help?

4. How might the challenges associated with teaching a student who is deaf in elementary school compare to those faced in middle school or high school?

5. If you were an administrator, how would you justify placing a student who is deaf in a regular/traditional classroom to a teacher? To the parents of another student within the class?

6. What problems could have resulted had this situation not be approached from a positive, constructive perspective? If you were an administrator, how could you provide assistance to a frustrated or overwhelmed teacher in this position?

WORLD WIDE WEB RESOURCES

American Sign Language Teachers Association (www.aslta.org)
American Society for Deaf Children (www.deafchildren.org)
National Association of the Deaf (www.nad.org)

CASE 6.4

CHRONIC ILLNESS AND THE ART OF JUGGLING MEDICATIONS, INSTRUCTIONAL ACTIVITIES, AND TRANSPORTATION
Yvette Q. Getch

This case presents the story of a mother and her young son and the struggles of accessing assistance for her child. Specific strategies used by the mother demonstrate how critical parental involvement is in managing a chronic illness.

I dreaded the thought of all the education I would have to provide and all of the juggling that would need to be done for Danny to enter public kindergarten. Danny has numerous health-related issues and also has a rare growth disorder called Russell-Silver syndrome (RSS). Danny is growth-hormone deficient, has an enzyme deficiency, has chronic asthma and allergies, has a poor appetite, and basically has no subcutaneous fat. At nearly six years old he weighed a mere twenty-seven pounds, stood thirty-six inches tall, and wore a toddler size three.

I'm a mom who is familiar with the public schools. As a college supervisor, I have taught university undergraduate courses in survey of exceptionalities and master's-level rehabilitation counseling courses. I have assisted students in field-based experiences in the schools, but none of that really prepared me to be the mother of a precious child who had to contend with so much. I was used to working with the school on a professional basis and now I was coming to a school as a parent whose child had a host of health needs.

With Danny, I had a variety of things about which to be concerned. We had experienced a rough year with his asthma and I was determined that his asthma medications would be with him at all times at school. Danny takes maintenance asthma medications (three different kinds) and has a rescue inhaler. He also has exercised-induced asthma so he needs to take a few puffs of medicine before recess or physical education. We keep track of his breathing by using a peak flow meter that he needs to check twice a day. As a child with RSS, Danny simply doesn't get hungry. He takes an appetite stimulant so that he will eat. Unfortunately, this also makes him quite hyperactive. Because he has a lipase deficiency (this is a pancreatic enzyme), he takes an enzyme pill right before he eats. Although the school does not have to administer Danny's growth hormone injections, I did want his teacher to be aware of what it must be like to take so much medication (plus a shot every day), be seen by several specialists, be constantly weighed and measured and encouraged to eat, and stick out because he was so skinny and short.

First, I sought advice from a colleague at the university. She was very helpful with ideas to approach the school. I didn't want to be seen as an overprotective, overdemanding parent but rather as a member of a team who had Danny's health as a major focus. During the summer, I made an appointment to see the elementary school principal. She was polite and accommodating, with one exception: She made it clear that state policy requires medicines to be stored in a secure location. I told her I understood that but that Danny needed his asthma medication (rescue inhaler) with him at all times. She said, "Well, we keep them [the medicines] in the school office." I explained that was not good enough. What if he had a severe attack on the playground? I relayed the fact that I had been in an area where two children had died from asthma attacks within months of each other, and one of those children had died on the school playground. She then became very serious and said we would work it out. I said, "Well, if we have to we can write a 504 plan." (A 504 plan is a document that allows children in agencies that receive federal funds to have access to services that they need in order to participate.) Her facial expression let me know that she now realized I had more information than she had anticipated. I said, "If we can work it out fine, but he will have his medication with him, and if that requires a 504 plan, then that is what we will do." She then basically told me to work it out with his teacher. I then asked her what we were going to do about transportation. She looked puzzled and said, "Transportation is your responsibility." I said that I worked full time and Danny would be riding the bus in the morning and also need after-school transportation. I requested a meeting with the bus driver to explain Danny's asthma medications to her. It was obvious that the principal had not given transportation a single thought. She told me to contact the transportation coordinator and work it out with him.

From previous interactions, I knew Danny's teacher would be supportive. Another mother had a child with chronic asthma who was also going to be in Danny's room. I did not hesitate to call Danny's teacher, Mrs. Richards, and say, "I know you are busy preparing for school but my son, Danny, will be in your class and he has asthma and some other health issues about which I'd like to talk with you. As you are aware, Russ will also be in your class and he has asthma too. Could Russ's mom and I talk with you about asthma and what you need to know to care for our children? If we come in together, the meeting will save you time and give you valuable information. Mrs. Richards was more than cooperative, appreciated that I was concerned about her schedule, and agreed to meet with Russ's mom and me.

In the meantime, I talked with Russ's mom, Angie. She was very nervous about the entry of her child into kindergarten. I shared with her an asthma care plan I had developed and she made one for Russ. We met with the teacher and the paraprofessional. I brought them easy-to-read asthma information from the American Lung Association and an asthma care plan for Danny. Angie brought Russ's plan as well. We then talked to them about asthma, triggers, early warning signs, and how to use the peak flow meters. Then each of us talked about our child's individual medication schedule. We looked at the classroom schedule, planned when the children would check their peak flow readings, and planned when they would take their medications. We tried to make it fit within the schedule with very little imposition on the teacher and the least amount of interference with class activities. We explained our desire to have the children do their peak flow readings and take the medications in the classroom rather than in the hall. This routine could then become a normal part of the day. We also worked out transporting medications from one place to another in the school. The paraprofessional would carry their medication bags from location to location and remind them to have their medications with them when they left for the day. Danny's teacher appreciated our willingness to work as best we could with the schedule and she appreciated being trained and getting written information that she could read and instructions that she could follow. After this conversation Angie left because Russ didn't have other health-related issues. Mrs. Richards and I talked about Danny's other conditions and his other medications. Danny must take an enzyme pill right before he eats, he must go to the office as soon as he arrives at school to take a pill before breakfast and immediately before lunch. Danny also needed to take his appetite stimulant during the day but it couldn't be within an hour of his enzyme pill. So we worked out a time that was convenient for everyone. I explained that his appetite stimulant made him slightly hyperactive and I'd like feedback about his behavior so we could adjust the time we gave this medicine accordingly. The paraprofessional and teacher were both supportive and cooperative.

Other issues we tackled were Danny's difficulty in regulating his body temperature. I explained that because I layer Danny's clothing, he always has a jacket or a sweatshirt. With little subcutaneous fat, he gets cold very easily. I explained that he may take off or put on his sweatshirt several times during the course of the day. Danny also gets really hot and needs to drink lots of fluid during outside play or gym.

As I left that day, I assured them that I was available if they had questions and if they were ever unsure about his condition(s) to give me a telephone call. I had also explained that either Angie or I would make ourselves available for any field trips because we knew each other's children well and their triggers. The teacher seemed supportive and concerned and seemed to appreciate our meeting and the information we provided. However, I felt she may have been somewhat overwhelmed. I felt confident we would have a good year.

I called the transportation supervisor and had to explain several times why I needed to get in touch with the bus driver. Finally, I was given her name. I telephoned her and explained Danny's medical problems and she said, "I'm so glad you let me know. Of course I will meet with you." I went to her house one evening, explained Danny's asthma to her, and showed her how his medications worked. She told me that she had a child on her bus last year and never knew that child had asthma until she had a problem right at the end of the year. I explained that I simply wanted her to know what to do and to understand a little about asthma, just in case there was a problem. She thanked me. I felt really good about Danny being safe on her bus.

What I didn't feel good about was the administration. Every once in a while a comment would be made about the asthma medications being placed in a "secure" location. One suggestion was for the medications to be put in locked boxes in the classroom. There were three children in Danny's class with asthma. I asked, "What's going to happen if an allergen is introduced into the classroom and all three children have asthma attacks simultaneously? Whose medications are you going to unlock first?" That comment closed the discussion of separate locked medication boxes.

Danny entered school and things went rather well. The paraprofessional called me a few times about Danny's condition or with questions about his medications. The medications were forgotten one or two times but backup medications were at the school and at the YMCA where Danny went after school. We worked on Danny becoming more responsible for remembering his medications and he did improve. By Thanksgiving, however, Danny started having problems at school. He wouldn't sit still. The teacher telephoned and we met. Danny was getting the appetite stimulant in the morning before he left for school but by 10 A.M. he was up and down, constantly. So I called his doctor and we worked out a different schedule and dosing for his appetite stimulant. Instead of giving him three doses per day, we gave him two larger doses per day. We set a time at school and agreed that we would change the time as needed as long as it remained within the 10 A.M. to 2 P.M. range. After several weeks of juggling the time, we found that in order for Danny not to become hyperactive, he needed the medication sometime between 1:30 P.M. and before he left school. That way he was headed to the YMCA when the medication side effects began. This worked out beautifully with one exception. Danny was starving by the time he got to the YMCA and he wasn't eating nearly as much breakfast or lunch. We then worked it out where a cafeteria worker would encourage Danny to eat his breakfast (she monitored it and reported to the teacher) and the teachers encouraged him to eat his lunch. He also was allowed to eat a snack. I called the YMCA and we worked it out so that he could eat a snack when he arrived. He also carried snacks in his book bag and was allowed to eat on the YMCA bus.

Another hurdle cleared. We had a good year! There were lots of notes, phone calls, a few extra meetings, but all went well until the last few weeks of school. Danny started having asthma problems. The first incident was met with some fear and anxiety on behalf of the teacher and paraprofessional, but they handled it wonderfully. They called me and we shared information. After the first incident, they met the other incidents with less apprehension. The teachers were amazing!

I wish I had documented all the time I spent coordinating, teaching, informing, and planning with the schools about Danny's condition(s). I spent a lot of time. The sad part is that every year I have to do the same thing. Information just doesn't get passed from one year to the next. So every summer I perform the same routine. Fortunately, Danny's school has a new administration that is much more supportive. Every year is met with a little uncertainty. Danny and I have been fortunate because all of his teachers, paraprofessionals, and bus drivers have been extremely supportive and cooperative. Unfortunately, my friend Angie hasn't had that experience this year. She is not confident Russ's teacher can handle an emergency and there have been several significant bus episodes. I've worked with her and the school to tease out some of these issues. After all, these issues really affect any child who has a chronic medical condition. I want my efforts to reach beyond my child so other parents won't have to jump the same hurdles that I've had to jump. Juggling medications to manage a chronic illness is definitely an art and a challenge. The more practice everyone gets, the less likely balls will be dropped when juggling.

QUESTIONS FOR REFLECTION AND DISCUSSION

1. What are the major issues in this case?

2. What could the teachers or school administration do to assist the mother and child in this situation?

3. Does Danny qualify for services under Section 504 of the Rehabilitation Act or under the Individuals with Disabilities Education Act as other health impaired?

4. What could be done to assist in the transfer of information from year to year so that the mother does not spend so much time explaining Danny's condition(s) and negotiating the necessary arrangements?

5. Discuss ways in which a teacher, paraprofessional, school counselor, or other school staff could advocate on behalf of Danny so that he is provided with the services he needs to succeed in school.

RESOURCE

Getch, Y. Q., & Neuharth-Pritchett, S. (1999). Children with asthma: Strategies for educators. *Teaching Exceptional Children, 31*(3), 30–36.

WORLD WIDE WEB RESOURCES

Allergy and Asthma Network Mothers of Asthmatics (www.aanma.org)
American Lung Association (www.lungusa.org)

CHAPTER 7

THE FAMILY

The picture of a "family" has expanded considerably to include a variety of configurations and lifestyles. The family structure is complex and often fluid, making it difficult for a teacher to always understand the various situations a child might encounter within a family unit. This section focuses on alternative ways to view a family with all of its complexities while addressing realistic issues and challenges that are common for a classroom teacher. To teach from a multicultural perspective, children and families are valued for their particular contributions and strengths regardless of previous stereotypes and expectations.

Because today families are more mobile for various reasons, the first case deals with the common scenario of a new child arriving at a new school. Teachers are concerned about meeting the individual needs of all children, and they care about the adjustment and acceptance of a new child. The authors, Martha Allexsaht-Snider and Nakheung Kim, provide excellent suggestions for teachers with new students in the case describing Susan Jordan's visit to Washington Elementary School to learn how the faculty and administration accommodate new students.

William, the Conquerer, is a resilient individual who has to combat the welfare system and school system to overcome the stigma of being a foster child.

Lola Finn presents a compelling case about Jonathan, a survivor and foster child, who continues to overcome adversity with the love and support of his caregivers and biological parent/grandparent.

A subject usually not addressed is the stigma associated with being the child in a same-sex relationship. Paige E. Campbell and Dee Russell describe this dilemma in their case of Emily, a first-grade teacher, and her student, Toby, who lives with his biological father and his "stepfather."

An increasing number of children are coming to school homeless, in poverty, and in poor health. A realistic and well-documented portrayal of homeless families is presented in three vignettes by Claire E. Hamilton and Xernona J. Thomas.

CASES

CASE 7.1

ANOTHER NEW STUDENT? SUSAN JORDAN LOOKS FOR HELP WITH HER HIGH NUMBERS OF MOBILE STUDENTS

Martha Allexsaht-Snider

Nakheung Kim

This case focuses on Susan Jordan, a fourth-grade teacher, who is concerned about how to meet the needs of new students, especially internationals. She visits another school to learn about appropriate strategies and resources. The Student Intake Center was a special room in the school for student diagnosing and for providing additional services to the new students. What do you think would be your reaction to any new student, but especially an international who does not speak English? How can ESL teachers and regular classroom teachers work together to be supportive of an international child?

"Ms. Singleton? This is Susan Jordan. I met you at the state educators conference last week and we talked about visiting your class to see what you're doing at Washington Elementary to address the large numbers of students coming and going all the time. I wondered if tomorrow is still OK for a visit? I just got another new student this week in the midst of Halloween and getting ready for parent conferences, and I'm really feeling swamped!"

"Hi, Susan—I have you on my calendar for tomorrow and it's good timing. A new student named Cindy Powell arrived yesterday and they'll finish the paperwork with her today at the new Student Intake Center. So you'll be able to see what her first day in our class is like and how I use some of the strategies I shared in the workshop at the educators conference. If you come a little early, around 7:30, I can share the new student intake summary with you before the students arrive. We have physical education at the end of the day so we can talk then about any questions you have. Don't expect everything you see will be smooth sailing—we've figured some things out but we've got a ways to go I think."

As Susan drove the hour-and-a-half trip to Washington Elementary, she wondered how her newest student, Carlos Guerra, would handle the day while she was gone. He had been withdrawn and quiet since he arrived three days ago and hadn't completed any of the assignments in math and social studies on which they had been working. She had written a short note to the substitute about keeping an eye on him and not worrying about expecting too much work.

Teachers are concerned about adjustment and acceptance of a new child. Fostering supportive relationships are key.

She wasn't sure he would even be in school though because he had looked ill and was coughing the day before.

When Susan checked in at the office of Washington Elementary School, she noticed a big WELCOME TO WASHINGTON ELEMENTARY SCHOOL bulletin board with photos of school staff and activities and messages in several languages including Spanish. Underneath was a display of brochures for parents, a school handbook, and photo albums illustrated and captioned by students of different ages. A colorful sign pointed to the new Student Intake Center down the hall from the office.

Ashley Singleton's first-grade classroom had similar inviting and colorful displays of photos and the word *Welcome* in Spanish, Russian, and a language Susan didn't recognize. "Hi, Susan. Come in and sit down. I set out the new student form for you to review while I go and talk to the curriculum director about her recommendations for Cindy for reading. There's a note about glasses too. I'll be right back."

Susan skimmed the sheets that Cindy's mother and the curriculum director had filled out the day before, noting that Cindy had been in a school in rural Texas and that the reason for relocation was divorce and job change. One of Cindy's favorite things to do had been to visit the horses at her grandparents' farm. The curriculum director had indicated that Cindy was at a preprimer level in reading and on grade level in math. Cindy also seemed somewhat restless and distracted during the day that she had spent in the intake center office and touring the school.

BEGINNING THE DAY

When Ashley and Susan entered the classroom, some of the children were painting a big *W* on a sheet of paper. Each group was working on a different letter, decorating it. Ashley explained that they were preparing a "Welcome Cindy!" sign. Ashley asked Latisha, who was assigned as Cindy's buddy, to go to the office to get her. The principal introduced Cindy and asked Latisha to introduce herself. "My name is Latisha. I'm glad to meet you. I'm six—How old are you? I came to take you to our classroom." Latisha held Cindy's hand as they walked down the hall. She asked her, "Do you have any brothers or sisters? I have a baby sister. She cries sometimes but she's cute."

When they entered the class, the children were doing calendar work on the rug. Ashley said, "Welcome to our class, Cindy. My name is Ms. Singleton. Latisha, can you introduce Cindy please?" "This is Cindy. She's seven—bigger than me. She just moved here with her mom and brothers. They are named Jim and Tom." "Thanks, Latisha, you did a great job with the introductions. Does anybody want to share something with Cindy?" "My brother's name is Tom too. He's my big brother." "I'll help you find the bathroom." "Our class is fun—we play kickball on the playground." After a brief conversation, Ashley continued the calendar activity.

As the children moved to their desks for reading, Ashley said to Cindy, "Latisha is going to help you find your cubby and coat hanger. She will be your buddy to help you with everything this week. I will help you too and, really, all the boys and girls in our class are good helpers. Latisha was a new student about a month ago. She'll tell you that she was very nervous and didn't know anything about our class. But, now she knows a lot and she can introduce you to all of her new friends. Don't worry—you are going to have fun in our class. After you hang up your backpack you can come and join me at the reading table."

STORY TIME

Ashley called the children to the rug for story time as they came in from recess. Susan watched Latisha invite Cindy to sit next to her on the rug. "Today we're going to read, 'The Lost and Found House.' It's about a family who moves to a new town. Remember that this week we have been reading and talking about moving—about children who move to new houses and new schools. Let's see what happens to the boy in this story who moves. We have a new person in our class who just moved, so maybe Cindy will have some stories to share about her family's move."

The children settled down and listened as Ashley read, turning the vividly painted pages of the book. She asked, "How do you think the boy felt when he left his old house?" "He felt bad." "Sad—I think maybe he was crying." Cindy listened quietly. "Why do you think he couldn't sleep well in the motel and kept waking up when he moved into the new house? Have you ever had trouble sleeping like that?" "I think he felt funny—he missed his own house." "He was thinking about his friends in his old school." "I think he was wondering if his new friends and school would be nice and warm." Ashley turned back to one of the pages in the book and said, "Yes, he was worrying about his new friends and the new school. But did his worries really happen?" "No!" Ashley asked, "What really happened?" "He met nice new friends who live next door." "They threw the Frisbee to him." "How did the boy feel about that?" "He was happy!" "He smiled." As they finished the story, Ashley asked her children, "When you moved to a new house or a new school, what things made you feel happy?" Ashley wrote their responses on a small white board and then asked, "Cindy, did this story make you think about your new house?" Cindy nodded shyly. "Do you want to tell us something that happened when you moved?" Cindy shook her head and didn't answer. "It's OK if you're not ready to tell us a story yet—later today maybe you can draw a picture about it during writing workshop. You all can choose what you want to write and draw about in writing workshop. But maybe some of you want to keep working on your books about moving and going to a new school."

WRITING WORKSHOP

The children were arranged around the room at small tables with their writing notebooks when Susan returned after the lunch break. She sat with some children as Ashley reminded the class that some people had editing conferences scheduled and others were going to work on projects they had begun earlier in the week. She held up the book they had read earlier and reminded them, "Some of you may want to write about helping people who are moving to a new house and school. You might want to work with a partner and draw some pictures about how you felt when you moved to our school. We have about a half an hour to work and then it will be time for PE." Susan watched as Shantay sat down with markers and paper next to Cindy, saying, "Cindy, let's draw a picture of your new house. We can draw me too because I am your friend now." Cindy answered, "I want to draw my old house too. My daddy is in it."

Sam shared his book titled, "Moving to a New School," with Ms. Singleton. "I like this part about how scared you felt when you rode the bus for the first time. You still remember that John was your buddy and he helped you feel better, don't you? Have you shared this book with him yet?" Sam shook his head no. "On this page you have a mad look on your face—can you tell me something about this?" Sam answered, "That's me in reading group. It was too hard—I couldn't read the words and I felt mad and sad." "Do you remember the tutor from the junior high who helped you when you first came? Her name was Rachel I think." "Yeah, we read that funny book about rockets!" "Maybe you could write about her on this page—what do you want to say?" "Rachel was cool. We read a rocket book."

TWO TEACHERS' CONVERSATION AFTER OBSERVATION

Susan and Ashley sat together in the teachers' workroom sipping iced tea and taking a few minutes to talk about the day. Susan reflected, "Wow, this day was packed—you never stopped all day long! I think I have a good idea of some of the things you do in the classroom to help children get oriented, but can you tell me some more about the intake process?"

Ashley explained, "When new students arrive, the secretary does an initial orientation to the school forms and provides the family with an information packet. She takes them to a small room that we use as an intake center, and, if the parents can stay, the curriculum director who does the intake interviews meets with them right away. The room is set up with books, computers, and activity centers so the children have things to do while the parents are interviewed. Some days there are no children, but many days we have from three to ten new students. The curriculum specialist has different informal and formal assessment instruments that she uses, depending on how much information the family has brought from the previous school. She has a simple form where she records a summary of the most important information about reading and math levels and the languages the child speaks. She also adds health and special education information. She includes a little bit of information about the family situation and the child's interests."

"How long do the students spend in the Intake Center?" "They usually spend only a day—in addition to the assessment work. Counselors take the students on school tours and arrange for lunch with a small group of students who work with the counselor as part of the school welcoming club. The school welcoming club is comprised of children who have moved recently and are receiving support from the school counselor. As part of her work with them, the counselor helps the children figure out how they might support other students who are new to the school."

"Are there other kinds of support for you, the student, and family after that first day?" "Yes—the curriculum specialist coordinates everything. So if there's important information about special needs or about health issues, either she'll follow up or she'll get other people to follow up with the family and the previous school. The curriculum specialist follows up with the teacher of a new student after the first two or three days, to see if any issues have come up. She also checks in the with the child and then with the family by phone after the first week. If the child seems to need assistance in mathematics or reading, the curriculum specialist helps secure Title I services or volunteer tutoring, a program she coordinates. She notifies the parent–teacher association (PTA) welcoming committee about new families and makes arrangements with the speech and language teachers. We have a teacher support team, comprised of all the school's resource people, including special education teachers, who meet every week to discuss concerns about particular students. Here we can brainstorm about resources and strategies to use with each student. It's important for me to know that I can go to my colleagues for help."

"I noticed a couple of students who had a really hard time following directions and paying attention—do you get any help with behavior problems?" "Remember, I told you that it isn't all smooth sailing? These children in our school who move a lot often have other stresses—outside of school and trying to make new friends. So students are dealing with lots of emotions and sometimes there are lots of behavior problems. I don't believe we have a very good support system set up yet for handling behavior issues. I think it's something on which we need to work. You saw that we are doing a unit about moving with books and writing workshop activities. So the next unit I am going to do is about families and changes in families. We're going to read some good books I found about families and divorce, because a lot of these children are experiencing that. There's a real need to help all the children understand their own feelings and the feelings that other children have. They need to know that all families go through changes."

"I got so many ideas today from watching you and your students but I'm not sure how I'm going to be able to apply them in my classroom and my school. It's different with fourth graders…and we don't have anything like the system you have set up with a curriculum director who seems to be such a big help. It seems like an important piece would be to work with the parents too—before they move, and then after they move, giving them some ideas about how to support their children." "Yes, that's another area that I think we really need to work on—maybe there's a way to get the PTA and other community groups to work with families on some of these issues."

"That sounds overwhelming to me. I think I need to start with my own children in my own classroom. I'm worried right now about my new student, Carlos, who doesn't seem to be getting any work done and hasn't really connected with any of the other kids. I think he's got some serious problems with reading, and I'm not sure really how much English he knows. And it's scary to think that while I'm thinking about him another new student might come tomorrow."

QUESTIONS FOR REFLECTION AND DISCUSSION

1. What strategies could Susan implement immediately in her classroom?

2. How would students benefit from an intake center?

3. How can a teacher help a new child feel more comfortable in the classroom?

4. What activities or discussion can a teacher use with the children in the classroom to make a new child feel more at ease?

5. What additional challenges might the international student face?

CHILDREN'S BOOKS

Aliki. (1995). *Best friends together again.* New York: Greenwillow.
Altman, L. J. (1993). *Amelia's road.* New York: Lee & Low.
Bunting, E. (1991). *Fly away home.* New York: Clarion.
Bunting, E. (1996). *Going home.* New York: HarperCollins.
Cadnum, M. (1997). *The lost and found house.* New York: Viking.
Dragonwagon, C. (1984). *Always, always.* New York: Macmillan.
Fiday, B., & Fiday, D. (1990). *Time to go.* San Diego: Harcourt Brace Jovanovich.
Moss, M. (1995). *Amelia's notebook.* Berkeley: Tricycle.
Rogers, F. (1987). *Moving.* New York: Putnam.
Stinson, K. (1985). *Mom and dad don't live together anymore.* Toronto: Annick.
Turner, A. (1991). *Stars for Sarah.* New York: HarperCollins.
Waber, B. (1988). *Ira says goodbye.* Boston: Houghton Mifflin.

STUDENT MOBILITY BIBLIOGRAPHY

Alexander, K., Entwisle, D. R., & Dauber, S. L. (1996). Children in motion: School transfers and elementary school performance. *The Journal of Educational Research, 90*(1), 3–12.

Beck, L. G., Kratzer, C. C., & Isken, J. A. (1997). Caring for transient students in one urban elementary school. *Journal for a Just and Caring Education, 3*(3), 343–369.

Evans, D. A. (1996). *The effect of student mobility on academic achievement* (Report No. PS 024-518). Chicago: Chicago State University. (ERIC Document Reproduction Service No. ED400048)

Fisher, T. A., & Matthews, L. (1999). *Examining interventions for highly mobile students and their families.* Paper presented at the annual meeting of the American Educational Research Association, Montreal, Canada.

Heywood, J. S., Thomas, M., & White, S. B. (1997). Does classroom mobility hurt stable students? An examination of achievement in urban schools. *Urban Education, 32*(3), 354–372.

Jalongo, M. R. (1994/1995). Helping children to cope with relocation. *Childhood Education, 71*(2), 80–85.

Kerbow, D. (1996). *Patterns of urban student mobility and local school reform* (Report No. UD 031-408). Baltimore, MD: Center for Research on the Education of Students Placed At Risk. (ERIC Document Reproduction Service No. ED353486)

Mehana, M., & Reynolds, A. J. (1995). *The effects of school mobility on scholastic achievement.* Paper presented at the biennial meeting of the Society for Research in Child Development, Indianapolis, IN.

Miller, Y. F. (1991). *On the move: Children in transition* (Report No. CG 024-704). Silver Spring, MD: National Association of School Psychologists. (ERIC Document Reproduction Service No. ED353486)

Nelson, P. S., Simon, J. M., & Adelman, H. S. (1996). Mobility and school functioning in the early grades. *The Journal of Educational Research, 89*(6), 365–369.

Stafford, M. E., Williams, T. A., Gutierrez-Lohrman, C. M., & Strickland, J. (1999). *School mobility: Child and family qualities and concerns.* Paper presented at the annual conference of the National Association of School Psychologists, Tempe, AZ.

Tucker, C. J., Marx, J., & Long, L. (1998). "Moving on": Residential mobility and children's school lives. *Sociology of Education, 71*, 111–129.

U.S. General Accounting Office. (1994). *Elementary school children: Many change schools frequently, harming their education* (Report No. PS 022-259). Washington, DC: General Accounting Office. (ERIC Document Reproduction Service No. ED369526)

CASE 7.2

WILLIAM, THE CONQUEROR

JoAnn Marshall
Mark Barker
Kathryn Barker

William is a six-year-old boy who has been in the child welfare system since age two. As a ward of the state, William has suffered under the "foster child" label and its stigma. He has tried to overcome that label and create an identity and a life for himself beyond it. The child welfare system and the school system have hindered his attempts. William wants to have more to call his own than the label "foster child." Research foster care and investigate its strengths and challenges.

William is an active six-year-old who loves to play his guitar, watch cartoons, and run with his dogs in the backyard. Unlike most little boys, though, William has his own case number and a four-page file that details his unpleasant childhood. He may not remember all that happened to him in his early years or what brought him to his new family, but all those events shape William's identity.

William's childhood, like the childhoods of many foster children, was filled with unthinkable episodes and much confusion. He was born to a drug-addicted mother who had the mental capacity of a thirteen year old and who, at the age of twenty-two, had already lost custody of her two older daughters. Her then-boyfriend, William's father, had an extensive criminal record for armed robbery and had spent more than twenty of his forty-one years in and out of prisons. Neither parent was able to adequately care for William, something that went unnoticed until William's mother traded him at a yard sale at the age of two for the use of the telephone. Once traded for the price of a long distance call, William became a foster child and spent the next five months in two different temporary homes. William's first foster family, the husband and wife running the yard sale, cared for William for four months. William's stay at his first foster home came to an abrupt end two days after Christmas when William's foster father became extremely intoxicated and took William hostage with a gun. The police arrived, calmed the situation, and removed William from the home. As a result, William has a fascination with guns and a fear of police officers. Next, William was placed in another temporary home for two weeks with a married couple and their children until another home could be found. Finally, at the age of two years and five months, William was placed in his third foster home, one that all concerned hoped would be permanent.

William could barely speak when he arrived at the Martin's home, but he was able to vocalize his urge to belong to a family and not to be abandoned, by screaming each time Mr. or Mrs. Martin went out of eyesight or failed to pay him attention. He began calling Mr. and Mrs. Martin "Daddy" and "Mommy" almost immediately. Additionally, he decided that two of the Martin's older children, Jack and Laura, were his brother and sister. As time went by and his communication skills developed, William introduced his new family to everyone, even the other members of the family. At breakfast, he would state emphatically to anyone at the table, "This is Jack. Jack is my brother. This is my brother Jack." Moreover, William insisted that Jack was his brother and only his brother, just as the Martin's daughter Laura was William's sister and only William's sister. William decided to adopt the Martin's name. When asked his name, he would proudly state, "I am William Martin." The Martin's corrected him by saying, "No, your name is William Philips." To this, William would respond, "My name is William Philips Martin." William reveled in his new family life and slowly created an identity for himself within the Martin's home.

The teachers and staff at the preschool knew William's status as a foster child because the state paid for his schooling. State workers picked up William for various appointments and visits during the school day. William soon became labeled as "the foster child" on paper and in front of him. As Mrs. Martin discovered, the term "foster child" rarely was used positively in conversation and was usually accompanied by an irritated or sad look.

"Hello, Ms. Ross, I'm here to pick up William. By the way, he won't be in school tomorrow. He has an appointment at the state building." [Mrs. Martin]

"The state building? Oh, is this part of his foster placement?" [Ms. Ross, a staff member, who looks sympathetically at William]

William did not understand the meaning of the label. He did understand that it meant something was different, or even wrong, about him. This label made him different from the other children and set him apart. William, like most children, wanted to belong. He did not want be different.

Even more damaging than the label, was the reaction William's new family received from both the state and his teachers. Although William's caseworker did not object to William using the Martin's name occasionally, she insisted he use Philips as his last name at school because the state, not the Martins, paid for his school. This created confusion for William. He had been part of the Martin family for half of his young life. He believed he was a Martin, not a Philips. Martin was not simply a name to him but part of his identity. Having a different name than his self-defined parents and his brother and sister brought additional attention to William's status as a foster child. William's primary teacher Miss Lee, who was an experienced prekindergarten teacher, was aware that William was a foster child and tried not to call attention to his situation. Yet, the other teachers and staff who came in contact with William were intrigued by the story behind his label and his family life, past and present. At times, they called unnecessary attention to what they considered an unusual family situation and fished for information regarding William's past. For instance, when the Martin's daughter Laura came to pick up William at the end of the day, one of the teachers questioned her relationship to William as he stood next to her:

"Hi, I'm Laura Martin. I'm here to pick up William Philips. I'm on the list of adults allowed to pick him up." [Laura, William's older sister]

"This is Laura, Miss Jeffries. She's my sister." [William]

"Are you William's *real* sister?" [Miss Jeffries, a staff member]

"Well, I'm Laura, Mrs. Martin's daughter." [Laura]

"Oh, you're his *foster* mom's daughter. So you're his *foster* sister." [Miss Jeffries]

"No, Miss Jeffries, Laura is my **sister**!" [William]

Miss Jeffries's motive for delving into Laura's precise relationship to William seems to be curiosity rather than concern. William's discomfort with Miss Jeffries's statement that Laura is not his *real* sister, but a *foster* sister is clear. To William, who only clearly remembers his life with the Martins and not the other families before them, the Martins are his parents and Jack and Laura are his siblings. The word "foster," that was usually used negatively in William's presence and placed in front of his sister takes something away from William's relationship with Laura. The word "foster" is almost a threat to William and, used in the same context with a family member's name, is a threat to his family and to his identity within that family.

William's identity was further challenged when he entered kindergarten. At the same time William began kindergarten, Mrs. Martin was battling cancer and was going through chemotherapy treatments. The Martins found themselves unable to work, to care for Mrs. Martin, and to provide William with the attention he needed. They agreed to relinquish custody of William to another family only if that family was willing to keep William permanently and to adopt him once all parental rights were severed. The Houstons, a young couple who had adopted a girl at birth, wanted more children and took an interest in five-year-old William. After an adequate transitioning period, William moved in with the Houstons. William stayed in touch with the Martins and reported he was happy with the Houstons and his new little sister. Unfortunately, William's living situation did not remain happy. Eight months after William joined the Houston family, the Houstons brought a four-year-old foster child named Roger into their home. William felt threatened by Roger's presence in his new home and soon developed a stutter. He began to act out in school after Roger arrived by refusing to do assignments and talking without permission. At the end of his kindergarten year, William was tested by the school for behavioral and learning disorders. The test results indicated that William had attention deficit hyperactivity disorder and was of low-average intellect. The Houstons were disappointed by the test results. They were afraid William might need special education and help they could not provide. Later that summer the Houstons informed the Martins that they decided to adopt Roger, not William, and no longer wanted William as a foster child. William returned to the Martin's home within a couple of weeks. Of course, William was confused and had many questions: "Who is my family? Why didn't Mr. and Mrs. Houston want to keep me? Why did Mr. and Mrs. Houston like Roger and not me? Will I live with you forever now that Mommy is better?" William no longer had a firm grasp of who he was.

The move from the Houston's home back to the Martin's home impacted William in another way. Foster children typically do not have many material possessions. When they leave their temporary homes, they are not always able to take many things with them. William arrived at the Martin's with two boxes of clothes that were too small and some broken toys. Foster parents are given approximately $200 a month for food, clothes, and essentials. At the beginning of each school year, foster parents are given an additional $100 for school clothes. The state also provides children with extra toys and clothes at Christmas. It is the responsibility of the foster parents to buy the children food, clothes, and necessities throughout the year with the money provided. Any extra clothes, treats, and toys are purchased at the expense of the foster parents. In William's case, he was spoiled. The Martins filled William's closet with clothes and shoes, the kitchen cabinets with nutritious food and snacks, and the living room with toys and books. When William left the Martins home to live with the Houstons, he took everything from his clothes to the posters on his bedroom wall with him. He returned to the Martin home with a few new clothes and toys, but several of his old toys and possessions were missing. Items, such as the baby book the Martin's assembled over the years, the stuffed bunny and blanket Granny Martin made for William, his favorite Batman toys, and other cherished possessions, were missing. William immediately noticed the missing items. He was distressed that several of his favorite possessions were gone. The Martins asked the Houstons to return the items to William as soon as possible, but all of the items were not returned. Months later, William still wondered why the Houstons would not return all of his things to him. William became upset with the Houstons when they did not give back his toys and told Mrs. Martin that he wanted to get rid of any toys the Houstons gave him. In essence, William wanted to forget his time with the Houstons. If they did not want him, he did not want their toys. He only wanted to be surrounded by things given to him by the Martins and he wanted to be a part of the Martin family. The toys given to him by the Houstons would take away from the life and identity he created with the Martins.

As William struggled to recreate an identity for himself, he entered the first grade at age six. His first-grade teacher, Ms. Black, had twenty years of experience as a teacher. Ms. Black knew William's status as a foster child and also knew that he acted out in his kindergarten class at the end of last year. In fact, she remarked to Mrs. Martin at the open house, "I've heard all about William." A few weeks after William began the first grade, Ms. Black called the Martins in for a conference.

"Mr. and Mrs. Martin, let me first say that William is a good boy. However, I believe that child needs more time and attention than I can give. I believe if he stays in my class that he will have a tough time."

"What do you recommend?" [Mrs. Martin]

"I do not believe that William is ready for the first grade. I recommend that he go back to kindergarten." [Ms. Black]

"William's report card from last year reflects that he was a good student. He passed kindergarten. Why didn't anyone recommend at the end of last year that he repeat kindergarten?" [Mrs. Martin]

"I am not sure. I can only tell you that he is not ready for the first grade. I think he should be taken out of my class and put into a kindergarten class." [Ms. Black]

"Are you sure this is the best thing for William?" [Mr. Martin]

"Yes, I do." [Ms. Black]

William was immediately removed from his first-grade class as advised by Ms. Black and placed in the same kindergarten classroom as the year before. His kindergarten teacher, Ms. Gideon, was a teacher with twenty-five years experience. She was happy to have William back in her classroom but did not understand why Ms. Black recommended that he return to kindergarten. William adjusted to the change well. Although he did not fully understand why he could not be in the same class with all of his friends, he was glad to be back with Ms. Gideon, a teacher with whom he was familiar and comfortable. For William, things were getting back to normal. He was part of the Martin family again and he was one of Ms. Gideon's students again.

William will have more adjustments to make to his life and to his identity in the coming years. Mr. and Mrs. Martin love William, but they are afraid that he will not thrive in their home. They are older than the majority of six-year-olds' parents and live in a neighborhood filled with many older couples. William has no friends his age to play with in the neighborhood and no young siblings at home. Therefore, the Martins are committed to finding a young couple to become William's parents and recently met an interested couple. The couple wants William to become a permanent part of their family as soon as possible and William likes the idea. After two years of subjecting William to disturbing visits with his biological parents, the state severed the biological parents' rights three months after William's fifth birthday. He is now able to be legally adopted and shed the "foster child" label. It is hoped that he will no longer hear comments such as: "To look at him you wouldn't know he was a foster child," "You must really have your hands full with that one," and "Does he act different from your real children?" Maybe now William will hear, "This is our son William."

QUESTIONS FOR REFLECTION AND DISCUSSION

1. As one of William's teachers, how would you have helped William feel more comfortable with his family situation?

2. What do you think is important to William?

3. What did William's story teach you?

4. What thoughts do you have about a child who is in first grade and then is removed and placed back in kindergarten?

5. What impact does moving and lack of consistency in one's home life have on student achievement and identity?

RESOURCES

Knauss, L., & Geroski, A. M. (2000). Addressing the needs of foster children within a school counseling program. *Professional School Counseling, 3*(3), 152–161.

Noble, L. S. (1997). The face of foster care. *Educational Leadership, 54*(7), 26–28.

Pelzer, D. (1995). *A child called "it": One child's courage to survive.* Deerfield Beach, FL: Health Communications, Inc.

Pelzer, D. (1997). *The lost boy: A foster child's search for the love of a family.* Deerfield Beach, FL: Health Communications, Inc.

CASE 7.3

JONATHAN'S STORY

Lola Finn

Jonathan's heart-wrenching story focuses on a young boy's experiences, resilience, and adjustments to multiple foster homes while continuing a close relationship with his biological mother and grandmother. The complexity of this case prompts numerous questions for consideration.

Jonathan was only three years old when the judge presiding over his divorced parents' contested custody case ruled he was to be removed from his home and placed in a foster home for "an indefinite time." The judge's stern face emphasized the chilling effect of his words, "My ruling must be to protect the child. Neither of his parents seems fit at this time to raise him."

Jonathan's parents and grandparents sat in stunned silence for a few moments. The quiet was abruptly broken when Jonathan's father, sobbing, rose to stand before the judge, pleading, "I lied about her using drugs. She's a good person; a good mother. Let her have him."

The judge, noted for his "no-nonsense" decisions, stared directly at the young man before him. "I do not know who to believe. I do not know what to believe. I stand by my decision."

Jonathan's mother was allowed only four hours from the moment of that decision to talk to her child, gather his clothes and his special toys, and prepare herself to tell him, "Good-bye." Reluctantly, unable to believe this was actually happening, she and her mother took him to the waiting Social Services worker assigned to deliver him to the approved foster home. As the stranger took Jonathan's hand from his mother's, the little boy immediately reacted, "No, Mama, No!" he cried, struggling to return to his mother's arms.

Mother and grandmother stood together, both weeping silently, as the Department of Family and Children Services (DFACS) agent, tightly holding Jonathan's hand, walked away from them. What the two grieving women could neither see nor hear were the other woman's tears, her heart also breaking for the two frozen figures she left behind, taking with her one's only child, the other's only grandchild. The worker silently vowed then she would do everything possible to return Jonathan to his family in the near future. She could not foresee it would be three families and fifteen months before his return.

JONATHAN'S PARENTS

Jonathan's parents came from dissimilar backgrounds. Jim had dropped out of high school while only in the ninth grade. Professional help for him was short term, although he was diagnosed as having dyslexia and manic depressive symptoms. His father and grandfather had each committed suicide during their individual bouts with depression.

Until his marriage to Alice, Jim lived with his mother, Grace, and an older sister, both loving, both overprotective. They would later admit to the judge presiding over Jonathan's custody hearing they had never held Jim accountable for misbehaving during his formative years. "We made excuses whenever he misbehaved. That was wrong!" his mother said.

Jim had found satisfaction working as a skilled laborer for a local business, but the drug habit he acquired while still in school continued to haunt him. He received treatment at drug centers on several occasions but was unable to be drug free for more than a few consecutive months. During the drug-free periods, Jim was a happy, likable young man. He had many friends. His job performance was rated excellent by his supervisor. As a result, his employer continued to support him even when he was away from his work while receiving treatment. Jim's job was held open for him until he was once more rehabilitated.

It was during a "good" period that Alice, Jonathan's mother, met Jim. Alice was still in high school and liked the young man, a friend of her older brother. Their early relationship was casual, not intensifying until several years later when Alice was attending college in another state. After a year of long-distance dating, Jim knew he must seek medical help again if they were to marry. This time he was the one who made the decision to check himself into a hospital known for its treatment of drug dependency.

"This time," Jim promised Alice at the end of the extended treatment, "I know I am cured. I am clean and I promise to stay that way. If you will marry me, we will have a good life together."

Alice believed him. She had been adopted when she was only seven weeks old. Her home environment was an excellent one. Alice's parents, Sarah and Todd, were well educated and supportive of Alice's interests, giving her opportunities to develop an early interest in horses. As she grew older, she decorated her room with ribbons and trophies, evidence of her successes at the numerous horse shows in which she competed.

Alice was an average student in high school. She studied hard and showed little evidence of a learning disability until she attended a private girls' college and her grades spiraled downward in the more demanding environment. Testing pinpointed the deficiency. The college faculty made the necessary adjustments in her studies and she eventually was able to graduate with a business degree. Immediately after her graduation, Alice announced to her family and friends that she planned to marry Jim.

Alice's parents, now divorced, were united in their concern about their daughter's marriage to Jim, a high school dropout and a recovering drug addict. Not surprisingly, Grace was delighted her son was marrying this young woman. She became defensive when Sarah attempted to share her concerns about the marriage in a private conversation between the two women. "My son should be given credit for checking himself into the hospital," Grace argued. "He was the one who sought help. No one made that decision for him."

THE EARLY YEARS

The first two years of marriage were good ones. Jim remained drug free. He and Alice had good jobs, saving enough to buy a small home after one year. It was a happy time for the young couple when they discovered they were to be parents. The pregnancy and birth were comparatively easy and without complications. The grandparents were all present when Jonathan was born and the future looked promising for the new family.

Jonathan was a healthy, happy baby. His physical development was normal, though it was noted in the doctor's records that "he was very energetic." The couple shared the responsibilities of caring for the baby and it was evident they both loved him. Alice returned to work, leaving her child in the care of a friend.

Abruptly, their brief, idyllic lifestyle changed. Jim returned to his cocaine habit, this time even more intensely. Arguments and threats of physical harm increasingly filled the small home until Alice, fearing for their safety, left their home with Jonathan to live with her mother. Alice soon filed for divorce, seeking permanent custody of Jonathan, now three years old.

Jim angrily retaliated and filed a countersuit, seeking custody of his own son. His suit stated Alice was an unfit mother who smoked marijuana and was addicted to other drugs. To strengthen his case, he showed a photograph of Alice standing beside a five-foot-tall marijuana plant, at the same admitting he was responsible for growing the plant in their yard. Jim assured the judge that his mother, who was always present during the extended hearings, would care for her grandson while Jim was once again in a rehabilitation center.

The judge listened attentively to lawyers, parents, and grandparents and then ruled. He made it clear there would be no appeals at this time.

FOSTER HOME CARE

Jonathan's foster parents welcomed the sad little boy with open arms and understanding when he frequently cried, calling for his mother. At first Jonathan believed his mother did not know where he was, telling the foster parents, "If my mama knew where I was, she would come and get me."

Eventually, the tears became less frequent and Jonathan began to respond to the two people who made every attempt to fill the void left by the separation from his beloved mother. The new environment was a peaceful, caring one and Jonathan found his smile again.

After one month, DFACS authorities agreed that Jonathan could be reunited with his parents and grandparents for a brief period. A date was selected; appropriately, Jonathan's fourth birthday. The foster parents brought Jonathan to a large park, a neutral, court-approved site. It was the first time Jonathan's parents and grandparents had all come together since the judge's decision. In addition, it was also their first time to meet the foster parents. Although they were excited at the prospect of seeing their little boy, they were all apprehensive about the visit, Jonathan's reaction, and the future.

It was a happy reunion. Alice, Jim, and their parents appreciated Jonathan's foster parents remaining in the background as the little boy and his family reunited. Later, after talking together, they reassured one another that this couple already loved Jonathan and would take good care of him, physically and emotionally.

After a short visit, the foster parents thoughtfully left the families alone to celebrate Jonathan's birthday. There were balloons, gifts, party favors, and a large cake. There were games and lots of hugs. When the foster parents returned for Jonathan several hours later, he did not want to leave his parents and grandparents but seemed to understand his Grandmother Sarah's reason, "We want to take you with us, but we can't until the judge says we can."

As Jonathan left with the two people who once more would make the decisions concerning his daily life, he looked back only once to wave at those he must leave again. Then, facing forward, he took each of his foster parents' extended hands and walked between them to the car.

MORE CHANGES

Three months later Jonathan faced another critical upheaval in his young life over which he had no control. His foster mother became very ill and it was discovered she must have a kidney transplant. She could no longer care for Jonathan and he must be relocated immediately.

His new foster parents, also childless, welcomed Jonathan into their home as though he were their own child. He, surprisingly, readjusted again, partly because of their caring manner, but also, perhaps, because of an innately resilient nature. Alice was later to remark to her mother, "Jonathan just seemed to realize he must do this. Since he was born, he always seemed to sense other people's feelings."

Jonathan's second foster mother was a kindergarten teacher who spent many hours after school with the little boy, helping him to grasp concepts that would prepare him for his first years in school. Though full of energy, Jonathan would sit and listen attentively, especially when she told him stories from the numerous picture books she brought home from school. Jonathan attended a nearby day care school while his foster mother worked.

The family lived on a farm where the foster father spent hours with Jonathan, letting him help with chores while teaching him about the animals and crops. Life in this rural setting was quite different from his other two homes and Jonathan seemed happier than he had for many months.

Soon though, Jonathan faced another change. His second foster parents, who had long hoped to adopt, unexpectedly received word a baby was at last available. One of DFACS's present regulations is that foster children can no longer remain with a couple who adopt. The couple's joy at the news of the adoption was dampened with the knowledge that Jonathan would have to leave their home. In less than a year, and for the third time, Jonathan faced the unknown.

Jonathan's new foster family was a single mother and her nine-year-old son. The three bonded quickly. Each unexpectedly found in the other two a fulfillment of individual needs. Jonathan found a stable environment, a loving but firm mother, and a sibling with whom he could play and share confidences. The nine-year-old was excited to have a younger "brother" whose needs exceeded his, one who looked to him for advice and comfort. The mother, also lonely, found in this little boy patience and a unique courage she had never expected in one so young. During these months, they became a family.

Jonathan was happy and thrived in his new environment. Again, he attended a nearby day care center while his foster mother worked the day shift at the police department. In the evenings, their laughter filled the small house as they shared stories of the day's activities during supper. Jonathan learned to play Monopoly, his favorite game of the many they enjoyed after dishes were washed and homework was completed.

WHILE HE WAS GONE

After the successful birthday party, Alice and her mother were allowed to see Jonathan twice each month at the local DFACS office. Those first visits in a small office were an especially hard time for the three of them. The hour allowed for the visit seemed brief and their time always concluded with the child's plaintive cry, "Please take me home with you!"

Their response sounded cold, robotlike, to their ears, "We can't. We want to, but we can't! The judge will have to tell us when we can!"

After several visits, Jonathan seemed to accept this explanation. He always asked, "Has the judge said I could come home?"

Increasingly, it required more effort for his mother to respond, "Not yet!"

Sarah, a respected and loved educator in a neighboring town, sought out the DFACS director at every visit to keep her appraised of her daughter's situation, which had changed significantly since the judge's stinging words and decision. Sarah assured the director that Alice had worked through the initial shock and anger, and was making every effort to provide her son with the proper home environment.

With family support and a new, more responsible job with the local hospital, Alice was able to sell the home she and Jim had purchased when they were married and buy a house in a family-oriented neighborhood. An excellent school was within walking distance. As in past years, Alice became actively involved at her church. Those qualities that once enabled Alice to overcome a severe learning disability and graduate with a business degree were once again apparent, enhanced by deeper maturity and an evident sense of responsibility.

Sarah assured the DFACS director during visits that Jonathan's father was no longer a part of Alice's life and that Alice would be able to provide a good home for him. She pleaded with the director that Jonathan be returned to his mother before the end of summer; thus he could enter kindergarten in the fall. The school was within walking distance and had an excellent reputation for its instructional programs and caring teachers, many of whom she knew well.

The DFACS director listened intently to Jonathan's grandmother during each visit and assured Sarah she would report this information to the same judge whose devastating decision had changed forever all their lives.

THE HOMECOMING

In August, two weeks before the first day of the new school year, Alice received the telephone call she would always remember, word for word. Jonathan was coming home to her. His room had been ready for him since she had moved into the new home and now he would be there to fill the empty drawers and closet with his clothes and little boy treasures!

Two days later Sarah drove her daughter to the same DFACS office where they had spent many hours. The only tears shed this trip were joyful ones as Jonathan ran down the steps into his mother's arms, hugging her as though he would never let go. Then he turned to his grandmother who waited patiently for the big hug that let her know how much he loved her.

"The judge said I could go home?" Jonathan asked, almost as though he could not believe it.

Their answer was almost a chorus, "Yes! Yes! Yes!"

It was time to leave behind, appropriate at this building, the pain of the past fifteen months and look forward to the future—a new home, a new neighborhood, new friends. Also changed, yet still the same, were Jonathan's wonderful mother and grandmother, the two who never gave up hope they would soon be reunited permanently.

Jonathan's transition to his new home was surprisingly smooth. He flourished in the supportive, exciting environment of his kindergarten class where his "handpicked" teacher knew "Jonathan's story" and cared for him as though he were her own grandchild. He made friends easily and quickly. There was little evidence of the past months—unless one looked into Jonathan's eyes at the same time a sad memory interrupted a happy moment.

He seldom spoke of his father who had been granted visiting rights, with the condition that it must be under the supervision of his maternal grandmother. But Jim was no longer a part of Jonathan's life. His drug habit had once again caught up with him and he was now in prison, convicted of armed robbery. The paternal grandmother, unable to cope with her son's problems, had moved to another state.

Jonathan spoke of his father only once during his first year in school. The children's were having "circle time," talking about members of their families. Jonathan suddenly raised his arm, waving it frantically, anxious to share his thoughts. He stood when his teacher called on him, and spoke with a strong voice:

"My daddy; well, you see, my daddy was a bad boy. So he just rode off into the sunset."

Relieved, Jonathan sat down. He had erased one of those bad memories—at least temporarily.

QUESTIONS FOR REFLECTION AND DISCUSSION

1. How much information should Jonathan's mother and grandmother reveal of the traumatic events in Jonathan's life to his kindergarten teacher and to the school administration?

2. What is the best learning environment for Jonathan's first year of school?

3. Describe the teacher, emphasizing her personal and professional qualities, you think would be most appropriate for Jonathan.

4. How do you think the teacher should respond to Jonathan's statement about his father?

5. What challenges does this teacher and Jonathan's future teachers face as he progresses through the grades?

6. What should be the family's expectations of Jonathan's progress and behavior in school? Discuss what you think the teacher should expect of Jonathan in both his behavior and academics?

7. What school resources would you use for support if you were Jonathan's teacher? What community resources would you recommend to his mother?

WORLD WIDE WEB RESOURCES

American Foster Care Resources, Inc. (www.afcr.com)
National Institute on Drug Abuse (www.nida.nih.gov)
National Resource Center for Foster Care and Permanency Planning (www.hunter.cuny.edu/socwork/nrcfcpp)

CASE 7.4

MY BROTHER SAYS YOU'RE A FAG

Paige E. Campbell
Dee Russell

The case takes place in a middle-class community in the Midwest. It involves Emily, a first-grade teacher, and her student Toby. Toby Tanner lives with two men. They are gay and they are his fathers. Tony is his biological father and Steve is his "stepfather." Tony and Steve had been a committed couple for ten years before they decided they wanted children. They approached their friend Nancy to be a surrogate. She agreed and was artificially inseminated with Tony's sperm. That's how Toby became a member of his family. They are a typical, middle-income family. Tony is a branch manager at a local bank, and Steve teaches English literature part time at the local liberal arts college. They live in a neighborhood surrounded by other families and are active members of their community board.

Emily has never worked with a gay family before and stumbles along until a terrible playground incident. Toby is teased by three children with very influential parents and Emily cannot decide how to handle the incident. She fears for her career. She isn't sure where she stands on the homosexuality issue, yet she hates to see this innocent child tormented about things beyond his control. Think about your own personal feelings about a child in your classroom who has homosexual parents.

Emily Shank is a new teacher at Honeywell Elementary School in Beachton, a midwestern middle-class community near a major metropolitan area. The children are mostly middle class and represent a wide range of ethnic and racial backgrounds. Emily teaches first grade and, although she is in her fourth year of teaching, she is really anxious about doing well in her new school. Honeywell Elementary School was built two years ago and Mrs. Caldwell, the principal, handpicked her staff from all over the state. Emily was hired this year because one of the teachers left to care for her ailing mother. Emily was thrilled but also a bit intimidated. Mrs. Caldwell had a reputation for being an excellent, yet demanding, administrator who did not tolerate opposing views very well. Emily just hoped she wouldn't get on her bad side.

FAMILY PORTRAITS

"OK kids! It's time to finish your family portraits!" Emily sang out to her first-grade class. The children were eagerly putting the finishing touches on their family pictures.

"Susie, I see that you have a pink house with your mommy and daddy. Do you have any brothers or sisters or pets?" asked Emily

"Nope. Just me and my mommy and my daddy. They getted a divorce but I like to have daddy at home so I drawed him in the picture. He gots his own apartment now."

"Keisha, your family picture reminds me of my own family. I see you've drawn mom, dad, Deshawn, Samson, and Eartha. I have one brother, too, and we had a dog and a cat, only their names were Rover and Tabby."

Emily enjoyed the children's family portraits. She really valued the relationships she'd developed with families in years past and always looked forward to meeting them at the open house every August.

"Jose! Your family portrait looks like a family reunion! I see twelve people in your picture. Do you all live together?"

"Only my grandma lives with me and my mom and my dad. I got lots of aunts and uncles and cousins who live on our street. We like to play together a lot." Emily can't even imagine having so many relatives so close all the time!

"Well, Toby, tell me about your picture." As soon as she says this, she wishes she could have swallowed the words.

Toby is a quiet, six-year-old boy. He seems very polite and well mannered and gets along well with the other children. But his picture! "That's Steve—he's my dad—and that's Tony—my other dad. And that's Rosie the cat. She doesn't really live with me yet but Daddy Steve says I can get a cat when I'm seven and my birthday's in March so I'm gonna get a cat in March."

As Emily collects the pictures she feels torn. Although Toby seems like a nice boy, she really feels uncomfortable putting his picture up. What would the other children say? And the other parents? Two dads! It just doesn't seem right. She decides to simply put all of the family portraits away in the children's folders now. Better to simply leave it alone.

OPEN HOUSE

Emily had never worked with a gay family before. She really didn't know what to expect and she was quite apprehensive about her first conference with them. Despite all of her fears, Emily found the first parent conference with Tony and Steve quite pleasant.

"I want to share with you the family portrait that Toby drew on the first day. He seems very comfortable with two dads."

"Well," Steve began, "We're his family. We've been his family since his conception and we're all he knows—"

Tony interrupted, "We really should have come to talk with you before school began but we were in Wales for the summer and barely had time to buy school supplies before the first day. We are very devoted to our son and I understand if you feel some discomfort with our family, uh, configuration. If there's ever anything you need, please don't hesitate to call. We're both very involved parents."

Emily felt oddly reassured by Tony's remarks. "I have to tell you, I felt really torn about whether to display Toby's picture. I don't want the other kids to tease him and, well, I guess I was afraid that some of the other parents might get upset with me. I'm sorry, but I finally decided to not display any of them. I simply didn't know what to do."

"Hopefully, you'll feel more comfortable contacting us next time. It's OK. Let's consider this a fresh start." With that, Tony extended his hand to Emily and gave her a firm handshake. Steve did the same and they left. Maybe this wouldn't be so bad after all.

THE PLAYGROUND INCIDENT

Emily watched it happen. She really couldn't believe it. Her heart sank.

Justin, a second grader, shoved Toby shouting, "My brother says you're a fag! He says it's true 'cuz you live with two faggots!"

Toby cried silently as he stared toward the ground.

"What's the matter, fag?!?" Tad, another second grader, had joined the melee. "See, I told you he was a sissy! Can't be a *real* man if you live with two *faggots*, can ya, Toby?" he spat.

"Ooo, yuck! C'mon, let's get away from him. He might try and kiss us!" Charles, another second grader, tugged at the other two and they ran away shouting, "Gross! Sissy boy! Faggot!"

She couldn't believe it! She walked over to Toby and put her arm around him. "Why don't you go in the room and feed the turtle for me? You can read a book until the class gets back. OK, sweetie?"

Toby nodded silently but still refused to look up from the ground. He slowly made his way into the building.

Emily felt nauseous. She knew that she should tell Steve and Tony. But she was terrified enough not to report it to Mrs. Caldwell the principal. After all, Justin Caldwell was her son! Justin, Tad, and Charles were "model" students in the school. Justin was the principal's son, Tad the PTA president's son, and Charles the son of the minister where Emily attended services every Sunday. "What on earth am I going to do?" Emily wondered to herself.

QUESTIONS FOR REFLECTION AND DISCUSSION

1. How would you resolve the situation? Explain your reasons for selecting a course of action and the outcomes you might expect.

2. Consider the values portrayed by Emily through her actions and thoughts in the case. What elements or events challenge those values? Why?

3. How do you perceive Tony and Steve's values? What are their goals for Toby? How do they portray themselves through their words and actions as parents?

4. Consider the way Tony, Steve, and Toby talk about their family. Consider Emily's thoughts about their family. Finally, consider the taunts of the children on the playground. How will the words used by the boys on the playground affect Toby's view of himself? What are the consequences of the language of identity as presented in this case?

RESOURCES

Benkov, L. (1994). *Reinventing the family.* New York: Crown.
Bialeschki, M. D., & Pearce, K. D. (1997). "I don't want a lifestyle—I want a life": The effect of role negotiations on the leisure of lesbian mothers. *Journal of Leisure Research, 29*(1), 113–131.
Cameron, P., & Cameron, K. (1997). Did the APA misrepresent the scientific literature to courts in support of homosexual custody? *Journal of Psychology, 131*(3), 313–332.
Crawford, I., & Solliday, E. (1996). The attitudes of undergraduate college students toward gay parenting. *Journal of Homosexuality, 30*(4), 63–77.
Gartrell, N., Hamilton, J., & Banks, A. (1996). The national lesbian family study: 1. Interviews with prospective mothers. *American Journal of Orthopsychiatry, 66*, 272–81.
Golombok, S., & Yasker, F. (1996). Do parents influence the sexual orientation of their children? Findings from a longitudinal study of lesbian families. *Developmental Psychology, 32*, 3–11.
Letts, W. (1999). *Queering elementary education: Advancing the dialogue about sexualities and schooling.* New York: Rowman & Littlefield.
Maney, D. W., & Cain, R. E. (1997). Preservice elementary teachers attitudes toward gay and lesbian parenting. *Journal of School Health, 67*(6), 236–241.
Patterson, C. J. (1997). Children of lesbian and gay parents. *Advances in Clinical Child Psychology, 19*, 235–282.
Pies, C. (1988). *Considering Parenthood* (2nd ed.). Minneapolis, MN: Spinsters Ink.
Sears, J. T. (1993–1994). Challenges for educators: Lesbian, gay, and bisexual families. *High School Journal, 77*(1–2), 138–156.
Victor, S. B., & Fish, M. C. (1995). Lesbian mothers and the children: A review for school psychologists. *School Psychology Review, 24*(3), 456–479.

CASE 7.5

MANY FACES OF HOMELESSNESS

Claire E. Hamilton
Xernona J. Thomas

Most often when we think of homelessness we picture adults panhandling on the streets. Yet, families with children are the fastest-growing segment of the homeless population and 40 percent of the individuals who do become homeless are families with children (National Coalition for Homelessness, 2001). Families become homeless for many reasons and the reality of being homeless varies. Some families, especially those in urban areas, find accommodation in shelters or welfare hotels, whereas others, living in more rural areas, may stay temporarily with one relative

An important part of teaching from a multicultural perspective is being aware of family complexities that can affect student learning. An increasing number of children come to school homeless, in poverty, and in poor health.

or friend after another, often in substandard or overcrowded conditions. Increasingly, teachers must find ways to support children in their classrooms who are homeless. A first step is beginning to appreciate the many faces of homelessness. We present three cases, illustrating both the child's and the classroom teacher's perspective. Each of these cases also represents some of the general statistics we know about children who are homeless. Investigate the homeless situation in your community. What resources are available for supporting their needs? Does there seem to be some common causes?

COREY AND TRAVONTE

After teaching first grade for four years, Corey Hill was beginning to see how early in the school year she could tell which children were going to have trouble. This year it was clearly going to be Travonte. She knew he had been retained in kindergarten and that he had already been evaluated once for special education services.

Late in August, Corey had sent out letters introducing herself, explaining her classroom, and welcoming all her new students and parents. Travonte's letter had come back twice because the address was wrong and the telephone number in his record had been disconnected. Corey was annoyed by the fact that some parents never took the time to update their children's records. When school started Corey sent home the usual list of basic school supplies she expected each child to provide. Corey believed that, unlike some teachers, her list really was basic—a box of crayons, three pencils, a box of kleenex, one glue stick, one notebook, and six colored folders. She had really pared the list down so that parents wouldn't be overwhelmed by buying a lot of materials. Still some parents, like Travonte's, even after several notes home, never provided the materials for their child and Corey ended up having to buy the materials herself. Corey was tired of having to pick up the slack; she didn't have much money herself on a teacher's salary.

Travonte was a sweet enough child, a bit hard to know, and sometimes a little dazed. He really did seem to try even though he obviously didn't seem to be at the same skill level as the other children. Corey knew she would have to keep an eye on him and was already considering referring him for student support services (a prereferral system for special education services).

Travonte, his mother, and two younger sisters were living in a mobile home with his aunt and three cousins. He didn't like living there as much as he had liked living with his grandmother. His mother and grandmother always seemed to be shouting about something so maybe it was better that they moved. Travonte's family had never really had a home of their own. When he was born, he and his mom had lived with his dad but that hadn't lasted very long. He hadn't seen his dad since his fourth birthday. As his sisters were born, he and his family seemed to move even more frequently, sometimes staying with friends, sometimes with other relatives. They stayed with his grandmother for almost a year and had been living with his aunt for the last two months. He really liked school and Ms. Hill was nice, but she had seemed a bit cross when he didn't bring in the right crayons. His sister's child care teacher had given his family some school supplies but they weren't the same as those the other children had. School seemed like a good place and he liked getting a desk of his very own where he could put his belongings. He knew it was important to pay attention but he was so sleepy sometimes.

TODD AND HARRISON

Todd Simmons was beginning his third year as a second-grade teacher. He had proven himself to the all female staff and had developed an excellent relationship with students and their parents. Todd was young, full of energy, and always looking for exciting ways to help his students learn. As Todd prepared the class for their lesson on Native Americans, pilgrims, and origins of the Thanksgiving holiday, he informed the students of the annual upcoming can-a-thon. Each student was given a letter to take home that explained when the drive would start, who the cans would benefit, and what the classroom incentives would be. The principal had announced that the class with the most cans would win a pizza party. Todd was a natural competitor and always wanted his class to win. To spur their interest, Todd helped the students create a race track. Each student was given a small car made of paper. As students brought in cans, they were allowed to move their car ahead on the track. The student who was furthest along at the end of the can-a-thon would be teacher's helper for a whole month! Harrison arrived in Todd's class just as this new segment was beginning. Todd noticed that this was Harrison's third school since the beginning of the school year. Harrison seemed like he was a good student. He dressed really nice and his mother always offered to help in the classroom. Todd explained the can-a-thon to Harrison and stressed that the class really wanted to win. There were two things that slightly bothered Todd about his new student. He had a croupy cough since he enrolled. After several conversations with his mother about the need to visit a doctor, Harrison still continued to come to school but he never brought any medicine. Todd was also aggravated because Harrison had only brought in one can. Surely a student who wore Hilfiger and Nautica everyday could afford to go to the doctor and could spare more than one can of food. Todd decided that even though this was apparently a wealthy family, they lacked some basic values. He would use his lesson to stress that it is not only good to have nice things but it is also good to share what we have with others.

Harrison, his mother, and his older sister are living in an area shelter that provides services only for women and children. His three-year-old twin siblings were staying with his grandmother because the shelter bedroom could not accommodate all of them. Harrison's father is temporarily staying with a friend. All of Harrison's family had lived with his grandmother, but they had to move because the large number of people violated her lease agreement. Harrison's family recently became homeless because of the closing of the factory in which his father worked. His dad had been a supervisor at this local plant. He made a generous income and had always been the sole provider for his family. After the closing, the family lived off savings until nothing was left. Harrison has had asthma since he was two years old and requires ongoing medication for maintenance of his condition. The medication, which was once covered by insurance, averages $90 a month. In addition, he has not been able to follow up with his doctor because of the cost of the visit. Harrison is really excited about his new school. He has never had a male teacher before and thinks that Mr. Simmons is cool. Harrison is also a natural competitor. He played tee-ball and baseball for his dad's company team for three years. He is miserable because his car is last on the track. He wants to be a part of the team effort and he really wants to be the class helper, but the only food that his family gets is from the shelter. His mother borrowed one can from his grandmother, but that was all that she could spare. He and his mother volunteered to stay after school to help count the cans. Mr. Simmons accepted the help, but his car still didn't get to move.

KAREN AND MARISSA

Karen was more than halfway through her first year as a third-grade teacher. She had become familiar with all of her paperwork requirements and felt fairly confident in her ability to teach. Karen was excited because most of her children had adjusted well and all had returned their necessary documents to school. Karen received a note in her box that a new student would be entering her class on Monday. She was excited about the new student and wanted to make sure that she felt comfortable in her classroom. After Karen introduced Marissa to all of the students in her class, she had them introduce themselves and told them about their next assignment. "This will really be fun," she exclaimed. Karen explained to the students that they would be creating a scrapbook about their life. This is your chance to tell the world about your life. Karen told the students that they would be putting together various assignments from throughout the year and that they were welcome to bring in other items that told something about them. They would share their creations with their parents during winter open house. She noticed that Marissa began to look sad. She also recalled that Marissa became really tense when she hugged her and that she did not reciprocate.

At snack time, Karen allowed the students to talk quietly with each other. Several students made efforts to talk to Marissa and to tell her about themselves. Stacy, one of the friendliest girls in class, asked Marissa where she lived. Marissa became angry, pushed Stacy, and yelled that it was none of her business. Karen immediately separated the two and Stacy tearfully said she only wanted to invite Marissa over to her house. Karen took Marissa out into the hall to discuss her outburst. Marissa would not talk to Karen. She told her the class rules and her expectations. Karen told her that she would give her a chance to start over and act like nothing ever occurred. Karen also reminded Marissa that she needed her to bring in her enrollment papers. The school secretary had told Karen that if the forms were not returned in a week, Marissa would be required to stay out of school until her mother could bring them in. Karen began thinking that this child would require close monitoring. When the students left for the day, Karen reminded Marissa to bring back her forms, pictures for her scrapbook, and a better attitude. As the days passed, Karen constantly reminded Marissa that she needed to bring in some items from home to include in her book. She told Marissa that she was willing to help her complete the assignment, but she needed some cooperation from Marissa.

Marissa, her mother, and her younger brother were residing in a domestic violence shelter. Marissa really liked her new teacher and was eager to please her. Yet everything was going wrong. She did not have her forms and there was no way for her to bring in the items needed for her project. Marissa and her family fled from their home while her father was at work. He kept all of their important papers in his car so that her mother would never try anything "crazy." All that Marissa's mother brought with them was a few items of clothes, her car, and a little money. The shelter staff had been wonderful. They had given Marissa school supplies, a book bag, and new clothes for her new school. The shelter worker was also trying to help her mother secure copies of their birth certificates, social security cards, and immunization records. Those things could be replaced. Many others never would be. There were no pictures or other items from her first years. All that Marissa had to remember her past were the marks on her and her mother's bodies. That morning before school, Marissa had been excited about her new start. She could hardly wait to show her teacher how well she could read and write. Now she was dreading returning to school because she could not even do the first assignment.

CONCLUSION

Almost 30 percent of children who, like Travonte, are homeless have been homeless more than once and more than half have never lived in their own homes (National Coalition for the Homeless, 2001). Often these children experience academic difficulties: A child who is homeless is nine times more likely to repeat a grade and is three times more likely than a child with a home to be in special education (National Coalition for the Homeless, 2001). As with Harrison's family, the typical homeless family has lived with other relatives before becoming homeless, and becoming homeless often leads to separation from family members. Regular school attendance is problematic, and within a given school year 41 percent of students who are homeless attend two different schools, whereas 28 percent attend three or more schools. At least one child in a family that is homeless is likely to suffer from chronic health problems (almost 42 percent have asthma or other respiratory conditions), and nearly 20 percent lack a regular source of medical care (National Coalition for the Homeless, 2001). Similar to Marissa, 50 percent of the children who are homeless have been the victim of or have witnessed violence in their homes. Twenty-two percent of mothers who are homeless report that they became homeless because of domestic violence. Teachers can support these children by modifying their own classroom practices and by helping students access services.

Services available to students who are homeless vary by school district but all are funded by the McKinney Homeless Assistance Act signed into legislation in 1987. The primary goal of this legislation was to ensure that children and youth who are homeless have undelayed, uninterrupted access to schools. Some schools have personnel specifically designated to coordinate services for this population. Other schools may not offer specific programs but serve these students through their counseling, social work, or psychology department. There are a variety of funded services that are authorized under the McKinney Act. The activities include personnel training, assistance with locating records, referrals to area agencies, transportation assistance, tutoring, psychological services, and the purchasing of supplies. Harrison, for example, would benefit from a medical referral to receive treatment for his asthma and to assist with purchasing medication. Marissa would be well served in a counseling group that focuses on anger management. The school social worker could also help her family locate the records needed for her to remain in school and could request an immunization waiver for up to ninety days while records are being sent. Travonte could use some school supplies and may need to meet with the counselor on a individual basis to discuss his frustrations.

QUESTIONS FOR REFLECTION AND DISCUSSION

1. How might teachers learn that children are homeless? Are there any signs that Corey, Todd, and Karen might have noticed?

2. What are some common misconceptions you have that might affect your interactions with and attitudes toward children and families who are homeless?

3. What changes in classroom activities and structure would you make to support children who are homeless? How could Karen include Marissa in the family scrapbook activity?

4. What do you think Travonte, Harrison, and Marissa found most challenging about being homeless? What do you think their parents and teachers found most challenging?

REFERENCE

National Coalition for the Homeless. (2001). Homeless families with children. Available at http://www.nationalhomeless.org/families.html. Retrieved May 30, 2003.

WORLD WIDE WEB RESOURCES

Better Homes Fund (www.tbhf.org/homepage.html)
Homes for the Homeless (www2.HomesfortheHomeless.com/hfh/)
National Coalition for Homeless (www.nationalhomeless.org/)

SUBJECT INDEX

Academic performance and expectations, 57

Advocacy, 152

African American, 35, 56

Alcohol, 97

Assessment, 26

Cases
  advantages, 5
  guidelines, 7, 8
  rationale, 1, 3, 4
  structure, 6
Catholicism, 35
Cerebral palsy, 156
Child abuse, 90, 95
Child welfare system, 176
Culture, 12
Constructivism, 4
Cultural therapy, 2

Deafness, 158
Death, 119
Diabetes, 114
Dishonesty, 130
Divorce, 181
Drugs, 96, 101, 114, 181

Families, 168
  communication, 27
  involvement, 29, 144
  meeting, 20
Foster care, 176, 183

Gender, 72
Gifted education
  Black children, 58, 76
  underachievement, 58, 64
Grade
  fifth, 35, 64, 72, 101, 114, 127, 130, 136
  first grade, 141, 188
  fourth, 41, 46, 54, 111, 147, 169
  kindergarten, 19, 84, 95, 145, 176

prekindergarten, 144, 152
  second grade, 98, 121
  third grade, 59, 92, 111
Grief and loss, 119

Homelessness, 191

Immigration, 50
Incarceration, 96

Jehovah's Witness, 141
Judaism, 127

Language
  native, 14
  English as a Second, 19

Mathematics, 58, 59, 72
Medical issues, 163
Mobility, 169
Morality, 130
Multicultural education
  ceiling effect, 35
  definition, 2, 3
Multicultural teacher education, 1
Muslim, 46

Neglect, 90

Philippines, 41, 51
Philosophical basis, 4
Planning, 20
Poverty, 41
Preschool, 18, 152
Profanity, 111

Religious celebration, 141
Retention, 58, 84

Safety and prosocial behaviors, 88, 106
Science, 23, 41
Segregation, 31